SHAMAN OF OBERSTDORF

Studies in Early Modern German History

H. C. Erik Midelfort, Editor

SHAMAN OF OBERSTDORF

Chonrad Stoeckhlin and the Phantoms of the Night

(Chonrad Stoeckhlin und die Nachtschar:
Eine Geschichte aus der frühen Neuzeit)

Wolfgang Behringer

Translated by H. C. Erik Midelfort

University Press of Virginia
Charlottesville

Originally published in German as *Chonrad Stoeckhlin und die Nachtschar: Eine Geschichte aus der frühen Neuzeit*, © R. Piper GmbH & Co. KG, München, 1994

The University Press of Virginia
Translation © 1998 by the Rector and Visitors of the University of Virginia

Printed in the United States of America

First published 1998

The paper used in this publication meets the minimum requirements of the American National Standard for Information Sciences—Permanence of Paper for Printed Library Materials, ANSI Z39.48-1984. ∞

Library of Congress Cataloging-in-Publication Data

Behringer, Wolfgang.
[Chonrad Stoecklin und die Nachtschar. English]
Shaman of Oberstdorf : Chonrad Stoeckhlin and the phantoms of the night / Wolfgang Behringer ; translated by H.C. Erik Midelfort.
p.   cm.
— (Studies in early modern German history)
Includes bibliographical references and index.
ISBN 0-8139-1788-3 (hardcover : alk. paper)
ISBN 0-8139-1853-7 (paper : alk. paper)
1. Witchcraft—Germany—Allgäu—History—16th century.
2. Occultism—Germany—History—Allgäu—16th century. I. Title. II. Series
BF1583.B43813   1998
133.4' 3' 094337—dc21   97-48497
CIP

Contents

Maps

Author's Acknowledgments

I HAVE DISCUSSED the story of Chonrad Stoeckhlin and his phantoms of the night on the following happy occasions: in a lecture at the University of Innsbruck at the invitation of Leander Petzoldt; in an advanced seminar at the University of Bonn at the invitation of Bernd Roeck; and in a lecture at the Royal Holloway College, University of London, at the invitation of Lyndal Roper. I thank my generous hosts and the participants at these events. I am also grateful to the following persons for ideas and suggestions: Andreas Blauert of Constance, Willem de Blécourt of The Hague, Peter Blickle and Renate Blickle of Bern, Rosalba Ciranni of Pisa, Gustav Henningsen of Copenhagen, Günter Kapfhammer of Augsburg, Gábor Klaniczay of Budapest, David Lederer of Dublin, Sönke Lorenz of Tübingen, Erik Midelfort of Charlottesville, and Manfred Tschaikner of Bregenz.

Wolfgang Behringer
Munich

Translator's Preface

THIS SPARKLING LITTLE book tells the story of a sixteenth-century mountain village caught in a panic of its own making. Four hundred years ago the Bavarian alpine town of Oberstdorf, surrounded by the towering peaks of the Vorarlberg, was awash in legends and rumors of prophets and healers, of spirits and specters, of witches and soothsayers. Some of these legends seem harmless enough to us, perhaps even picturesque in their evocation of invisible forces, ghosts, raptures, and revenants who brought back tales of the land of the dead. But Wolfgang Behringer's story is hardly one of a merely colorful folkloric culture of odd survivals and strange superstitions. Once the episcopal authorities caught wind of the rumors emanating from Oberstdorf, the story turned serious indeed.

The translator is faced with problems in trying to convey readers to this distant land of legendary figures and forces. English has no proper terms for some of Behringer's main characters, beginning with the spectral shapes referred to in his title. Chonrad Stoeckhlin spoke of traveling with the *Nachtschar*. We might say that these were the "armies," "legions," or "squadrons" of the night," except that the word *Schar* need not have military connotations at all. We might speak of hordes, except that a *Schar* need not be very large. We could use words like "night people" or "night folk," except that Behringer later compares the notion of *Nachtschar* with other notions of the *Nachtvolk*, which almost has to be rendered as "night people." Fifteen years ago, the translators of Carlo Ginzburg's classic account of the *benandanti* found themselves in a similar predicament, and opted to introduce the reader to the Italian word, rather than suggesting an English equivalent.[1] Perhaps I should have done the same, but I have tried, whenever possible, to find evocatively equivalent terms, even when no literal synonym could be found. And so we have "phantoms of the night."

That world of sixteenth-century Germany also enjoyed a highly differentiated language with which to describe witches. Latin terms were sometimes deployed to emphasize the similarity of witches to blood-sucking monsters (*lamiae*), screech owls (*strigae*), poisoners (*veneficae*), or to harmful magicians (*malefici*). The Germanic term *Unholde* (with connotations of idolatry and impiety) survived in the German Southwest while other regions preferred the modern word *Hexe* (witch), and still other sixteenth-century Germans preferred to worry about *Zauberer* (magicians or sorcerers), *Zauberinnen* (sorceresses), or *Giftmischer* (poisoners). Because of their relatively sheltered position in the history of witchcraft, the English never developed a witchcraft language of equal resonance. So once again the translator must try to convey a realm of nuance in an English that is sometimes strangely impoverished. In certain instances I have found no other solution than to introduce readers to odd German words or to add a translator's note.

As an introduction to modern German witchcraft research, a study of the local impact of the Counter Reformation, and as a historical investigation into popular culture, Behringer's book has the advantage of telling a compelling story, while taking off on tangents to inform us of peasant raptures, magical healing and unfamiliar alpine notions such as the "furious army," the "wild hunt," popular bonfire festivals, and eerie echoes of pagan Wotan. In other chapters he responds to the important work of Carlo Ginzburg, who has uncovered an Italian peasant culture in which notions of shamanism and of fertility cults survived, while still other excursions connect with the history of peasant rebellions or remind us of the deeply suspect anthropological and folklore studies conducted under the auspices of Hitler's Third Reich. Wolfgang Behringer has become one of the best historians of German witchcraft, not only because of his mastery of the subject at the regional level,[2] but because he also writes movingly, forcefully, and with an eye for the telling anecdote. With his help and with the many friendly suggestions of Kathy Stuart, I hope that this translation succeeds in conveying some of these qualities. This edition has corrected a few minor errors and cites English translations, when available, for works that Behringer cites in German.

H. C. Erik Midelfort
Charlottesville

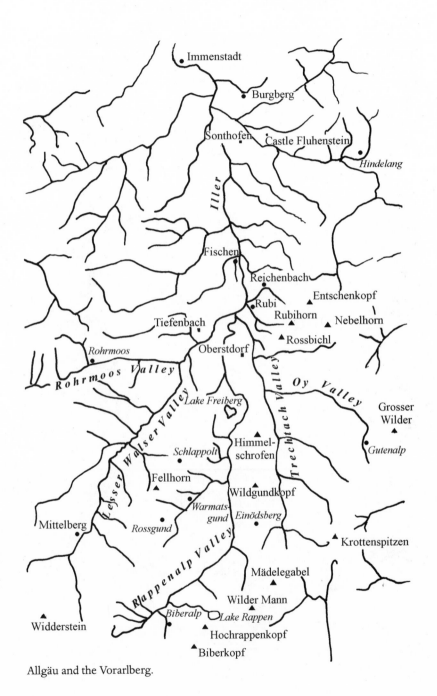

Immenstadt

Burgberg

Sonthofen · Castle Fluhenstein

Hindelang

Iller

Fischen

Reichenbach

Rubi

Entschenkopf

Rubihorn

Nebelhorn

Tiefenbach

▲ Rossbichl

Rohrmoos

Oberstdorf

Rohrmoos Valley

Trechtach Valley

Oy Valley

Grosser
Wilder

Lake Freiberg

Lesser Walser Valley

Schlappolt

Himmel-
schrofen

Gutenalp

Fellhorn

Wildgundkopf

*Warmats-
gund*

Einödsberg

Mittelberg

Rossgund

Rlappenalp Valley

Krottenspitzen

Mädelegabel

Wilder Mann

Widderstein

Biberalp

Lake Rappen

Hochrappenkopf

Biberkopf

Allgäu and the Vorarlberg.

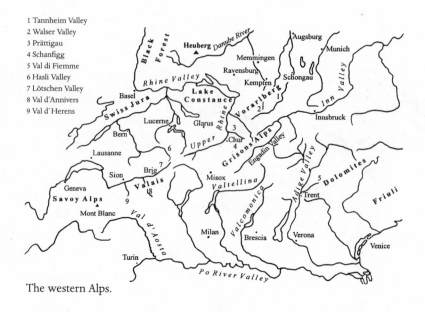

1 Tannheim Valley
2 Walser Valley
3 Prättigau
4 Schanfigg
5 Val di Fiemme
6 Hasli Valley
7 Lötschen Valley
8 Val d'Anniviers
9 Val d'Herens

The western Alps.

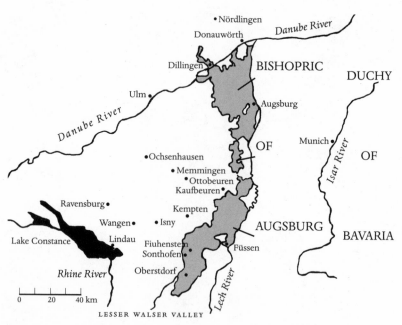

The Prince Bishopric of Augsburg in 1600.

SHAMAN OF
OBERSTDORF

1.

Herdsmen

ONE EVENING, EIGHT DAYS before Shrovetide, Chonrad Stoeckhlin and Jacob Walch were sitting together. Both of them were herdsmen, the horse wrangler and oxherd for the town of Oberstdorf in the mountains of Allgäu, and they were drinking, which was reckoned a "manly" pleasure. Although more or less on the margins of their rural society, they were still able to afford wine. There was little work for herdsmen in winter, and so they were swapping tales, and not just trivial stories about the events of the day or ordinary village gossip. Instead they were discussing serious topics, metaphysical matters,—specifically the "last things" in a person's life. Their conversation veered far from what faithful Catholics or Protestants, or any manner of Christians for that matter, were supposed to believe in that age. One of these men wound up paying for these stories with his life. And with him were executed a large number of other inhabitants of the Oberstdorf Valley. These stories were no simple children's fairy tales. These words were deadly.[1]

The place and the actors in this history are easily sketched. Oberstdorf in the Allgäu belonged to the judicial district of Rettenberg, the most southern of the sixteen administrative districts of the prince-bishopric of Augsburg, a territory belonging to the prince-bishop of Augsburg.[2] This little principality of roughly a thousand square miles had fewer than a hundred thousand inhabitants, stretching along the rivers Lech and Iller from the alpine Oberstdorf Valley in the south to the banks of the Danube in the north. There it bordered on the principality of Palatinate-Neuburg; to the east was the great duchy of Bavaria; and to the west and north lay a scattering of tiny territories, the largest of which were the county of Königsegg-Rothenfels and the imperial abbey of Kempten. The prince-bishopric of Augsburg was not an integrated territorial state like the county of Tyrol, over on the south side of the Allgäu Alps, but rather a conglomeration of episcopal holdings, each obtained under different legal titles and broken up by the competing legal rights of monasteries, knights, and cities. Above all, the mighty imperial city of Augsburg, with its almost fifty thousand inhabitants, stuck like a thorn in the flesh of the prince-bishopric. The famous city of the financial houses Fugger and Welser had long since freed itself from the jurisdiction of the bishop, who paled in financial significance compared to the wealthy city. And because of its resistance, the bishop, for his part, had long since abandoned Augsburg, transferring his residence north to Dillingen on the Danube. There he founded a small university with faculties of theology and philosophy because the educational facilities of the now mainly Protestant imperial city seemed to him thoroughly polluted.[3] The prince-bishop of Augsburg residing in Dillingen during the years in which our story takes place was a nobleman from the region of Ulm, Marquard vom Berg (1528–1591), a strict and zealous proponent of the Counter Reformation.[4]

But this is not a story about a spiritual overlord or about a judge in his administration or a theologian at his university. This is a story about a man at the other end of the social hierarchy, the horse wrangler Chonrad Stoeckhlin (1549–1587), who was discussing life and death with his friend the oxherd Jacob Walch. In general, of course, we know less about horse wranglers than about bishops. In this case, however, because of the more or less voluntary tales of the herdsman, as transcribed by the clerk of the court of Rettenberg, we actually know a few facts. Stoeckhlin was born in 1549 in the little mountain town of Oberstdorf, and he spent his whole life in that region. He had surely visited the horse markets in Sonthofen, Mittelberg, Oberstaufen, and Immenstadt, but it is unclear that he ever went farther, for example to Lindau or Bregenz on the Lake of Constance, thirty miles to the west, to Füssen on the Forggensee to the east, or to Kempten, twenty-five miles north.

Stoeckhlin's life did not revolve about the towns or villages of the alpine foothills. Instead he lived his life in the high valleys of the Alps themselves.

Herdsmen

In the valley of Oberstdorf, a name that refers to the "uppermost village" of the Ill Valley, eleven smaller valleys come together, and cattle and horses were driven up into these valleys during the warmer months of the year. Up on the high alpine meadows, at elevations of 5,000 to 6,500 feet, we find the real home of these herdsmen. From the best-known peaks of the Allgäu Alps—Rubihorn, Nebelhorn, Himmelhorn, Grosser Wilder, Rauheck, Krottenspitzen, Mädelgabel, Wilder Mann, Biberkopf, Hammerspitzen, and Fellhorn[5]—views opened south toward the great scenery of the central Alps, the 13,000-foot-high snow-capped roof of Europe.

With its uplands, Oberstdorf was one of the more important regions of the alpine chain. It had been given a parish structure already in the days of the Carolingians, and in 1422 it became the jurisdictional center for the knights of Heimenhofen. Stoeckhlin's ancestors had belonged to the official association of Heimenhofen subjects and were thus some of the oldest inhabitants of the village. In a list of the serfs of Heimenhofen recorded in the year 1440, we find the name of a certain Chonradt Stoeckhlin, presumably the same man who bought his freedom from serfdom (and that of his wife Auffren Ursellerin, along with all their children) in 1448. First names were often handed down in a family, and so we can be fairly certain that this man was an ancestor of our horse wrangler. Yet another Chonrat Stöcklin, perhaps the son of the first one, is mentioned in 1478 as a shoemaker in Oberstdorf, a citizen and an artisan. By then, clearly, the family had risen into the circle of "free citizens."[6] In the late Middle Ages, the lords of Heimenhofen, who had grown wealthy by entering the service of the Italian city of Pisa and had bought up the old holdings of the lords of Rettenberg, were increasingly overshadowed by even mightier feudal lords. In 1453 they lost the Lesser Walser Valley to Austria, and in 1477 they lost Oberstdorf and all the rest of their holdings to Bishop Johann of Augsburg. In 1495 Oberstdorf was elevated by King Maximilian to the rank of market town and transferred as a fief to the bishop of Augsburg.

The bishop of Augsburg in turn named Oberstdorf as the seat of an episcopal high court, but that court existed only in theory, just as with the high courts of Rettenberg and Wertach. Actually, the judge and district governor resided only in Sonthofen, which was therefore, de facto, the seat of criminal jurisdiction for the district of Rettenberg within the bishopric of Augsburg. Sonthofen, which had fallen into the hands of the bishopric of Augsburg only a few years earlier than Oberstdorf, was far and away the most important town in the episcopal district of Rettenberg because it was both a mining center and a market for the trade in cattle and linen. Even so it numbered hardly more than six hundred inhabitants.[7] Like Oberstdorf it never had city walls and was separated from its hinterland only by a fence. To be sure, Oberstdorf was legally entitled to fortifications, but because of its well-protected location, walls were unnecessary. Oberstdorf possessed some 227 houses, or 348 houses counting the surrounding villages in the district: one might estimate the total population at some 1,925 inhabitants.[8] What moneys they had, the proceeds from licensed businesses (such as taverns, mills, etc.), for example, might have been spent more prudently, for the community of Oberstdorf had built itself a "dance house" in 1476. It was there that the town court and the communal assembly met. The town claimed extensive rights of self government and could afford to employ several communal workers, including the herdsmen.[9]

The post of horse wrangler was the most eminent in the hierarchy of herdsmen, well above the more numerous herdsmen for oxen, cows, goats, sheep, and geese.[10] In the Allgäu as in many other places horses were regarded as prestige animals, whose care demanded the greatest attention and the highest qualifications.[11] Whoever held the highly responsible position of horse wrangler usually tried to pass on the job to his heirs just as if it were a trade. This was also the case with Chonrad Stoeckhlin. His father, Hans Stoeckhlin, had been Oberstdorf's official horse wrangler for almost thirty years before him, from 1539 until 1567. The economy of the Oberstdorf valley depended to a large extent upon raising cattle and horses, although others raised flax, cut wood, and tended the forests, as was typical in the Allgäu. Among the trades we find linen weavers, cloth bleachers, beer brewers, sculptors, fiddlers, locksmiths, potters, coppersmiths, and nail makers.[12] The chief citizens of the town were drawn not only from among the artisans but also from among the managers of the episcopal manors. These leading citizens included families such as the Kapellers, the Schraudolphs, and the Straubs. Innkeepers, too, played an important role in the life of the town, and we must not forget the pastor, who tended to the salvation of souls but also represented the bishop's government. Like every decent Catholic priest, including the prince-abbot of Kempten and the bishop of Augsburg, the pastor of Oberstdorf in the 1580s had a "concubine." It was only at the end of that decade that the decrees of the Council of Trent regarding priestly celibacy were actually implemented. The fact that this change (at least in this region) came so suddenly had—like so many other events of the late 1580s—something to do with the strange stories told by Chonrad Stoeckhlin.

Breeding horses was a specialty of the Allgäu, and horses were raised not just for local use but also for export to Graubünden and Italy, to the Tyrol and Württemberg. Count Marcus Fugger (1529–1597), the owner of a stud farm in the neighboring village of Hindelang, wrote in 1584 in his book, *On Horse Breeding* (the first German book on raising horses), "From ages ago the horses of the Allgäu and of Switzerland have been highly valued, especially because they are excellent war horses, durable and hard-working."[13] Around the region of Oberstdorf there were high pastures set aside just for horses: to the southeast the Rossgundalp at the end of the valley of the Warmatsgund;[14] to the northeast the Rettenställe on the Rossbichl and the Rossgehren on the Rubihorn. Old field names like Rossgund and Rosshag and Rosshof testify to other old horse meadows. The hooves of horses could easily damage the thin layer of humus and soil on these high meadows, and in the fifteenth century special alpine ordinances began to establish exactly how many horses were allowed in each meadow. In the region of Oberstdorf, therefore, most of the meadows were used by a mixture of cows and horses, in exactly regulated ratios. We know that the following meadows were used for horses: the Seealpe on the Seealpsee above the anterior Oy Valley and the Gutenalp up in the farthest reaches of the Oy Valley (in 1629 the ratio was 149 cattle to 34 horses); the meadows of the Einödsberg and Mädele, lying on the slopes of the high Mädelgabel at 8,500 feet (140 steers to 19 horses); south of Oberstdorf, the "Ringatsgrund" between Himmelschrofen and Wildgundkopf; southwest of Oberstdorf, the Sölleralpe and the meadow of Schlappold on the Söllerkopf; the meadow of Warmatsgund (141 cattle to 15 horses) and the two meadows lying in the valley of the Warmatsgund, called the Bierenwang; the meadows of Taufersberg and Rossgund at the entrance to the valley of the Rappenalp; the Linggersalp and the Rappenalpe in the distant parts of the valley of the Rappenalp, up on the slopes of the Hochrappenkopf at an altitude of almost 8,200 feet; and finally the Biberalp and the meadow of Haldenwang in the farthest reaches of the valley of the Rappenalp, in the main ridge of the Allgäu Alps.[15]

When Stoeckhlin's father went blind in 1567 and could no longer care for the town's animals, Chonrad took over this communal job, being then eighteen years old. Presumably he had already helped out with herding duties, as was customary, because herdsmen were skilled employees with several helpers, usually including their own sons. Chonrad was therefore well prepared for his new tasks. After taking over his father's position, the Stoeckhlins continued for a time to dwell together, because the new official herdsman did not yet have his own household. It was only after the death of his mother that his family life changed completely. Ursula Stoeckhlin, who was generally known by her maiden name, Ursula Schedlerin, died in a year of great famine, in 1571.[16] Chonrad's blind father then moved into the spital in neighboring Sonthofen, and so at the age of twenty-two Chonrad took over his parents' house in Oberstdorf and married a girl from the village, Anna Berchtoldin, of a family that had just moved in from the Walser valley to the south.[17] In the course of fifteen years of marriage, Anna and Chonrad had seven children, of whom only two survived. One child was stillborn, and four others died shortly after their birth. The Stoeckhlin house lay on the edge of Oberstdorf, probably toward the south in the direction of the Stillach valley (most of his testimony mentions places in this direction). That would not be too surprising because most of the horse meadows were also in this direction—in the valleys of the Warmatsgund and the Rappenalp. Stoeckhlin expressed satisfaction that he was able to keep a cow over the winter at his house, for in this way he had a guaranteed supply of milk and cheese, on which their lives depended, as well as manure for their garden. They could not live extravagantly, but they had enough. The herdsman had a home and a hearth, a wife and children. That fateful conversation with his friend, the oxherd Jacob Walch, seems to have taken place in Stoeckhlin's house.[18]

The cosmographer and geographer from Basel, Sebastian Münster, reported in his *Cosmographia* of 1544 that the Allgäu "is a land of rough win-

Herdsmen

ters, but it has handsome and sturdy people, both women and men."[19] We have no idea, however, of how Stoeckhlin actually looked. We do have pictures of most of the princes and bishops of the sixteenth century, but for simple people that is almost never the case. We do get an impression of how a typical herdsman from the Allgäu looked from an altar painting finished in the same year that Stoeckhlin took over his father's position, an altar painting for the wooden chapel of St. Anna in Rohrmoos, near Oberstdorf. Over their tight leggings herdsmen wore a tunic or poncho belted at the waist, sturdy shoes, and a hooded jacket. They might wear a hat with a rakish feather and carry a bagpipe or a long-bladed knife, a so-called "stag killer," much like those we can still admire in the Walser Museum in Riezlern. But can we trust this altar image in Rohrmoos? Although this panel painting was commissioned by the Truchsess Jacob von Waldburg and by his wife Johanna von Zimmern, and even though it betrays the clear influence of Dürer's woodcuts, the artist's care in rendering local details is unmistakable. The peaks of the Allgäu Alps rise steeply against the sky and in the background of this Christmas theme, the "Adoration of the Shepherds," we can recognize a man blowing an alpenhorn, possibly the first one recorded in art history.[20] The modest costume of these herdsmen might have been just what Stoeckhlin wore, for, as we shall see, he belonged to the society of herdsmen, although he was among the more successful of them. We know less about his drinking companion, the oxherd Jacob Walch, whose family name first appears in the records of Oberstdorf in the years around 1500. It is not to be found in earlier lists of hearths and serfs. Walch was a Walser name, and it seems likely that his family also came into Oberstdorf from the Walser valley.[21]

Stoeckhlin enjoyed a certain level of respect in Oberstdorf, but not just because of his employment and the usual supplementary jobs it provided. Herdsmen served, after all, as veterinarians; like blacksmiths, midwives, and executioners, their help was much in demand for human sicknesses, too.[22] Herdsmen exchanged medical recipes, but other occupational groups also shared in the healing trades. A bathhouse owner in the Tannheim valley, for example, owned a book of magic and exchanged his horse-blessings for money.[23] Stoeckhlin must have supplemented his income by using his knowledge of animals and of nature, and thus in addition to his communal salary he received extra pay in goods and money. And yet his abilities were not based only on his professional experience or on the magical recipes and ceremonies he had learned. In fact it is most unlikely that he could actually read magical recipes, for he had never attended school. And yet he had obtained abilities that went far beyond those of his rural neighbors. And it is these special abilities of Stoeckhlin—and their dire consequences—that even today whet our appetite to know more about this particular wrangler.

2.

Shrovetide Conversations

So it came to pass that Stoeckhlin and his comrade, the oxherd Jacob Walch, were sitting, drinking wine at the home of the horse wrangler "eight days before Shrove Tuesday" in 1578. On a freezing night during that snowy winter, they were discussing a grim subject, and the exact time of their conversation was not insignificant for their choice of topic.[1] This example, however, also illustrates how approximate our reconstruction of these and other events must be. "Eight days before Shrove Tuesday" would have been the Monday evening before the Sunday known as Estomihi, the Shrovetide Sunday (9 February 1578). And so the exact date of their meeting would have been 3 February 1578.[2] But we must take all such dates with a grain of salt because they rest on a written record of oral testimony, which in turn rested only on memory. On another occasion Stoeckhlin remembered the night of drinking as a Wednesday, which would have made it 5 February.[3] And on a third occasion he mentioned Thursday (6 February), which was known in Allgäu folklore as Hopping Thursday (*Gumpige Donnerstag*), an important holiday on which all the normal rules of daily conduct were suspended. It was a day for the games of "the world turned upside down".[4]

Fortunately for our interpretation of events, these details are not crucial. The weeks before and after the Sunday of Estomihi, the seventh Sunday before Easter, were recognized as a special time not only by the church year (as the beginning of Lenten fasting) but also by folk beliefs.[5] Up to the Sunday known as Invocavit, the sixth Sunday before Easter and the first Sunday of Lent, known in the Allgäu as the Fire Sunday (*Funkensonntag*), the deadly forces of winter wrestled with the forces of life to determine the fertility of the coming year. Certain ancient rituals were connected to these ideas, rituals that were often opposed by the church, such as the burning of annual bonfires. On the evening of Fire Sunday in the Allgäu a life-sized effigy was symbolically burnt.[6] At this time of struggle between life and death, just as on Twelfth Night between Christmas and the Day of Three Kings, spirits circulated in great numbers; devils might rub elbows with the masked revelers, as many legends recounted, and at night one might see the "wild horde," the society of the unquiet dead.[7]

And so it was no coincidence that at this time of year the two herdsmen were talking about death. Or, to speak more precisely, about death and about whatever came after death. This question fascinated the two herdsmen, as it has many others, but it was prudent to talk about such matters only in small groups, within the family or among good friends. One was never well advised to discuss such topics on Sunday outside the church, where then as now men of the Allgäu passed the time during divine services. After all, the doctrine of the Roman Catholic Church prescribed exactly what one was supposed to think about the time after death. Curiosity about it might imply that one did not accept the crystal-clear teachings of the church about the hereafter, even though there seemed to be so many unanswered questions about the period between one's death and the last judgment. How did official doctrine fit with the common stories about the People of the Dead,[8] the Wild Hunt, the Unquiet Dead, revenants and specters? The French scholar Claude Lecouteux has pointed out the difficult problems medieval Christian theologians had in dealing with these non-Christian ideas.[9] But if official churchmen had their difficulties, how much more difficult must it have been for simple people? Artisans and peasants were accustomed to boast self-confidently of their own experiences, and people in the Allgäu were certainly not used to believing blindly everything their rulers told them to believe.

And yet how could one obtain knowledge about conditions in the hereafter? How could one experience a world that one could not enter as a living person? Theoretically, one could force a spirit or a dead person to talk, but necromancy was not only a difficult art, it was dangerous as well as strictly forbidden,[10] as Johann Hartlieb (1400–1468) had written: "The very worst part of necromancy . . . is the art of awakening the dead in order to ask them about the future and the past."[11] And besides, it was not supposed to be just any dead man but rather someone whom one had known and trusted. So it was that the oxherd Walch finally made the following proposal, as Chonrad Stoeckhlin later testified:

"Jacob spoke to him and pressed him hard that he should agree and promise that whichever of the two should die first should come to the other one (as long as God did not forbid it) and [should] show him what it is like in that world."[12] Naturally, Stoeckhlin presented his story to the magistrates as if it had taken great powers of persuasion to convince him of this proposal. Be that as it may, he did agree to the proposal, and the two herdsmen turned their mutual promises into a contract[13] and probably sealed it the way cattle dealers still do in the Alps today, with a handshake.

3.

The Specter's Message

CONTRACTUAL THINKING HAS always played an important role in European culture. So even though Roman Law said nothing about contracts that required someone to return from the dead, the agreement between Chonrad Stoeckhlin and Jacob Walch was not without consequences. Exactly eight days after their agreement, on Shrove Tuesday (11 February 1578) or according to two other versions of this story on one day later, on Ash Wednesday at the beginning of Lenten fasting, the oxherd Jacob Walch died suddenly.[1] On this day Christians have for centuries strewn ashes on their heads, "For thou art dust and to dust shalt thou return." In the local folklore, dying at so significant a time could hardly be an accident and certainly must have heightened Chonrad Stoeckhlin's expectations.[2] Ash Wednesday was a day of death, and yet his comrade could not turn into mere dust for he was now under contractual obligation.

After another eight days, on Thursday, 20 February 1578, on the day after the spring Ember day, Chonrad was walking in a woods to cut down a fir tree, probably for firewood. He described what happened next in the following words: "When he was just about done, he looked around, and there at . . . [a placename], about one gunshot's distance from him he saw something standing. He concluded that it was the above-named Walch. Then he got up and came as close as two yards to him, unafraid and without any horror, and spoke to him, asking, 'Jacob, is that you?'"

This ghostly visitor from the hereafter, who inspired no "horror" in Stoeckhlin because it was his best friend, answered, "Yes." And after identifying himself, the dead man passed on the information he had promised to the horse wrangler. Jacob Walch spoke in the following words:

The Specter's Message

Chonrad, we are common herdsmen, and we occasionally get totally drunk. Give it up! Behave yourself well toward God, toward the world, and toward the magistrates. For whoever lives in drunkenness, adultery, blasphemy, avarice, pride, anger, envy, and hatred and does not teach his children to fear and obey the Lord, will not enter into the Kingdom of God.

Pay attention and confess, repenting your sins here on earth so that you do not come to that place where I am, for I now must walk about the earth for three years and then suffer four years of pain and torture in the fires of purgatory.[3]

Stoeckhlin may have found this an astonishing message, but it may also have been just what he was expecting. In any event, there was little difference in its substance from what the priest had been preaching, except for the bit about the three years of restless walking about. The revenant spirit had recited the whole list of deadly sins, which had been sedulously cataloged by the Christian church for centuries in order to give the faithful some conception of their sins.[4] Returned from death, the oxherd thus confirmed several central teachings of the Roman Catholic Church concerning life after death, the connection between sin and repentance, as well as the existence of purgatory, that third place which stood as a barrier between one's starting point and one's goal.

It is also possible, of course, that Stoeckhlin merely made up this part of his story in order to impress the magistrates. But his steadfast insistence upon its details makes this unlikely, and his story also contained certain unorthodox details he should never have brought to the attention of the episcopal authorities: for example, his doubts about the doctrine of the afterlife, the contract that obliged one of them to return from death, the very possibility of returning from death, which the returning ghost confirmed in both word and deed, but which would have offended almost any theologian. Such a ghostly return was conceivable as a miracle, to be sure, if God gave someone a special task to perform, but in this case—and among mere herdsmen!—it had to seem most unlikely for contemporary theologians. Here one herdsman was speaking to another, and with a special appeal to their very status as herdsmen: "We are common herdsmen." The ghost had fulfilled his part of the bargain in returning, a fact worthy of serious theological reflection. And so were the other assertions of the horse wrangler. He testified that since the initial visitation, Jacob Walch had appeared several times to him, five times in all. At each appearance he had warned him "to behave righteously and reasonably." And he was told to pray nine rosaries a day, of which three should contain the Lord's Prayer and the Ave Maria, three the Ave Maria alone, and three the simple creed. Since then, Stoeckhlin and his family had adopted these prayers.

The idea of a dead person returning from the hereafter to instruct those left behind, and especially returning after making a mutual agreement or contract, is well known to scholars who study narratives. In international motif indexes it is classified as no. 470,[5] while the German catalog of legends places it in Class X, "Death and the Dead," Group F, "Unfulfilled Obligations," no. 29.[6] And one can easily see that this motif was not only alive in folktales but already had a long tradition in medieval theology. The church fathers Ambrose, Jerome, and Augustine, and many others wrote about it and mentioned examples, but always with the proviso that such miracles were possible only through the power and special permission of God. It is no wonder then that this theme returns in late medieval sermon collections.[7] Roman Catholic theologians living at the time of Stoeckhlin, and specifically the Jesuits Peter Canisius (1521–1597) and Gregory of Valencia (1550–1603), who were active at the episcopal university of Dillingen, the first purely Jesuit university in Germany, and downstream at Bavarian Ingolstadt, argued within this tradition.[8] Other contemporary demonologists employed the same theme.[9] We can assume that zealous village pastors throughout the bishopric of Augsburg tried to impress their flocks with such stories, too. We know for certain how earnestly these priests tried in their sermons to have an effect on their rural congregations and how this forced them to take the prejudices and ideas of their listeners into account.[10]

The motif of the agreement to return is also well known in medieval literature. A folklorist at the University of Innsbruck, Leander Petzold, has shown that a passage in the *Gesta regum anglorum* (*Chronicle of the Kings of England*) by William of Malmesbury (d. 1142) served as a prototype and was picked up in exemplum literature, and from there made its way into folk tradition.[11] The prolific seventeenth-century writer from Nuremberg, Erasmus Francisci (1627–1694), however, quoted a story from the *Speculum Historiale* of Vincent of Beauvais (ca. 1184/94–1264), giving it the new title, "Appointment with an Apparition."[12] The most widely known collection of legends in the Middle Ages was the *Legenda aurea* (*Golden Legend*), composed before 1267 by Jacopo da Voragine. There we find a story that was supposedly derived from an experience of Magister Siger of Brabant (1235–1282), one of the most renowned scholars of his age, who taught at the University of Paris until 1270, when his brand of Aristotelianism, much influenced by Averroës, brought him too near to outright heresy because it made too sharp a distinction between theology and philosophy.

> Master Silo asked one of his students, who happened to be very ill, to return to him after his death and report how things stood. After a few days he did appear to him, dressed in a hooded gown of parchment that was inscribed on the outside with all kinds of deceptive pieces of wisdom while the inside was lined with hellish fire. Silo (that is, Siger of Brabant) asked the apparition who he was. "I am he whom you invited to return." So then Silo asked how things were for him, and he received the following answer: "This cowl weighs heavily on me and oppresses me more weightily than if I were crushed beneath a tower."

Moreover, the returning ghost described how heavy were the penances imposed because of his earthly life and displayed them to the Master in such a way that he decided to renounce the world and to enter a monastery.[13] These stories did not illuminate merely theoretical truths, as we can see from the warnings that Johann Hartlieb gave to Margrave Johann von Brandenburg, that trying to make such contracts often invited the devil to put in an appearance.[14]

In the folklore of the alpine region, this motif of making a contract for someone to return after death survived until just a few years ago, as we can see, for example, in a systematic collection of legends from the German-speaking Upper Valais [in Switzerland] at the beginning of the 1960s.[15] In a typical example taken from the Glödnitz valley of Carinthia (in southern Austria), moreover, we find the following story:

> In Glödnitz there were two peasants who were extremely close friends. Often they talked about what it would probably be like in eternity, and

they came up with one idea after another. Once they promised each other that whoever should die first would return and tell the other what it was like in the hereafter. And one did in fact die shortly thereafter, and just when the fire in the hearth flickered out, he did indeed appear as a spirit to his neighbor, murmuring: "It isn't like what I thought, and it isn't like what you thought. But one can tell that the rules there are followed exactly." And with these words the ghost disappeared.[16]

Again and again herdsmen appear as the protagonists in these stories, for example in this legend from the Lower Valais, which took place on the meadow Rouaz in the Val d'Annivers (called the Einfisch Valley in German), a locality that was part of the alpine pastoral economy.[17] Here we find a contract to return from the dead that involved two herdsmen, a tale that survived in the narratives collected in the nineteenth century and that represents a case just like that of Chonrad Stoeckhlin and his friend Jacob Walch.[18]

4.

An Angel Appears

THOSE TWO SHROVETIDE weeks of 1578—a period lasting from the fateful agreement to return from the dead, through the death of his friend Jacob Walch, to his return—changed Chonrad Stoeckhlin's life. With his family the herdsman now embarked on a new way of living. He did penance according to the instructions he had received so as to avoid the pains of purgatory. His new religious orientation, with penances and continuing communications with the revenant dead man, was by no means the end, however. Instead they marked only the beginning of a psychological evolution away from his earlier life. In many respects these outward signs look like a rite of transition, not some collective "rite of passage" to a new stage in the life cycle, but rather an initiation into a new and individual stage of existence.[1] These new works of penance had the character of a highly individualized ritual purification, signaling the transition from Stoeckhlin's old life to the new. The religious usages of the church, of course, also prescribed ascetic exercises, but for Chonrad Stoeckhlin his reorientation did not serve to initiate him into the mysteries of the Christian faith.

Rather, the herdsman used his purification from worldly lusts to establish continuing contacts with the "other world." Four times his former friend, the oxherd Jacob Walch, appeared to him as a messenger from the hereafter. But this served only as a preparation for much more intensive encounters with the supernatural. The folk culture of the sixteenth century taught that after strenuous efforts one should obtain a reward, and after a year of penance, this period of transition was over. An angel appeared to Chonrad Stoeckhlin, but not just any angel, for this was now his personal angel. This spirit had nothing in common with Christian ideas of a guardian angel, whose existence the Roman Catholic Church had preached ever since the early Middle Ages.[2] This one had a totally different function. Here is what investigators recorded of Stoeckhlin's first encounter: "After this, a year later, a vision appeared to him one night around Our Lady's Birthday at Reicherberg Lake, over above Oberstdorf in the Holzmäden, a vision of a person dressed in white with a red cross on his (or her) forehead. And it spoke to him: 'If you would learn that Jacob Walch did not mislead you, and where he is, then follow me.'"

Criminal investigators have learned to regard such references to an exact time and place—Reicherberg Lake (known today as Freibergsee) above Oberstdorf; and Mary's Birthday, that is, 8 September 1579—as marks of authenticity. We must allow for the fact that this testimony was given in criminal proceedings directed by professional jurists, but that does not mean that it is necessarily all false. Our suspicion that he was telling the truth is bolstered by the fact that Stoeckhlin's description of the apparition was not at all what the episcopal authorities wanted to hear.

Angels of the Lord had appeared to shepherds in the time of Jesus' birth, as the Gospel of Luke clearly testified.[3] And of course some of the churches of the region possessed pictures of the "Annunciation to the Shepherds." After a thousand years of Christianity, however, and especially in a spiritual territory of the Holy Roman Empire, far more highly qualified recipients for divine messages were available. The jurists and theologians of the bishop of Augsburg, in any event, did not want to hear so much as one word about a shining angel with a cross on its forehead. The famous French advocate, Jean Bodin (1530–1596) maintained that these kinds of shining angels could actually be the devil.[4] So with his description of the angel, even such a stereotyped angel as this, Stoeckhlin revealed a piece of his own mental world. And he repeatedly insisted on this image even though it must have become quickly obvious to him that the authorities rejected it. With this confession Stoeckhlin began to place his own life at risk.

Stoeckhlin's story of his encounter with the angel was only the beginning, for this angel had no message like the one conveyed by the angel of the Lord in the Gospel of Luke (Luke 2:8–12). This one had no glad or sad tidings; instead he commanded the herdsman to follow him. And the herdsman followed him in a strange way, as investigators recorded: "And so he fell as if unconscious. And thus in a rapture he went with him to a place where he observed pain and joy, which he took to be purgatory and paradise. There he saw many people, but recognized no one."

With these words Stoeckhlin claimed nothing more or less than that in a state of unconsciousness he had been carried away, suddenly and without his doing anything himself, to a strange and distant place. Later he repeatedly said more precisely that this "rapture" had not been a bodily flight. Just like anthropologists of the twentieth century,[5] the inquisitors of the fifteenth through the seventeenth centuries were keen to learn whether the body or only the soul had flown through the air. Although informants often find this distinction unimportant, their answer has usually been that the soul leaves the body, which stays behind as a kind of husk or shell. The soul then travels out of the body and goes to distant places. Students of comparative religion have found many cases of this kind of description. Religious specialists in many cultures establish contact in this way with the regions of the "other side," with the upper world or the lower world, or just with distant territories. And the traveler must then report back to those who have stayed behind.[6]

Stoeckhlin's soul journey took him to places that seemed similar to the Christian purgatory and to paradise, where one could see "joy and suffering." But how did Stoeckhlin know how paradise and purgatory looked? At least with respect to purgatory we can answer this question. The idea of purgatory, invented in the twelfth and thirteenth centuries as a response to social changes brought by the beginnings of urbanization, was elaborated by mystics and synthesized in the early fourteenth century, for example, by Dante Alighieri (1265–1326) into a grand vision,[7] which then dramatically influenced folk beliefs. In addition to sermons about purgatory, altar paintings had a decisive impact on the reception of these ideas. This form of graphic representation was common around 1500 in southern Germany. Usually the "poor souls" in purgatory were depicted on the predellas of altars, that is, under the middle panel of the high altar.[8] An inventory of the art works from the district of Sonthofen shows that these pictures were by no means rare in Oberstdorf and its surroundings, but because of major town fires (in Oberstdorf most recently in 1865), surviving depictions all date from later periods. We can assume, however, that they usually replaced older pictures portraying the same motifs.[9]

If we compare Stoeckhlin's experience of rapture with the mystic visions of saints from the early and high Middle Ages, we find nothing especially "original" except for the fact that a common herdsman was claiming an experience usually reserved for saints.[10] But for that there was the precedent of the New Testament's annunciation of Christ's birth to humble shepherds. And so Stoeckhlin's story followed mainly orthodox channels, if one grants that angelic visions containing personal information might be religiously tolerable.

> But when he came back from there, the vision told him that he should charge his wife and children with the obligation to pray thirty thousand Ave Marias (which is said to be Our Lady's Robe) during each Ember season. And if he with his wife and children were able, they should attend Holy Mass eagerly. And they should hold the Sacrament in honor. And then he returned, he knew not how, to the same place where he had been lifted up.

This initiation by the appearance of the angel, along with the rapture and the experience of what he saw on his trip, could have been overwhelming for a herdsman. But that might have been true too of the penitential exercises demanded of him, for they required truly superhuman acts of piety, which were surely not meant as a parody but must have signified Stoeckhlin's naive readiness to undertake a profound change in his way of life, a new Catholic regimen of faith. Praying thirty thousand Ave Marias in just three months would have meant more than three hundred prayers every day if we do not regard these quantities as merely symbolic. In the realm of magic and of faith, after all, it was probably prudent to take such demands literally. But what was such an impossible demand supposed to mean?

The answer to this question was revealed to Chonrad Stoeckhlin in yet another apparition from the hereafter. Shortly after the epiphany of the angel, in the Ember days of autumn, 1579, his departed partner Jacob Walch came again for a fifth and final time and lent the following interpretation to what Chonrad had seen: "After this, when Jacob Walch came to him again, he

An Angel Appears

asked him what it was that had taken him away. To this he answered that God Almighty had created an angel for him so that he might realize that he had not been and would not be misled."[11] The angel thus confirmed the message of the ghost from the hereafter, the realm of the dead, but at the same time made it more specific. And now his departed friend confirmed the legitimacy of the new messenger from the beyond. Such an explanation was quite timely because from then on this angel, dressed in white and with a red cross on his forehead, became Stoeckhlin's soul-guide.[12]

5.

The Phantoms of the Night

For our herdsman, this initiation by God's angel was not without serious consequences, both psychological and physical. If we take Stoeckhlin's tales at face value, he now changed both his behavior and his thinking. Obviously he and his family intensified their works of penance. And communication with the "other world" now became regular. The ghost had fulfilled his role as messenger from the beyond. Starting in autumn 1579, the angel of the Lord appeared to Stoeckhlin regularly during the four sets of Ember fast days each year, that is, at times that were of great significance to current folk beliefs, for they were generally associated with the appearance of spirits. Those Ember days fell in the third week of September and the third week of Advent; the first week of Lent (between Estomihi and Invocavit), during which Stoeckhlin had first seen the revenant oxherd Jacob Walch; and, finally, during the week of Pentecost.[1] Of course we have to be skeptical about this precision as to dates because the first apparition of the angel had apparently taken place eight days before the autumn Ember days, which would have been 16 September 1579.[2] But it was at least true that the apparition came regularly four times a year in the period around the Ember days, in the cycle that was important for any agrarian society: spring, summer, fall, and winter.

Whenever his guide appeared, Stoeckhlin would fall into a kind of trance. His body would remain motionless wherever he had been, while his soul separated itself from his body and followed his psychopomp, the angel. He evidently had no choice about participating in these travels, and they were not always pleasant. They traveled long distances and for many hours, in groups that included both men and women. And Stoeckhlin had a precise notion of this group and a specific name for it that he stubbornly held on to: "the phantoms of the night" (*die Nachtschar*). He testified as follows:

> He had no choice about taking part in his trip with the phantoms of the night. That is each Ember week on Friday. And Saturday after Ember Wednesday and mostly at night. Shortly before he was·to go off traveling he would be overcome by a lethargy, an unconsciousness. And then, as he thought, his soul would leave his body and travel thither, remaining separated for two or three hours. This would occur sometimes painlessly but sometimes with pain. But his body would remain wherever the trip seized him.
>
> And he confessed that whenever his soul was out on its travels, if his body was turned over on its other side, his soul could only reenter his body with difficulty or with great pains.[3]

Angels here, angels there! With this story Stoeckhlin clearly left the firm basis of Christian visions behind. Theological literature knew nothing of such night phantoms, and demonologists and jurists were no more familiar with the concept. In such cases, they tried to grasp any concept they did not fully understand by deploying the explanations that demonological theory offered. Seen from the perspective of ethnological theory and in comparison with other cultures, Stoeckhlin's experiences are easy to interpret. The phase of transition in Stoeckhlin's "rite of passage" was over and had concluded with his "incorporation" into a new position.[4] He had been accepted among the phantoms of the night.

Even modern scholarship, however, has difficulties with the terminology the horse wrangler used so stubbornly to describe his "journeys." It turns out that throughout the German language area there are precious few references to these "night phantoms" (the *Nachtschar*) And the few citations found in legend collections assembled between 1840 and 1940 present an interesting pattern, for they are geographically restricted to a small and well-defined area. The folklorist Klaus Beitl from Vienna has clarified this by pulling together all the regional legend collections. According to his mapping, the term *Nachtschar* can be found only in the area of eastern Switzerland in the valley of the upper Rhine, in the immediate surroundings of the old Rhaetian episcopal city of Chur,[5] and in the two side valleys on the east side of the Rhine that empty into the Rhine there, the Schanfigg and the Prättigau (also known as the Val Partens), which were two formerly Rhaeto-Roman and later Germanized[6] valleys of the Canton of Graubünden.[7] There the appearance of the night phantoms often announced a death. And to that extent there is a close connection with the idea of the people or tribe of the dead (*Totenvolk*), perhaps encouraged by an idea of the "poor souls [in purgatory]," which was peculiar to that bishopric and which prompted a peculiar form of pastoral practice there.[8] When a questionnaire was circulated around 1940 for the *Swiss Folklore Atlas* there were still two places that knew the concept of the phantoms of the night: Zizers in the Rhine Valley and St. Antönien in the Prättigau.[9]

With Chonrad Stoeckhlin's 1586 reference to the phantoms of the night we have by far the earliest specific mention of this particular notion. And yet it is hardly likely that our horse wrangler invented it or that it was invented all over again in another place but with a different meaning. Confronting the unexpected appearance of this concept, we must ask the methodological question of how far this oral tradition extended, a problem to which we will have to return.[10] Tales that connect the night phantoms to the "people of the dead," however, are dramatically different from the reports that Chonrad Stoeckhlin made about his "travels." Usually in Graubünden it is black-clad figures who proceed at moderate speed and in orderly processions at a low height above the ground through the villages, and whoever can see them receives a warning from them of his or her impending death. Stoeckhlin's stories do have much to say about death, beginning right off with the contract to return that he had made with his friend Jacob Walch, but obviously his trips were very different. Stoeckhlin flew at great speed over vast distances to "another world," guided by an angel clad in white. And quite apart from the angel, his was a journey of the living, a flight of the living to the realm of the dead, in order to observe purgatory, limbo, and the gates of hell, or paradise. Stoeckhlin too differentiated conceptually between the travels of the "poor souls," which he called the "righteous journey" (*rechte Fahrt*), and his own journeys with the phantoms of the night. It is also noteworthy that his participation in this journey did not announce a death at all, but rather was useful because the herdsman could ask his angel questions while under way and obtain important information about things that mattered to him. Except for the pains that he occasionally felt in his ecstasies as his soul left his body, his impressions of the night phantoms were thoroughly positive. Stoeckhlin saw himself as one of the chosen.

But because the concept of the phantoms of the night has never been found by narrative researchers outside of that small area described above, we have to take their findings about its provenance seriously. And we will have to pay attention to the differences between the myth of the night phantoms and that of the people of the dead. Georg Luck once wrote the following about the relation between the people of the dead and the phantoms of the night:

> The phantoms of the night are the more uncertain and more fantastic beings and in their peculiar form much less well known than the people of the dead. The former are also different from the people of the dead in that with them the usually grim ceremonies of death are replaced with uninhibited joys. These wild phantoms appear on lonely mountain meadows, participating in a joyful roundelay, like the witches. And an invisible music plays movingly beautiful tunes. This music of the night phantoms has been especially praised, being played not only for dances but also for the nocturnal journeys through mountainous gorges and ravines. Whenever a living person hears these wonderful tones, a nameless yearning seizes his or her heart, and he or she must follow the grim procession over mountain and valley until the bells of morning or the first cock's crow breaks the magic.[11]

These impressions of the phantoms of the night obviously contain motif elements that cannot be easily combined. The annunciation of death and the "nameless yearning" for an easier life stand in a dialectical relationship, but they also contradict each other as antitheses. The fear of death and the joy of life make up the biggest contradiction imaginable in the life of mankind, incarnating two opposing liminal experiences of just the sort that anthropologists often study. The phantoms of the night stand between these two poles, between heaven and hell. But where do their positive aspects come from? Whence the utopian notions of a better life? These appear in studies of regional narrative traditions under yet another name: "the people of the night."

6.

The People of the Night

IN THE LEGENDS OF Graubünden, the notion of the night phantoms is inextricably intertwined with the notion of a night people. Wherever the concepts are used, they are practically interchangeable.[1] The specific idea of a "people of the night," however, is found in a broader though still clearly definable geographical area. We find it in the legend collections of the Austrian state of Vorarlberg as well as in the neighboring Tyrolean Valley of the Paznaun and in the Oberstdorf basin going north into Germany, as well as in the legends of Liechtenstein, and in the Swiss cantons of Appenzell, St. Gallen, Graubünden, and Glarus.[2] Remnants of the notion also survive in the cantons of Uri, the Upper (German-speaking) Valais, the Lower (French-speaking) Valais, as well as in the Bernese Oberland. Indeed the earliest known reference to the German concept of *Nachtvolk* comes from the shores of the Lake of Brienz in the canton of Bern: in 1572 the Bernese District Governor Zehnder reported from Interlaken to the Small Council in Bern that a certain Barbara Rappold was claiming that she had herself traveled with the people of the night.[3] At that time Interlaken was the largest district of the canton of Bern, lying at the foot of the high Alps between Lakes Thun and Brienz. It bordered on the cantons of Lucerne and Valais and also on the other Bernese districts of Oberhasli, Thun, and Frutigen. Just as in Oberstdorf, there was a well-traveled path from Interlaken up into the high alpine valleys with their pastoral economy.[4] Ideas about a night people can in fact be found right across the Swiss Alps, from the Allgäu Alps in the northeast down to Lake Geneva in the southwest.

   Legends concerning the people of the night have been collected systematically ever since the mid nineteenth century. They appear first in the legend collections of Franz Josef Vonbun (1824–1870) from Vorarlberg,[5] of Alois Lütolf (1824–1879),[6] and Arnold Büchli (1885–1970) from Graubünden,[7] and of Johannes Jegerlehner (1871–1937) from Valais,[8] and of the Oberstdorf local historian Karl Reiser from the Allgäu.[9] Ever since Vonbun was introduced to this myth by his great aunt, a myth that even the brothers Grimm did not report, it has assumed a place of importance in regional research on story telling, even though it has been little noticed outside the region. In Switzerland the preliminary work that went into the *Swiss Atlas of Folklore* took account of these ideas, cataloged under the categories "Procession of the Dead and the Army of the Spirits" (*Totenzug* and *Geisterheer*), and yet the density of citations was inadequate because too few informants were questioned, and the categories used were not sufficiently differentiated. And so right from the start the notions of night people, phantoms of the night, and people of the dead were all jumbled together into one complex (question 136), while the notions of the wild hunt, the army of the spirits, and the witches' dance were thrown together into another (question 137). Asking the questions this way made it easy to confuse neighboring but different ideas, because informants were not asked specifically what they understood by such notions as "night phantoms" or "night people".[10]

In valleys that have been longer protected from tourism and from the collapse of the old village social structures,[11] as folklorists and legend collectors have long recognized, the myth of the night people remained strong well into the twentieth century. Georg Luck, for example, wrote in 1935 that in the German-speaking valleys of Graubünden there was hardly a single village that did not claim to have seen them occasionally.[12] And Karl Ilg reported as late as 1956, in his study of the Walsers in Vorarlberg: "Almost every community tells of the people of the night."[13] It was only in the succeeding generation that the notion appears to have disappeared. Or perhaps it is true that these days the authors of local history refuse to listen to such mythologically charged stories. Thus in 1980 Ludwig Vallaster, in his local history of Montafon, spoke with considerable distaste about "that string of stories about spirits in our valley" recounted by "Dr. Beitl in his books," using a skeptical tone of voice, as if to suggest that the well-known expert on legends had actually invented these stories instead of merely reporting them.[14]

In the meanwhile, the varying interpretations of the myth concerning the night people have gathered their own history, and this aspect of our story is so fascinating that it deserves a short discussion of its own. We can obtain a good impression of the problem through the article entitled "Nachtvolk (Nachtschar)," or, "People of the Night (the Phantoms of the Night)," published in the *Encyclopedia of German Superstitions*, a large scholarly enterprise put together by Swiss folklorist Eduard Hoffmann-Krayer (1864–1936) and his student Hanns Bächtold-Stäubli (1886–1941).[15] The author of this article not only equated the night phantoms with the night people, but also identified them both with the people of the dead, equating them explicitly: "the people of the night and of the dead."[16] Moreover, basing his conclusions on the then current dissertation by Jacob Endter,[17] he equated all of these ideas with the notion of the "wild hunt" and the "furious army" (*die wilde Jagd, das wütende Heer*), which he in turn connected with the late Teutonic king of the gods, Wotan. It was 1934 after all, and Teutonic gods were highly prized, even in German-speaking Switzerland. Werner Lincke claimed that the mutually contradictory elements within the idea of the night people was evidence for the degeneration of a supposedly once-consistent myth, which of course must have had its origins in Germanic mythology.[18]

Arnold Büchli, a student of legends from Graubünden, argued more cautiously that it was hard to distinguish between the wild hunt (or as they called it in the Upper Rhine valley around Chur and in the Prättigau, "the flying army" [*ds flügend Heer*]) and the night people because "popular notions coming from both groups of legends have been mixed together."[19] Teasing apart elements that had grown together was obviously difficult. Even Klaus Beitl, who has argued in favor of a typological procedure, concluded dogmatically that Lincke was right and that the people of the night are "a leaderless army of black, sometimes horrible figures."[20] But the findings from the collections of legends from Vorarlberg are at sharp variance with this conclusion. There clothing is not usually mentioned at all, whereas in the *Swiss Folklore Atlas* we find regularly the explicit statement that the participants in the night people and in the night phantoms are dressed in white.[21]

The image of the night people, although it is more widespread than the idea of the night phantoms, means more than one thing. In essence the current conception of the people of the night pulls together two large and mutually contradictory groups of ideas. In Graubünden there are stronger

The People of the Night

hints of a gruesome people of the dead, who show themselves in the villages and warn individuals of their impending death or even foretell a great mass dying. Whoever tries to block the way of this people of the night will suffer harm just as do those who resist the "wild hunt" or the "furious army."[22] In Vorarlberg, in the Greater and Lesser Walser Valleys, and in the Bernese Oberland, however, the night people are more similar to fairy people, who do not bring harm to human beings but instead promise good fortune. The common element between these two conceptions is that these fairy people can also take up arms against troublemakers, as we know, for example, from Irish fairy stories. So here there are, indeed, points of connection between the people of the night, the wild hunt, and the society of witches, known as "striegen" in the Romantsch-speaking valleys of Graubünden.[23] But still they are not identical.

Beitl has tried in his most recent report on the literature concerning the legend of the night people to explain more historically why it spread where it did. Proceeding on the basis of the supposed fact that a cultural border runs through Vorarlberg, north of which one find regional narrative variants on the "wild hunt" (*Wuetas*, *Muetas*, etc.; see chapter 10), while to the south of this line one find the spirits of the people of the dead, the people of the night, or the phantoms of the night, Beitl concludes that this folkloric borderline corresponds to the early medieval language border between German-speakers and Romance-speakers, and that it was also the same as the borders (as of A.D. 600) between the bishoprics of Chur and Constance. He connects the diffusion of the *Wuetas*-myth therefore to the immigration of the Alemanni during the great period of Germanic migrations, but maintains that the fairy version of the night people myth was older, regionally more diffused, and possibly contained layers of Celtic tradition, which survived in Romanized Rhaetia. He theorized that this tradition was later taken over and handed down by specific immigrant groups, especially the Walsers. This would mean that during the high Middle Ages the myth of the people of the night was adopted by the Walsers in Graubünden and incorporated into their own traditions. Then with the migrations of the Walsers, the legends of the night people spread "beyond the area of Chur-Rhaetia," for example into the Lesser Walser Valley above Oberstdorf.[24] Beitl argues that in Graubünden especially the myth of the people of the night was disguised by the mythologem of the procession of the dead (an idea deeply influenced by Christian ideas) and claims that this disguise had its origins in the Reformation, which came into most of the valleys of the canton of Graubünden in the 1520s. In Beitl's words,

> I would like to suggest that this religious change in the sixteenth century altered the appearance and the distribution of the legends about the night people in Switzerland in such a way that under the influence of the Reformation, with the rationalizing spirit that came along with the Reformation, mythical and demonic elements in this group of legends were repressed. . . . The idea of a maleficent night people may thus have facilitated the spread of ideas concerning a people of the dead who presaged death.[25]

Beitl's attempt to explain the spread of legends historically is worth taking seriously even if he does not pay sufficient attention to the complexities of Swiss and Vorarlberg history,[26] for he did at least recognize the changeability and contingency in how legends get handed down. Many questions, however, remain unanswered. Looking at the whole, huge cultural area of the Celts, which extended during the five pre-Christian centuries from Ireland to central Anatolia, it is not at all clear why a conception of the night phantoms should have developed only in southern Switzerland or why the night people should arise only in the little region of the later bishopric of Chur, which after all had a partially Rhaetian and therefore non-Celtic population.[27] At the very least, the regional specificity of this myth requires explanation. Beitl's suggestion that it could have been a development of Rhaeto-Romantsch ideas that were adopted by the Germans, and that this process must have taken place after the year 1000 cannot be persuasive in the absence of even a shred of evidence. It is also highly problematic to connect the notion of *Wuetas* to the Alemannic "people," for this is a racial (*völkisch*) explanation of a set of beliefs.[28] As early as 1935 Karl Meisen expressed his opposition to the Teutonic mythologists by showing that ideas about a dangerous army of the dead also existed in Greek and Roman antiquity.[29] Analysis of the information submitted in the 1970s for a new *Swiss Atlas of Folklore* also showed that these kinds of myths transcended the borders of the four Swiss languages: German, French, Italian, and Rhaeto-Romantsch.

The People of the Night

In the light of modern conceptions of early medieval ethnogenesis, moreover, such racial and *völkisch* explanations are obviously faulty.[30]

In spite of these criticisms, however, Beitl's effort at separating myths and motif-combinations into their various roots in one restricted region remains striking. We know that pre-Roman ideas or abstractions survived in the region because some names for places and rivers have Celtic roots: the place-name "Cambodonum" survives as "Kempten," and "Brigantium" is "Bregenz"; the Argen, Iller, Wertach, Lech, and Isar Rivers are further examples of that sort.[31] We know of similar examples from the southern edge of the area through which the myth of the night people was diffused. The Roman "Vallis Poenina," the valley of Jupiter Poeninus, memorialized a union of Jupiter with a local god, but after the Christians demonized the pagan gods, the high alpine pass protector became the Great Saint Bernard, but a fragment of the old pagan name survived in the designation "Wallis" (in German) or "Valais" (in French).[32] Such concepts of *longue durée* usually testify to the continuity of population, and therefore to the potential continuity of traditions even in times of turbulent change. These examples were attached to fixed, material objects like mountains, rivers, and places, not to immaterial notions of the hereafter, but here too the possibility of continuity in cultic or religious conceptions should not be ruled out a priori. For certain periods we know of solid examples, as in the Christian continuity of worship from late antiquity to the early Middle Ages, or in the case of heathen religious continuities in various parts of Rhaetia. Archeological investigations into the early medieval gravefields of Bonaduz in Graubünden, where the anterior and posterior branches of the Rhine flow together, provide evidence for the survival of the practice of burying corpses with mortuary gifts (such as tools, food, and weapons) even after the region became Christian, strong evidence for what has been called the "stubbornness of old traditions, which were knitted together with new beliefs for as long as was possible."[33]

Of course one should not insist too strenuously on connections between prehistoric, ancient, or early medieval settlement patterns and patterns found as late as the nineteenth century. Just checking certain cultural forms against the patterns of political or settlement history should make us aware of the pitfalls. Take as an example the decisive rupture of burial practices in the Rhine Valley during the late third century, the transition from cremation to burial in the earth or the move to "orienting" the corpse so that it pointed toward the east, as was common from the fifth century onward. The addition of Christian memorials to the martyrs, the transformation of Alemannic grave fields into regular, walled-in Christian cemeteries with their own cemetery-churches, and the appearance of Christian priests as part of the burial ritual—all these must have dramatically changed the relationship between the living and the dead,[34] especially the newly central position of the Christian cemetery, which must have prompted everyone to think of a new solidarity between the living and the dead.[35]

It is even possible that burying the dead in groups in cemeteries evoked the first ideas of a people of the dead,[36] even though the purpose of building walls around cemeteries was originally a different one, namely the "pacification" of the restless dead, hindering their return from the hereafter.[37] The "presence of the dead" during the Christian Middle Ages testifies, on the one hand, to a kind of "dream time" that we usually associate with so-called primitive peoples, for whom the ghosts of ancestors remain ever-present; but on the other hand such ghosts were also supposed to be kept at a distance; they had to stay where they belonged.[38] The very intensity of the measures taken to pacify the dead, the cult of the dead, the cult of graves and sepulchers, and of Masses said for the soul prove that they were never quite sure that the dead would behave themselves. In this way we can see that heathen traditions lived on within the Christianity of Central Europe. Three additional developments had an impact on notions of ghosts and of life after death. The introduction of the Feast of All Souls (2 November) by Abbot Odilo of Cluny (994–1048), a feast that spread rapidly, the elaboration of the doctrine of sin during the high Middle Ages, along with the above-mentioned formulation of the idea of purgatory with its literary and artistic visions during the late Middle Ages, must all have strongly influenced the then-current notions of life after death, in which a reciprocal influence between popular and learned traditions must have been at work.[39]

Finally, we should ask whether we are dealing with a fully integrated myth at all when we take up the myth of the night people. Perhaps the notion was more a set of conceptual building blocks that could be and actually were

The People of the Night

combined in different ways, although within a restricted region, to make up distinct mythical concepts. Already in the sixteenth century certain observers were ready to ignore all the differences between conceptually distinct popular beliefs. For example, Theophrastus Bombastus von Hohenheim, known as Paracelsus (1493–1541) simply merged the idea of the "furious army" (*Wütende Heer*) with that of the "flight of the witches" because both of them flew through the air and belonged to the devil.[40] Regardless of these facts, one can tease out several characteristics of the night phantoms (*Nachtschar*) that clearly distinguish the notion from neighboring ideas. Thus, for example, the night people (*Nachtvolk*) had, in contrast to the wild hunt or the furious army, no leader whom an observer could recognize. And Büchli should have recognized that even in Graubünden "the flying army" (*ds flügend Heer*) wafted leaderless through the air, and so in this respect was similar to the conception of the night people.[41]

Another contradiction may be found in the fact the people of the dead were a society of the dead, as the name itself reveals. They moved about in procession, an idea that is known in Italian Switzerland (Misox) as the *processione dei poveri morti*, in francophone Lower Valais as the *procession des morts*, and as the *procesiun dals morts* among the Romantsch speakers of Graubünden.[42] In the Upper Valais, where processions of the dead also occupy the center of legends, they are also sometimes called a "mountain procession" (*Gratzug*) because of the notion that the penitent souls of the dead have to wander past nine mountain peaks and ninety-nine cemeteries along firmly prescribed paths. These paths were designated noisy (*Tschingel*), or processional (*Schwalt*), or "people's" paths, the routes taken by the people of the dead.[43] We can also tell that the notions of "people" and "phantoms" were interchangeable here, because in the Upper Valais the People of the Dead (*Totenvolk*) were also called the Phantoms of the Dead (*Totenschar*). Other terms for this idea were also used: "peoples' walk (*Volkgang*), symphony, synagogue, *Tschinigoo* [a corruption of synagogue]; and in the Lower Valais, *Senegouga*, or *Sabbat*, or *Chenegoda*."[44]

These peculiar terms deserve our special attention because they contain clues for dating them. Many of these names are obviously derived from the Jewish word *synagogue*, the very term with which inquisitors in the late fourteenth century labeled the witches' sabbath that they had just then newly discovered in the mountain valleys of Dauphiné and Savoy.[45] The first reports of massive witchcraft prosecutions in the area of modern-day Switzerland, hunts in the late 1420s in which more than two hundred men and women lost their lives,[46] come to us from the French-speaking Lower Valais, or more exactly, from the two relatively isolated side valleys of the Rhone, the Val d'Annivers (in German, the Einfisch Valley) and the Val d'Hérens (in German, the Eringer Valley) near the episcopal city of Sion (Sitten), which is the capital of the canton of Valais.[47] Sophisticates referred to the witches' dance as the Synagoga Satanae (the synagogue of Satan), and this conception, under the obvious pressure of the early witchcraft trials made its way into popular traditions.[48] We find here a perfect example of the relations between popular beliefs and learned interpretations, for the notion of a synagogue of Satan was derived from the learned tradition and served from the end of the fifteenth century onward to designate a procession of the spirits (Geister). But the reciprocal relation between learned and popular anxieties and fantasies is also demonstrable because the specific idea of the witches' sabbath was developed by learned demonologists in a region where intensive non-Christian popular beliefs were still thriving.

Adopting a word, therefore, does not fully determine what the word will be taken to signify. Because the noisy procession of the dead was known in Valais by a name that originally was used to designate the witches' sabbath, we can see that the original concept and what it came to mean have to be kept distinct in almost nominalistic fashion. And what it came to mean must be taken apart into its constituent parts because otherwise the meanings of the many different combinations of separate motifs and motif-complexes cannot be differentiated and understood. To do this, conceptual contents have to be analyzed as if they formed a binary code. What can be combined should indeed be combined, but those things that cannot be combined should be kept separate. Good and evil, heavenly and diabolical can serve as a simple set of ordering principles for analyzing these symbolic systems.[49] In the last analysis this is a question of whether these spirits, these alien beings, were helpful or harmful to human beings. This too turns out to be a question of life or death, but the first question we must answer deals with another unexpected topic, namely music.

7.

Music of Unearthly Beauty

THE APPEARANCE OF the night people or of the night phantoms was usually accompanied by delightful music of unearthly beauty, which placed human beings under a spell and summoned forth a nameless yearning. This music was described as "heavenly music," or as music so beautiful "that it was as if the angels were playing," as this legend recorded in Raggal (in the Great Walser Valley of Vorarlberg) has it:

> Once my wife was standing before her house on a bright moonlit night, and to pass the time she looked out into the "world." At once she heard in the distance a music so lovely that she had never in all her life heard anything like it, just as if the angels were playing. She went away from the house and inched, bit by bit, farther and farther, in order to hear the music better, and the farther she went the more lovely it sounded. At last my wife could no longer stand still, and she walked and walked, and came, just by hearing and listening, all the way to a mountain ravine. There she saw the people of the night traveling through the ravine as if they were in a cloister, and making such magnificent music that it seemed to the foolish woman that she could never get enough of it.[1]

Another example from Vorarlberg shows the people of the night, but in such a way that the tale demonstrates the mysterious power over nature exercised by a secret observer:

> Once a hunter was resting overnight under a dead tree. At midnight he awoke suddenly from his sleep and saw the night people coming toward him. And he thought, "one can't be too careful" with this kind of people, and so he walked a bit over to one side. The people of the night came closer and

closer and took up positions under a small tree, and suddenly the little tree began to play delightful music. One little branch sounded as if it were playing a flute, another as if it were the clarinet, and one little twig made the sound of a small pipe. And the night people began to dance around the tree in pairs so energetically that dust rose up in the wind.[2]

The phantoms of the night danced joyously on remote meadows and mountain pastures, met in certain houses for sumptuous dinners, sometimes in isolated alpine cottages, but sometimes in houses designated for them. In contrast to the wild hunt, which preferred to avoid human settlements and was associated with remote ravines and mountainous crevices, the people of the night sought to be near to people. A typical legend put it this way: "In Schruns (in Montafon, in the Vorarlberg) there is a house in whose atrium four gates were laid out in a cross, and this house was long ago much visited by the people of the night, as everyone knows."[3] Not every person could see the people of the night, who moved through the air just a little above the earth. But whoever received a visit from them was blessed with good fortune, and whoever was allowed to take part in their meetings instantly obtained special abilities he did not otherwise have. He could play instruments he otherwise could not or see things no person could ordinarily see.[4]

In the Upper Valais several legends tell of herdsmen who learned music at some unspecified nocturnal society, called "a joyous society." According to one legend from the parish of Turtmann (in the valley of Turtmann or Tourtemagne, a side valley of the Val d'Annivers),[5] a young herdsman, whom the chief shepherd had sent back up to the mountain pasture, met the night people there.

Having arrived up there, he opened the door of the hay barn and in the main room he saw a joyous society, who cordially invited him in to join them in eating. He thought they were tourists [!] and because he was hungry he fell to with an appetite. After a while they asked him if he would like to learn to sing or play the fiddle. He said he'd rather learn to sing because he was too poor to be able to afford a violin. The next morning he left this society and walked, singing and yodeling, down the mountain. And everyone came out to listen to his beautiful voice. The chief shepherd asked him, however, where he had learned to sing so beautifully all of a sudden. And the herdsman told him everything so that the shepherd grew jealous and decided that he would exploit the opportunity himself to learn to play the violin.

This wicked shepherd, however, was severely punished by the good society, and his corpse was found "bearing the deep impression of a violin on his chest."[6] The myth of the night people was also widespread throughout the Bernese Oberland, where they too were characterized by a music of unearthly beauty. Up in the high valleys, where the economy was pastoral, it was the herdsmen who got to hear it most often. "In the village of Loib, down under Mount Loib, there were three mountaineers who were sitting of an evening next to their hut, endlessly conversing and gossiping, and they reported this: 'They heard them singing. It was a Psalm: 'O Lord be gracious to thy true servants.' They listened and listened and listened, for they had never heard such a beautiful choir singing." That is how it was described in the Bernese Hasli Valley,[7] a valley with a purely pastoral economy that borders on the cantons of Uri, Unterwalden, the Valais, and the Bernese district of Interlaken.[8]

To emphasize this point once more, it is obvious that this happy troop could not have been clad in black for their festivities, for the contrast between colorful dancing with elaborate banquets on the one hand and deadly black clothing on the other would surely have found mention in these stories. Now and then, the members of this troop wore white coats, which was, as we know, also a costume of the hereafter.[9]

In Montafon, however, the night people appeared "in a long black train," as several legends from Tschagguns report, indicating a possible mixing of legends. For here among the members of the procession are also some terrifying figures, who stand in contrast to their delightful music.[10] In the Montafon valley of Vorarlberg, as in Graubünden, the fantasy of the people of the dead was very deeply imprinted. In the Rhaeto-Romantsch valleys of Graubünden special terms are used for them: *pievels da noatg* (people of the night) and *procesiung digls morts* (procession of the dead). And in the canton of Glarus, in the anterior Rhine valley, and in the Engadin (the Upper Valley of the Inn) too, the local legends are dominated by the "people of the dead."[11] There was also a definite connection here between death and music, as the illustrations of the dance of death, common from the fifteenth century onward, make clear.[12]

From this point on there is a linkage to the devil as well, because death and the devil have been closely related for ages, and there is also a theological tradition that has regularly condemned music.[13] There is reason enough, however, to follow conceptually the music of unearthly beauty played or sung by the people of the night in other directions, as well.

8

The Miracle of the Bones

Although the delightful music of the night people appealed to the human senses, another aspect of this fantasy had to do with the material basis of life itself. This was the "miracle of the bones," which runs like a leitmotif through the myth of the night people.[1] It speaks of the restoration of the dead to life, presented through a freshly slaughtered animal. The "resurrection of the dead" was represented narratively by use of the largest animal found in this part of the world. Cows and oxen also played the most important role in alpine agriculture, without whose production of milk, meat, and manure life in the Alps would have been scarcely conceivable. In one characteristic version of the myth, taken from the Greater Walser Valley, dominated as it was by an intensive pastoral economy, the miracle of the bones takes this form:

> Once a cowherd forgot his black cow on the alp Alpila [above Thüringerberg in the Greater Walser Valley] when he was driving the other cows down from the mountain pasture in the fall. When he went back up to retrieve her, he found his cow lying down at the alpine camp, but since night was falling, he moved the cow into the hut while he himself lay down in the bunkbed. Around midnight he was roused from his slumbers by a big noise, and saw around him in the hut a group of strange people who were busy cooking, boiling, and roasting. The herdsman watched for a while, but the longer he did, the more unsettled he became. Suddenly one of the strangers shouted to him, "Hey, you up there in the bunk, don't you want some meat?" The cowherd replied, "Yes, I'd like some," and so he came down from his bed and joined in. The meat was good, but he was surprised to notice that his black

cow out in the stall had a huge hole in her body, and he thought, "These fellows have cut the meat from the body of my cow, and they will have consumed her completely by morning." But wisely he decided not to reveal his anger to these strange guests. Then after a while the people began to dance and make such music that the alpine hut almost fell apart. The cowherd watched silently until one of the strangers asked, "Don't you want to learn to make music?" And he said, "Yes, I'd especially like to learn to play the flute." So someone gave him a flute and told him simply to blow hard. He did as he was told, and behold, he could play the flute delicately and beautifully, as if he had been learning for years. He had never known that he was such a musician. But in his joy over his newly achieved musical ability, he completely forgot his cow in the stall. At dawn's early light the strangers departed and the cowherd looked after them, and then he saw on the door of the hut a cowhide stretched out and hanging on the door. It looked like the hide of his black cow, but when it was full daylight, the cowhide on the door had vanished, and the herdsman saw his cow standing unharmed in the hut and the flute which he had played so well in the night was there too. He took it and his black cow back home.[2]

The flute he found was proof that the whole event and the delightful music were real. It is obvious that here, as in other Swiss legends of the Alps, for example those from the canton Uri, the point was that another world exists in addition to this one, not somewhere else, but parallel to ours.[3] The unexplained motif of the hide, stretched out to dry, was understood by listeners who would supplement it with the idea that the bones, too, had to be carefully collected. The night phantoms slaughtered and roasted a beef, but the hide and bones were carefully gathered up and put together again through magical forces. Next morning the cow stands uneaten in its stall, as they say in the legends of Graubünden.[4]

Essentially the same story is also told in the Lesser Walser Valley, although there the story has a different beginning:

In a house in the Nearer Meadow of the Walser Valley, during an afternoon church service honoring the Virgin Mary, the night people showed up in broad daylight. No one but the baby-sitters were at home. Those were the peasant's children, who were alone tending the babies. The night people made themselves at home, got out the most beautiful cow from the stall and began to slaughter it and skin it. They became very busy boiling and roasting and then devoured it, while also "dancing and jumping, singing and rejoicing, and playing most delightfully on the drums and stringed instruments." And the children got to eat "to their hearts' content," too.[5]

Typical in this story is the way the watcher gets drawn into the action. This is a motif that we also find in stories of the witches' dance and of the wild hunt. There, however, it is always linked to great terror and continuing harm for anyone who "interrupts." The night people, in contrast, do not see their "guests" as meddlers, at least as long as they do not behave with hostility. Indeed, they welcome the interrupters. They are encouraged to learn to play musical instruments or to take part in a meal. The Lower Valais tells the same story: When the cowherds descend from the alp of L'Allée (west of the Durand Glacier) down into the valley, they realize that a cow is missing. A cowherd goes back up, finds the cow, but it is too late for him to come back down. So he spends the night in the alpine hut with his cow and is awakened by noises around midnight. Strange men and women are dancing and celebrating in the hut. The cowherd barely dares to breathe. The strangers slaughter his cow and roast it over their fire, but when they discover the herdsman, they offer to share their food with him. The meat of the cow is completely consumed. And then we come to the miracle of the bones: "Now the cowhide was stretched out. One of the strangers collected the bones and threw them in the middle, folding the skin around them in a bundle, and then he shouted: "Rosina, arise," and the cow stood up. The spirits disappeared. When the sun came up the cowherd led his cow down to the village."[6] Around the Lake of Brienz in the Bernese Oberland there are surviving traces of this characteristic legend of the night people.[7] The miracle of the bones has a variant there in which the bones are lost, which sounds like this:

On one occasion the night people set up a sumptuous feast on Near Field in the Lesser Walser Valley, in broad daylight, during the church service on a feast day of Mary or of the apostles. They took the most beautiful cow from its stall and made a big to-do as they slaughtered it, cooked it, roasted it, and consumed it while they danced and hopped, sang and rejoiced, and while playing most delightfully on drums and stringed instruments. They also gave the children plenty to eat, but warned them not to gnaw on the bones or to lose any of them. And in the end, they tried to gather up all the fragments, but despite their best efforts they could not find one of the bones. So they bound up the remaining bones in the skin and said that the cow would simply have to limp. And so it was. For she was found standing in her stall, just as good as before, except that she now dragged one foot behind her.[8]

This miracle of the bones, which we have now identified as a fossilized leitmotif of the myth of the night people, was not at all restricted to the region in which we find the myth of the night phantoms or of the night people. We find parts of it in connection with nameless phantom "squadrons." In the South Tyrolean Val d'Ultimo, for example, there is a story about the miracle of the bones in which "men and women" came into the hut and began consuming the cow that they later put back together again.[9] We find parts of it, too, in a version that is of great interest from the perspective of gender, in stories of groups of women who travel about. At the end of the fourteenth century the *podestà* (mayor) of Milan condemned a woman who asserted that a certain Madona Horiente revived the oxen slaughtered by her followers by touching the ox bones wrapped up in hides with her magic staff.[10] In the South Tyrolean Val Passiria, it was "three wild women" who were roasting a mountain goat and invited a goat hunter to their banquet. Despite their warnings, he swallowed one of the small bones and later saw the revived goat limping.[11] In the neighboring Tyrolean valley of the Upper Inn River a certain Lady Hulda was supposedly regarded as the queen of the Blessed Maidens.[12] If this legend had not obviously been influenced by the Grimm Brothers' fairy tales, it would be a most interesting finding.[13]

These stories of the miracle of the bones, which have survived as narrative elements throughout the Alps down to our century, obviously are part of a long and sturdy tradition in European history. As early as the *Historia Britonum (The History of the Britons)* by the Welsh Nennius we can read that Saint Germanus of Auxerre (378–448) performed an "ox miracle" in the early fifth century while converting the Celts to Christianity.[14] A "goose miracle," in which the bird was put together out of skin and bones, was attributed to Saint Pharaildis ("Veerle" in Flemish), the patron saint of Ghent, whose cult has been documented as early as the ninth century. She carries a wild goose as her insignia.[15] In Christian hagiography "ox miracles" are attributed to Thomas of Cantimpré (ca. 1201–1270) and to the Brabantine monk, Wilhelm of Villers.[16] And all of these stories may be connected to the vision of Ezechiel, who in a literal ecstasy wrote

> The hand of the Lord was upon me, and carried me out in the spirit of the Lord, and set me down in the midst of the valley full of bones. . . . And he said unto me, Son of man, can these bones live? And I answered, O Lord God, thou knowest. Again he said unto me, Prophesy upon these bones, and say unto them, O ye dry bones, hear the word of the Lord. Thus saith the Lord God unto these bones; Behold, I will cause breath to enter into you, and ye shall live. . . . and ye shall know that I am the Lord. So I prophesied as I was commanded: and as I prophesied, there was a noise, and behold, a shaking, and the bones came together, bone to his bone. And when I beheld, lo, the sinews and the flesh came up upon them, and the skin covered them above. (Ezechiel 37:1–8)

This story from the Hebrew prophets of the Old Testament—was this the first of all these legends of the miracle of the bones? Could the European legends derive from Christian stories of the saints, which then simply returned as travesties in popular tales, "misunderstood" perhaps and applied "wrongly," as a well-respected academic interpretation puts it?[17] That does not seem very likely. For why else would Burchard of Worms in the early eleventh century wage war against the doctrinal error that involved night-flying women who were supposedly killing Christians, cooking, and eating their flesh, but then restoring them to life again ("iterum vivos facere et inducias vivendi dare")?[18] Heide Dienst recently showed with a few examples that the decrees of the Corrector Burchardi, which targeted magic and at magical practices, referred to real practices in his day.[19]

It is naturally harder to prove the antiquity of beliefs and ideas, and any such argument is easily challenged. And yet Celtic stories, too, tell of deer and geese revived from their bones, and it was only natural that the Christian church in the early age of missions needed saints who could compete with them. Just as the Irish monks developed an epistolary style full of strong expressions, which make palpable their sense of competition with the Celtic bards, so the Irish saints were said to be able to fly, in order to compete with Celtic druids, whose stories say that they could fly to heaven dressed in winged costumes.[20] Because of this tough competition, it is not surprising that in Celtic Brittany the missionaries, too, had to present themselves as "lords of the animals." The biography of the Irish Saint Patrick also shows how important it was to describe the saint as a hero "who could defeat the druids using their own [magical] arts, or even surpass them."[21]

There are, of course, miracles of the bones in areas well beyond the region of Celtic and Christian influence. In the Icelandic Edda of the poet Snorri Sturluson the Germanic god Thor could awaken goats from their bones to a new life by applying his magical hammer. We should not, however, be overhasty to connect this to some new "Teutonic thesis," for the geographic distribution of this motif and also of subsidiary motifs concerning lost or broken bones is amazingly wide.[22] Among the Abchases of the Caucasus is the god of the hunt, who can revive a recently killed animal.[23] And even farther to the east on the Eurasian continent one can find peoples who observe the custom of not breaking the bones of any game animals, but who instead gather them carefully together and deposit them at specific places in order to facilitate the return of game. It is possible that at the basis of this custom is the idea that the soul of an animal lives in the bones.[24] Beyond the Eurasian continent the myth of animals being resurrected from their skin and bones can be found, for example, among some peoples of Africa, which immediately poses the familiar alternative explanations of either cultural diffusion from one place to others or structural genesis, in which similar situations and structures prompt similar myths.[25]

Scholars used to assume that there were stages of culture, and on that assumption they would try to connect a particular myth to a specific stage in the evolution of human society, in this case to the culture of hunters and herdsmen. The trouble is that this miracle story has survived in peasant societies and in certain "high" cultures such as the European, the Iranian, and the Indian.[26] And so the spatial and temporal distribution of these tales of bone miracles prompts us to ponder fundamental questions about the coherence and tradition of myths in general.[27] Methodologically, with these

The Miracle of the Bones

stories we can demonstrate just how thoroughly Eurocentric is the dear old notion that "culture trickles down," a theory that was refined by Hans Naumann in the 1920s.[28] It is worth stressing the amazingly wide distribution of ideas about bone miracles, ranging from the Arctic Circle, through Siberia to Japan, which goes well beyond the cultural reach of Christianity. And not only in spatial terms, but also temporally, for the miracle of the bones has European origins that predate Christianity, and the memory of this miracle of the bones survived in non-Christian narrative contexts in the middle of Christianized Central Europe, from at least the eighth century into the nineteenth century.[29]

However widespread ideas of the bone miracle may have been, and however much we may believe or reject as too speculative Carlo Ginzburg's thesis concerning a prehistoric forest god or lord of the animals,[30] it is perfectly clear that in this case the miracle was closely connected to the myth of the night people. Since this myth can be found only in a relatively restricted area, one could speculate on the basis of archeological remains that the myth might have had early roots in our alpine region. Arguing *ex negativo,* we would not expect evidence from bronze age sacrificial sites because burnt offerings destroyed the skeleton.[31] Looking at the Celtic grave goods left at grave sites in modern-day Liechtenstein, we can find no direct evidence of the myth.[32] Whether one can connect a few Celtic-period depictions of a "mistress of the animals" to the myth of the night people seems dubious even though it does offer a possible foothold and cannot be absolutely excluded.[33] Let it be marginally noted also that both in Oberstdorf and in the neighboring parish of Tiefenbach there was a "bone house" (*Ossarium*) where the bones of the dead from open graves were meticulously gathered and laid atop one another. This was, of course, nothing more than a Christian usage documented for Fulda as early as 820 and completely customary in the alpine lands from the twelfth century onward.[34] But might it be useful to explain this custom by connecting it to the realm of ideas surrounding the bone miracles, which were preserved so tenaciously in the legends of this region?

Starting with a legend from the Walser valley of Vorarlberg, Johann

The Miracle of the Bones

Nepomuk, Knight von Alpenburg, interpreted the people of the night as a society of elemental spirits, who because of their "elf or fairy nature" would "enjoy dancing and music."[35] Whatever the case, many elements of the night people myth give us reason to think that they were indeed a society radically different from the society of the witches or of the wild hunt. The motif of the miracle of the bones can actually be used as a criterion with which to distinguish the two, for it symbolizes in the most extreme form the benevolence of the night people. They could bestow on human beings the best thing in the world: life itself.

9.

The Good Society

Motifs such as the "heavenly music" or the "resurrection of the dead" were obviously also Christian ideas, and yet that does not exhaust their range of meanings. For despite the strength and institutional spread of Christian mythology, a set of ideas circulated through the whole alpine region that cannot really be called "Christian." Another of these ideas was the myth of a "good society" that existed parallel to the evil condition of this world. On the basis of the geographical distribution of ideas about the night phantoms and the night people, and about the mysterious people with their music of unearthly beauty and their ability to reawaken the dead, we can demarcate a region that spread in a sweeping arc from Vorarlberg over Graubünden to the Upper Valais and the Bernese Oberland. Throughout this region the observations of Renward Cysat (1545–1614) assume a remarkable importance, for he was one of the most careful observers of his day. He was the son of Leopold Cysat, a member of the Milanese patriciate (the Cesati) who had emigrated to Switzerland and obtained citizenship there in 1549. After an apprenticeship in Italy, Renward opened an apothecary's shop in Lucerne.[1] As an enthusiastic supporter of the Counter Reformation he founded a Jesuit establishment in 1574 in Lucerne, and from 1575 on until his death he served at the city clerk and called himself the "chancellor" of Lucerne. Cysat stood out among his contemporaries because of his extraordinary energy. He was as well known for his extensive botanical garden as for his mountain climbing and for his interest in the stories of simple people, the peasants, hunters, and herdsmen.[2]

This "universal man" of the Renaissance wrote a twenty-two-volume *Collectanea Chronica und Denkwürdige Sachen pro Chronica Lucernensi et Helvetiae* (Chronicle collection and notable materials toward a history of Lucerne and Switzerland) in which he repeatedly dealt seriously with the peculiar beliefs and notions of ordinary people. In these matters it was not so much his joyful discovery of curiosities that inspired him but rather his religious concerns, and it was precisely his disapproval that prompted him to be such a sharp observer. In contrast to nineteenth-century collections of legends, we find here evidence from the very time in which Chonrad Stoeckhlin lived. And these were no mere fairy tales, but instead accounts of experiences that seemed entirely real to people like Barbara Rappolt of Interlaken or to our horse herdsman of Oberstdorf, Chonrad Stoeckhlin. The clerk of Lucerne writes of a "night ghost" (*Nachtgespenst*), which regularly troubled the phantasies of the "common, uneducated rabble" (*gemein einfältig pöffel*) and which they called "the blessed [i.e., dead] people or the army of God (*Guottisheer*)," words that here betray clearly a popular etymological reinterpretation of Wotan's army (*Wuottisheer*). Although the army of Wotan was usually associated with rage (*Wut*) and terrible noise, that would not have been compatible with notions of beings who danced charmingly and played music, bringing good luck to men. Quite the contrary: these night spirits were not harmful; they were useful and their presence was "good." The appearance of this army of God was "entirely friendly and pleasant to human beings."

According to Cysat, this phenomenon involved "the blessed souls" of men who had died too soon—in other words, the dead. And yet it is not clear that everyone accepted this interpretation. As an activist in favor of the Counter Reformation, Cysat was opposed to these popular notions as "heathen" forms of religion. Whenever he dealt with such matters, and that was often, he would work himself into a righteous fury, and he became especially exercised when living persons claimed to have had contact with these spirit-people, and even more enraged that these stories were obviously believed by his fellow townsmen in Lucerne. Worse yet, those who claimed to have such contacts had a reputation for special luck and sometimes even for special abilities. In the eyes of their supporters they enjoyed a reputation for semi-sanctity.

Many wanted to hear [them], or even to join their company, and the folly was so great that they believed that still-living men and women could go out wandering with them, keep company with them, and even obtain special luck. And when they suspect that someone has done such things, they hold him in great honor and believe that he is much more pious and decent than other men, being almost a saint. As an example, I remember a married couple in this city, who had this reputation and whom the uneducated honored highly, believing that they had been in just such a blessed fellowship.[3]

Again and again in his successive volumes Cysat returned to the theme of the "blessed people" [the dead], revealing in the process further details of a notion that seemed incredible to him. When he referred to learned authorities, such as Vincent of Beauvais with his explanations concerning the nocturnal excursions of women with the goddess Diana,[4] he provided an important clue to the learned interpretation of these popular beliefs and notions in the framework of his own time. Like all authors of that day, Cysat also depended on the *Canon Episcopi*, the most important source in canon law for the interpretation of such nocturnal flights. Whether one was dealing with the "night phantoms" or with the flight of the witches, no one could escape this *Canon*, which got its name from the first word of its text: "Episcopi" [Bishops]. An extensive scholarly discussion has continued to deal with this text right down to today, and in a way that affects our interpretation of Stoeckhlin's night phantoms.[5]

What was the point of this *Canon Episcopi*, and where did it come from? During the late Middle Ages and early modern period it was commonly believed that this text originated in the early Christian council of Ancyra in the fourth century, but we now know that it was first cited in the *Liber de disciplinis ecclesiasticis* composed by Bishop Regino of Prüm (814–915), that it probably had its origins in a Carolingian capitulary, and that it was therefore a decree stemming from the great period of Christian missions in Central Europe.[6] The *Canon* prescribed ecclesiastical penalties for various kinds of unbelief and superstition, but it was later famous mainly for one specific passage in which the following false belief was condemned: "Some wicked women . . . believe and profess themselves that in the hours of the night they ride out upon certain beasts with Diana, the goddess of the pagans, and an innumerable multitude of women, and in the silence of the dead of night traverse vast spaces of the earth." This strange notion was condemned as heathen, "because it suggests that there is some divine or miraculous power besides the One God. Therefore, priests must earnestly preach to the people in the congregations entrusted to them, so that they will know that this is false in every way." At most, the devil, "who can transform himself into an angel of light," might take over a sleeping person's senses and delude him or her with deceptive visions.[7]

In the high Middle Ages, this *Canon Episcopi* was taken up in several important collections of canon law, for example in the *Penitential* of Bishop Burchard of Worms (965–1025) and Ivo of Chartres (1040–1115). Around 1142, with its reception in Gratian's *Decretum*, the most famous medieval collection of canon law, it became an authoritative text in church law. All of these works were connected in a common textual tradition, and numerous late medieval penitential books took over the language of the *Canon Episcopi*, either verbatim or in vernacular translation.[8] In each we are aware of differences of accent. In the earlier texts, the ideas of the *Canon* were categorized under "dreams" and punished mildly.[9] But no later than the time of John of Salisbury (1120–1180), the false belief in these nighttime travels was connected to the idea of common banquets and the notion of *lamiae*, creatures who kidnapped children and ate them. Moreover, authors now saw a connection with sorceresses, who used various known techniques, such as palmistry, to predict the future, sinful ideas that Burchard in the early eleventh century had dealt with as part of a different category.[10]

Among the most interesting new accents is the version of the *Canon Episcopi* found in the penitential of the Bishop Burchard of Worms, who around 1020 wrote that certain women went out at night with the goddess Diana, but then explained that "here" (i.e., in his bishopric) people, in their stupidity, called such a woman "striga holda" (quam vulgaris stultitia hic strigam holdam vocat). In several manuscript copies of this passage, the text speaks only of "Holda" (hic holdam vocat), whereas in others the "striga holda" is counterposed to a "striga unholda," a notion that now set up the "good" night-traveling women over against "evil" women or demons.[11] The philologist Claude Lecouteux has investigated the early and high medieval glosses to such texts and has concluded that the concept of "Holda" had its origin in ideas about fairies. Etymologically, "hold" meant "well disposed," "gracious," or "benevolent," a positive meaning that survives in many names such as Berchtold, Berthold, and Withold. Lecouteux argues that adding the negative prefix "un" to the word was part of a process of demonization. The good "Holden" became in Christian interpretation "Unholden."[12]

Carlo Ginzburg has pointed out that the *Canon Episcopi* actually stood at the end of a historic development, during which Christian missionaries struggled to overcome the cults of the heathen gods, among whom Diana or other similar divinities played a serious role.[13] In the Celto-Roman area of alpine foothills, one of these was certainly Epona, known as the Mistress of the Horses, but also known as a fertility goddess and the female lord of the cult of the dead. To her fell the task of carrying the dead or their souls over to the other side. In ancient Roman times she had been honored as the patroness of the cavalry, and 18 December was dedicated to her cult.[14] A limestone relief of the mounted Epona (according to the interpretation most often preferred by scholars), dating from the third century, was found in the neighborhood of Bregenz [in the Vorarlberg], and an altar dedicated to her has been recovered in Kempten [in the Allgäu].[15] Ginzburg considers the Diana of the *Canon Episcopi* to be the specifically Roman incarnation of the Celtic Epona,[16] but there is little reason to think that the term should be interpreted so narrowly.

The originally Italic goddess Diana, with her various local manifestations or avatars (Isis, Artemis), belonged to the most attractive divinities of the Roman world of late antiquity. She protected women, children, and the poor. She was goddess of the forests and lord of the animals and therefore also goddess of the hunt.[17] It is no wonder then that we can find her characteristics surviving in Christian iconography relating to Mary, Mother of God, who was sometimes portrayed as the lord of the animals and the preserver of fertility (cf. Mary as the "corn goddess"[18] and as *Maria lactans*, i.e., nursing her baby). The iconography that displays Mary standing on a crescent moon probably derives this attribute directly from the heathen goddess.[19] But of course during the Frankish period of Christian missions there were still actual heathen cults throughout Central Europe. One of the most evocative examples of this struggle against the cult of Diana is the story of the destruction of "Diana's shrine" near Trier by Saint Wulfilaich in the year 585, as reported by his contemporary Gregory of Tours (538–594).[20] To take another example, Saint Kilian (d. ca. 689) supposedly found that Diana was the chief goddess of Würzburg, the center of his work as a missionary. A manuscript from Tegernsee, in Bavaria, dating from the twelfth century, refers in jest to the "family of the abbesses and their flock," namely Pallas [Athena], Diana, Juno, and Venus.[21]

One trait of the ancient Diana-Artemis seems to survive especially in texts such as the *Canon Episcopi*. The renowned classicist Ulrich von Wilamowitz-Moellendorff described this aspect as the "mistress of the beyond," the queen of woods and wilderness, a characterization that reminds us conceptually of the *donne de fuori* (ladies from outside), whom Spanish Inquisitors later discovered in parts of formerly Greek Sicily. With her bow and arrow, Artemis could send instant death, but she was also the goddess of nature and fertility, in whose honor young people celebrated with round dances and annual bonfires. Even in antiquity this Artemis was thought of as highly mutable. The spectrum ranges from the Asiatic "Magna Mater" (as in the Artemis of Ephesus) all the way to the horrible sorceress Hecate.[22] In opposition to many historians who see nothing more in the *Canon Episcopi* than a traditional text that simply and mechanically passed on topics borrowed from late-antique traditional material,[23] some historians have more plausibly regarded it as an essential and key text for seeing how Christian priests and theologians understood popular religious ideas.

According to this interpretation, we can see that repeatedly in various remote parts of Europe theologians gathered together notions of night flight under the summary title of the goddess "Diana." This is the case with a supposed goddess "Bensozia" (good society), to whom the diocesan council in Couserans in the Ariège (south of Toulouse) referred in the year 1280.[24] It may not be misguided to connect this term to the heretical concept of "good things" (bonae res), as detected by the Inquisitor of Toulouse, Bernard Gui (1261–1331),[25] who as a member of the Dominican Order had access to its records and traditions. As early as 1250 his fellow Dominican Steven of Bourbon (1190–1261), who was Inquisitor for the south and east of France from 1230 onward, and Vincent of Beauvais had also spoken of heretical "good things,"[26] and in both of these cases it is surely not far-fetched to see the mental connection with their fight against heretics. The heretical movements of the Middle Ages obviously had a tradition of using such concepts. The "perfecti," the "perfected ones," among the Cathars of southern France were described as "bonshommes," as "good persons," or "good people," or even as "boni christiani," that is, "good Christians."[27] This conception, which can be found at the very beginnings of heretical movements in the West,[28] survived into the late Middle Ages as a self-description for certain heretical groups, such as the Waldensians, who called themselves "good people."[29]

In the *Practica Officii Inquisitionis*, composed in 1315 by Bernard Gui, we have a most influential handbook for inquisitors, one that concerned itself chiefly with the dualist heresies of the Cathars and Albigensians. In this manual the concept of "good things" received an astonishing interpretation. Gui urged inquisitors to ask persons suspected of sorcery and of having a pact with the devil "about the fairy-women who are called 'bonas res' and who, as they say, go out at night" (de fatis mulieribus quas vocant 'bonas res' que, ut dicunt, vadunt de nocte). Here he referred explicitly to those night-traveling women of the *Canon Episcopi*, who are called "fairies." Just before, he had been speaking of the souls of the dead and of predicting the future, and after this passage he dealt with magic using fruits and herbs, as well as with collecting herbs on bended knee while facing east and praying the Lord's Prayer (versa facie ad orientem cum oratione dominica).[30] One origin of these ideas in the case of this active inquisitor was probably rooted in his practical experience as an inquisitor, but another lay perhaps in the internal traditions of his religious order or in the common knowledge of inquisitors working in southern and eastern France as well as in northern Italy.

The assertions of such handbooks were reinforced in a most peculiar way by actual confessions in inquisitorial heresy trials: the records of the Milanese inquisition mention a certain Madona Horiente, for example, who served as a kind of personification of the fairy figure mentioned by Bernard Gui. The worshippers of Madona Horiente, who were condemned in 1380 in Milan, and then again in 1390, called their fellowship the "bona gens," the "good people," or the "good society." It was only natural that this night-traveling society would be interpreted in the light of the *Canon Episcopi*. In its details, the confession extracted by the Milanese inquisitor Fra Beltramino da Cernuscullo from a certain "night-traveling" Petrina from Bripio concerning the meetings of the "bona gens" of course went far beyond the text of the *Canon Episcopi*, and for that reason it must be presented here in full. We will see that it contains many similarities to the idea of the night people.

> We, the brethren of the Order of Preachers, teachers of Holy Scripture and Inquisitors into heretical depravity in Milan, as appointed by the Holy See, have conscientiously analyzed a certain confession set forth by you, Petrina, the daughter of the late Zambellus of Bugatis and wife of Petrus from Bripio, [a confession which you] laid down before Brother Rugerius de Caxate of good memory, member of the said Order, and stating that you, Petrina, from the time you were sixteen until the date of this confession have continually taken part in a certain game of Diana, whom you call Herodias, and that you have come before the eyes of this Mistress and have always given her your devotion, in the following manner: that you have bowed down to her and spoken these words, "May you fare well, Lady Horiens." And in answer to you she herself has said, "May you fare well, good people." And you have said that they go to the game in the form of animals, or more exactly as a donkey, a fox, or as human beings, as living or dead persons, and that those who were beheaded or hanged display a deep sense of awe and do not dare to lift up their heads in that company. And you also said that in that society they kill animals and eat their flesh, but that they place the bones back into the skin, and the Mistress herself strikes the skin of the slaughtered animals with the staff that she holds in her hand with the apple,[31] and that these animals at once revive, but that they are never much good for work thereafter. And you said that they go with their Mistress through the houses of various persons and that they eat and drink there and that they rejoice in finding houses that are spacious and well ordered, and that the Mistress then gives her blessing to this house. And you said of this society that you do not mention God in the afore-mentioned society, nor do you invoke Him when you want to go to this society. And you have said that the Mistress teaches you members of this society the efficacy of herbs and shows you through signs everything you want to be shown and teaches you everything you want to know about sicknesses, thefts, and bewitchings, and also that she teaches you

the Art [*das Werk*] and you find out the truth about everything she shows you. And you have said that the Mistress does not want you to tell about all of the above mentioned, and [out of loyalty to] that same [Mistress] you have never confessed any of the above mentioned, even though your confessor has specifically asked you about these matters, and that in any of these afore-mentioned matters you do not believe that you commit any sin by conceal-ing the truth in the sacrament of confession. And that you have said that you believe that that Lady Horiens, Mistress of her society, will be like Christ, who is Lord of the World.[32]

The "game of Diana" is here equated with a certain "good society," under the direction of a hitherto unknown incarnation of the goddess, and we find the following characteristics: flying through the air, metamorphosis into an-imals, a banquet, the miracle of the bones, the visit to strange houses, re-wards granted for good housekeeping, the teaching of healing arts, learning to prophesy the future, and learning to diagnose bewitchings (*maleficia*). It is an amazing repertory of wondrous qualities or abilities, which were here assembled, well *before* the late medieval notion of the witches' sabbath was cobbled together. It is not all that surprising that such notions found their way into the literature through specifically Milanese treatises. The miracle of the bones, for example, appears to have been transferred directly from Mi-lanese trial records into learned demonology. In the treatise on witches, *Lamiarum sive striarum opusculum,* that he dedicated to Francesco Sforza around 1460, Dominican friar Hieronymus Visconti (d. ca. 1478) discussed not only the question of whether witches could fly but also the miracle of the bones, which took place according to the women's testimony at the "ludus" or game. Visconti denied the reality of the miracle of the bones because, ac-cording to the views of the theologians, a demon could not effect a resur-rection of the dead.[33]

These examples from Lombardy are astonishing enough in that they provide detailed accounts of the miracle of the bones in connection with a so-called "good society," but there are parallels to these ideas in the South-Tyrolean Alps. In his capacity as bishop of Bressanone, the famous philoso-pher Nicholas of Cusa (1401–1464) undertook an inquiry in 1457 against two women from the Val di Fassa, who claimed that they went traveling with the good Mistress Richella: He translated the name "bona domina" Richella (good Mistress Richella) into Latin as "quasi Fortuna," and into German as "Hulda," and he interpreted her theologically as the same as that demon whom the *Canon Episcopi* had called Diana.[34] In the stories told by these two women from the Romantsch-speaking region of the Dolomite Alps, according to Nicholas of Cusa, they followed their mistress "to a place full of dancing and festive folk. . . . For several years they went to this place during the Ember days."[35]

Fifty years later and just a few valleys away, there was a witchcraft trial in Völs on the Schlern (Fié a Sciliar), which was managed much less gently. Triggered by the witch doctor Zuanne (Giovanni) delle Piatte from Altrei (Anterivo), who had already once before come to attention for carrying on his person crystals and "many signs and diabolical formulas in the German language" (molti caratteri e formule diaboliche in lingua tedesca), these trials resulted in the fiery deaths of woman after woman convicted of supposed witchcraft between 1506 and 1510.

The quality of the stories told by delle Piatte was in no way inferior to that of those told by Chonrad Stoeckhlin. He spoke of travels to the "beyond," of being snatched away to the Mountain of Venus, where the night-traveling goddess Herodias lived ("el monte de Venus ubi habitat la donna Herodiades"); he described the loyal Eckhart ("uno vecchio con la barba bianca che dize el fidel Eckhart," i.e., a white-bearded old man called 'loyal Eckhart'), and Tannhäuser as well ("uno homo vecchio . . . che dize el Tonhauser"). On the Venusberg, the fairy society ("ragazze bellissime," i.e., the most beautiful girls) feasted with their leader, and human beings were also there as guests ("Et ibi erano donne et donselle et la donna Venus et anchora homini"). At these gatherings there was eating and drinking. Once, on a Thursday during the Christmas Ember days ("una nocte Jovis quatuor temporum de Nadale"), he supposedly flew off on a black horse after the gathering on the Venusberg together with this Lady and her society for five hours, traveling all around the world.[36]

This notion of the Venusberg, which was connected to receiving the gift of prophecy,[37] must have been widespread, because in 1508, three years after the Ladinian[38] magician Zuanne delle Piatte made his confession, the Strasbourg cathedral preacher Johann Geiler of Keisersberg (1445–1510) asked in his sermon intended for the Wednesday after Reminiscere (the Sunday after the spring Ember days, the second Sunday in Lent): "Now you will ask, What do you say to us about the women, who travel at night and gather together? You ask if it is credible when they say they travel to Lady Venusberg." This was from Geiler's sermon, "On the *Unholden* and the Witches," and it is not surprising that the eloquent preacher pulled out all the stops, touching on the *Canon Episcopi*, the legend of Germanus, and the "furious army of the *Unholden*" (witches), "the ghost-image of the devil," to say nothing of "wild men," and "werewolves."[39]

By mentioning the legend of Germanus, the Strasbourg cathedral preacher hands us a clue to the "good society" that is just as valuable as the more frequently discussed portion of his sermon dealing with the *Canon Episcopi* on the night flights of certain women. Here we have another key text in which popular notions such as the myth of the night people were absorbed by the learned. In the famous "Golden Legend" (*Legenda Aurea*) of the Dominican Jacobus de Voragine (ca. 1230–1298), director for his order in the province of Lombardy and later archbishop of Genoa, this story had found wide distribution. In an early German translation, the *Alsatian Legenda Aurea,* the episode was retold:

> Saint Germanus was staying one night in the house of an honorable man. In the evening he ordered a table to be prepared, even though they were getting ready to go to sleep. This surprised Saint Germanus. Thereupon the man said that it was customary for the women who traveled at night to come into the house, and in this way the table would be ready for them. Then Saint Germanus stayed awake and watched as many devils in human shapes came in and sat at the table.[40]

Who were these "women who traveled at night"? In a continuation of the *Speculum Morale* by Vincent of Beauvais, they are called "good ladies" or "good wives," and there are not only many stories about them but even satirical travesties of them. In one, for example, impudent youths exploited the belief in "good ladies" and, dressing up as ladies, they visited a rich peasant one night. There they danced and shouted out, "We take away one thing and restore an hundredfold." With these words they began to carry off all the goods and possessions of the peasant, and yet the simpleton was well pleased, saying to his wife, "Keep quiet and shut your eyes; we shall be rich. These are the good women, and they will increase our wealth a hundred-fold."[41]

The legend of Germanus leads us further in several different ways. First, it connects seamlessly with the notion of the night-travelers of the *Canon Episcopi*. Second, it changes the point of view by describing the arrival of the night-travelers at the houses that they visited. Third, it calls attention to the custom of preparing food offerings for the night-travelers and thus connects folk beliefs with actual ritual practices. Bishop Germanus of Auxerre was the missionary to the Celts, well known for his druidic miracle of the bones. In this miracle tale he unmasks the society of the fairies as a gathering of demons. The importance of this story is obvious, and it is no wonder that in the context of the myth of the night people this particular exemplum found wide distribution. Johannes Nider cited it in his discussion of night flights,[42] as did Mathias Widmann from Kemnath[43] and many other authors, including Geiler of Kaisersberg, from whom it was adopted by Johann Weyer in the later sixteenth century.[44] Even though Geiler regularly tried, as a zealous preacher, to demonise all non-Christian conceptions of the hereafter, it is still clear that folk beliefs possessed an amazingly labyrinthine arsenal from which, over and over, new concepts could be cobbled together or created.

The women of the Dolomite valleys accused by Zuanne delle Piatte as witches recounted in their confessions stories that appear archaic. In fact, we often find archaic details in the earliest witchcraft trials because of their less stereotyped interrogations: details such as traveling during the Ember nights and the feasting on oxen or cows up in the high meadows of the Dolomite Alps. And regularly they were restored to life again. In her very first hearing, Orsola la Strumechera from Trodena, one of the first women to be accused, told of how numerous men and women came together. In her fifth hearing she finally produced a full-fledged story of the miracle of the bones: "And when they have cooked and eaten, they gather all the bones together, and afterward the animals come alive and return home." Widow Margherita Tessadrella and others too followed her example in 1505, and nothing seemed more natural for these women from Cavalese, Kastelruth, Klausen, Salurn,

Predazzo and other villages of the Dolomite valleys, to confess that they had come together with "Lady del Bon zogo (Lady of the Good game) and a large company of people."[45]

Like Chonrad Stoeckhlin, these women from the Val di Fiemme distinguished clearly between different sorts of nocturnal travels. Answering a question about the witches' flight, for example, Margherita Vanzina from Tesero mentioned the "game of the devil" (*zogo del diavolo*) and "the one of incubi and of night fears" (a game involving the "poor souls" of the dead), but then she spoke of yet another: "and the other one, the one of the Lady." This Lady was the "Mistress of the Good Game," "la donna del bon zogo."[46] The maidservant Anna Jobstin, who had come from the Valley of the Upper Inn and had worked as a dairy maid in the high meadows of the Siusi ("Seise" in German) confessed that she had participated in nocturnal "travels," which had taken place mostly during the Ember nights. On the Meadow of the Villander they had supposedly eaten an ox, a detail that did not fit well with the normal stories of the witches' dance but which was perhaps a normal characteristic of the "good society," even though this time it did not result in a "miracle of the bones." Jobstin had finally been chosen Queen of Angel Land (also Queen of the Angels, Queen of the Elves), which was certainly not a typical notion in witchcraft trials, but which was probably not so unusual in a region where the myth of the elves had developed into the medieval German epic of King Laurin of the Dwarves with his Rose Garden.[47] Indeed, "Rose Garden" was the name of the mountain peak around which all of these villages can be found: in the Valley of the Fassa, the Val di Fiemme, the Val di Tires, and the high meadows of the Schlern. A certain Juliana Winkerin from Ums (Umes) on the Schlern told of traveling to dances that offered good food and beautiful music. There she had supposedly met people from Campitello in the Valley of the Fassa, from around on the other side of Mount Rose Garden. Once she said they had cooked and eaten a baby, but Maid Jobstin had fulfilled her role as queen of the fairies and had gathered the bones together and had brought the child back to life. In such matters they had to be extra careful, for if just one little bone was missing, the child would be crippled and deformed. Katharina Haselriederin confessed that the devil had offered to bring her thither, where she would be able to see all the joys and pleasures of the world. And together with Katharina Moserin, up on the meadow of the Val di Tires, they had consumed two oxen, and two years later, during the autumn Ember days, at Welschnofen (Nova Levante), at the foot of the Karer Pass (the Passo di Costalunga), they had even devoured three oxen. In 1510 Anna Miolerin confessed that it was customary to travel to the dancing places during Ember nights; and she doubted whether the government would be able to abolish "the game" by holding witchcraft trials.[48]

We have found a "good people of the night," who according to testimony opposed the evil game of the witches. Such stories crop up again and again in the records of the inquisition, in treatises, and in collections of exempla and of sermons. Moreover the connection between the different kinds of texts is obvious, for example, when practical men transformed their ethnographic results into literature. The author of the *Malleus Maleficarum*, Heinrich Kramer, sang the praises of the Dominican inquisitor Bernard of Como (d. ca. 1510), who in 1485 had burned forty-one women as witches in Bormio, high in the remotest reaches of the Valtellina;[49] this same Bernard of Como had encountered the "game of the good society" (ludum bonae societatis) in his hearings, and immortalized it in his *Tractatus de strigibus*.[50] As an inquisitor he was one of the very first to discuss the old *Canon Episcopi* using a "rigorously inductive method" on the basis of what he had found out in the latest trials. According to Bernard of Como, the old canon legal text had nothing to do with the new heresy, which had only arisen in the Valtellina about the year 1360. It is possible that for this dating Bernard of Como actually used the Milanese Inquisition records of the Madona Horiente trial from the years between 1380 and 1390. The inquisitor regarded the long tradition of such trials (going back more than one hundred years) as well as the numerous variations in the confessions, the precise and sometimes exactly parallel details (which he called their *conformitas*) in the witches' confessions concerning places, times, and accomplices, as irresistible proof that the witches' sabbath was real.[51]

Methodologically, we will not go wrong in reading the various regionally diverse demonologists in such a way that requires us to pay special attention to whatever provides a different emphasis or perhaps even something completely different from the well-known and standard *topoi*. And it is hardly surprising that with this method we can make real discoveries in those demonologists who collected enormous treasuries of anecdotes and examples. What sort of witches were Nicolas Rémy (privy counselor and attorney general for the duchy of Lorraine, 1530–1612) and Henry Boguet (Burgundian witch judge, 1550–1619) describing when they reported finding witches who healed and helped others?[52] Some unconventional witches confessed that at their gatherings they heard instrumental dance music, took up contact with angels and with the dead, and worked a magic that made animals begin to speak, as reported by the Dominican Bartolomeo Spina (ca. 1479–1547) and the Milanese theologian Francesco Guazzo.[53] And strangest of all, what kind of witches were those who revived the dead—both animals and human beings—instead of killing the living?[54] Here it was imperative to be cautious and to avoid raising false hopes and aspirations. The demonologists generally hastened, therefore, to insist that these "druids" and "witch societies" only "entertained themselves with false and illusory amusements."[55] But was this charge credible if they had already noticed that even their choice of meeting place suggested remarkably good taste? For the demonologists had also noted that "their meetings take place . . . mostly on high mountain tops, where beautiful and pleasant fields are found, or in delightful broad valleys . . . or in large palaces or in extensive wine cellars."[56]

Even though the demonologists tried to reinforce their findings with a host of classical citations, one should still take their concerns seriously. Humanistically educated jurists such as Rémy and Boguet were well aware of methodological dangers and tried hard to avoid retelling just any old stupid and newly fabricated stories. They hoped to describe only what they knew from experience, as the new Renaissance idea of knowledge and of true historical reporting required.[57] From the Dominican inquisitor Bernard of Como down to the Reformed theologian Bartholomäus Anhorn (1616–1700), son of the reformer and chronicler of Graubünden with the same name,[58] we find in all the demonologists anecdotes and exempla that were verifiable because they named the precise places, times, and names of those involved. Of course, that does not mean that their stories were the "objective" truth, but only that these reporters appealed to the credibility of eyewitness accounts.[59] And so it is that even the *Disquisitiones Magicae,* a huge scholastic treatise on the demonic world of wonders and magic published in 1600 by the influential Jesuit scholar Martin Delrio (1551–1608), a work that wove together the first coherent description of the witches' sabbath, still retained a trace of popular ideas. Even Delrio invoked the idea of the game of the good society (ludus bonae societatis) and conveyed a vague impression of banquets, dancing, and music, even if they were perverted now into a demonic phenomenon and even if his account was based completely on "written authorities."[60]

In addition to these anecdotal stories found in the demonologies, there are countless examples that never found their way into print. That does not make them less significant, for writers had no special criteria for testing the empirical reliability of what they reported. If one looks at the production of anecdotes and exempla during the age of the Baroque, one can see in the case of Delrio just how fragile the empirical base of sermon topics often was.[61] Their ancestry and meaning in their original context were forgotten in the transparent effort to use them to make religious polemics. Often one cannot even tell where they come from. With the *ludus bonae societatis,* however, we can see that Delrio was borrowing mainly from Bernard of Como, and that the above-mentioned Anhorn was borrowing in turn from Delrio.[62] Often enough the origin of an exemplum was cited only vaguely or not at all, as in Anhorn's description of an English fairy society, "a big house filled with candle light and full of men and women, who were enjoying a banquet with fine things," accompanied by "lusty singing, jubilation, and rejoicing," in the middle of the night, far from the nearest village.[63]

Keith Thomas has reminded us that the fairies of popular medieval belief "were neither small nor particularly kindly;" they bear little resemblance to the picture we get of them from later "fairy tales." The Anglo-Saxon idea of "elf-shot," which corresponds to the later German idea of *Hexenschuss* (witches' shot), indicates that such fairies were by no means harmless.[64] The English tried to classify these beings and to distinguish singing, dancing, and celebratory fairies from protective spirits, house spirits, mermaids, and water nymphs, as well as from other monstrous figures,[65] but these were in the end just speculative distinctions because there were still other ideas of ancestral spirits, sleeping heroes, and fertility spirits, who continued to be recognized. And if we ask how strong the belief in fairies was, many questions remain. In Geoffrey Chaucer's *Canterbury Tales*, the Wife of Bath says

> In the old days of King Arthur . . . the whole land was filled with troops of fairies. The Elf Queen and her joyous company danced many a time on many a green field. That was the old belief, I've read. I speak of many hundred years ago. But no one sees the fairies any more, for nowadays the prayers and over-flowing Christian charity of mendicants and other saintly friars, who go about every nook and corner of the country thick as motes in a sunbeam. . . . Where elves used to go, there now walks the begging friar.[66]

And yet we may ask how credible such witnesses are. In the famous trial of Joan of Arc (ca. 1410–1431), the Maid of Orleans reported that she had once called upon an angel to drive the English out of France, but the evidence against her also included allegations of dancing around a "fairy tree." To her inquisitorial questioners in the third public session held on 24 February 1431, Joan answered

> Yes, near to Domrémy there was this tree. They called it the Tree of the Mistresses or sometimes the Tree of the Fairies. Nearby was a spring. Sick people are supposed to go there to scoop up water to drink, in order to get well. I have seen that myself. . . . Often I amused myself there with the other girls. I braided wreaths for the picture of Our Dear Lady of Domrémy. The old people used to say that long ago—before my time—the fairies carried on there. . . . I have seen the girls hang bunches of flowers over the limbs of the tree, and occasionally I did it with them. . . . I don't know anymore if I danced near the tree once I was grown up; it is certainly possible that I danced there with the other girls; but I sang more than I danced. . . . My brother told me that in Domrémy they said: "Joan received her commission under the Fairy Tree."[67]

Her fairies, her asceticism, the appearance of the angel, the message for the king, her prophecies for the future, wondrous healings, a promise from the angel to show Joan paradise, her conviction of being the chosen one—many traits of Joan of Arc were characteristic of a peasant prophetess, one who obviously borrowed from a broad repertory of popular motifs. And the more closely the Inquisition asked about her notions of the fairies, the more astonishing were the confessions from the peasant maid. On 17 March 1431: "Don't you know anything about those beings who came on the winds, accompanied by the fairies?" Joan's answer: "I was never there and knew nothing about it. I heard tell that they went there Thursdays, but I don't believe it."[68] On 30 May 1431, we will recall, "Jehanne," as she signed her confession, was burned to death in Rouen as a heretic and a conjurer of the devil. But the prophecy did not die, and after the partial expulsion of the English from France, her trial was opened again in 1450. Several Dominicans who had sat on her original Inquisitorial tribunal now found themselves answering questions, and in 1456 witnesses from Joan's hometown were finally heard. Of course the topic of the fairies came up again (in question 9). A seventy-year-old peasant testified that even today the youth regularly went out to the fairy tree, where they danced and picnicked, and this testimony was confirmed by all the other witnesses. But no one claimed to have actually seen fairies anymore.[69] As early as 1456 we can see that many had begun to regard the Maid of the Fairy Tree as a saint. She was indeed rehabilitated but was not officially declared a saint until 1920.[70]

The mendicant friars in Chaucer's *Canterbury Tales*, who supposedly drove out the fairies, may have been a disguised reference to the impact of the inquisitors, who mainly came from the mendicant orders. But why did fairies play such a large role in these trials when supposedly no one believed in them anymore? Writing in 1584, the Kentish gentleman Reginald Scot (1538–1599) claimed that fear of fairies had been replaced by fear of witches. But at the end of the seventeenth century William Temple claimed that belief in fairies had dwindled away only in the previous thirty years: "When I was a boy, our country people would talk much of them." And Keith Thomas has pointed out that for centuries the English have relegated their belief in fairies to the past, or to country people, or to the memories of one's childhood. But when folklorists of the nineteenth century began to search systematically for such beliefs, they found that these notions were still very much alive.[71]

Trial documents from the British Isles demonstrate that in the sixteenth century magicians not infrequently claimed that it was fairies who had given them their magical powers—their abilities to heal and to foretell the future.

Joan Tyrry of Somerset for example testified in 1555 that she could recognize bewitchments "because the fairies told her so."[72] Despite the scorn cast upon such ideas by intellectuals, we can tell that fairy beliefs were still intensely alive in early modern Britain because con artists could actually exploit belief in the existence of fairies. They sometimes inveigled their fellowmen to give up their money, promising to "invest" the money with the fairies, or they stole game from the forests and tried to explain the strange disappearance as tribute for the Queen of the Fairies.[73] And in Wales there were folk magicians who claimed to go traveling regularly on certain nights with the fairies.[74]

If one treated the fairies well, keeping one's house neat or offering them food, one might be rewarded by them. But if they were neglected, they could cause the same sorts of damage as witches. Just as in the Alps, medieval English theologians were quick to condemn as demon worship the common custom of leaving out nighttime food for the fairies.[75] But why did people cling so tenaciously to the dangerous belief in fairies? Functionalist ethnologists and folklorists have pointed to the social function of fairy belief in the peasant society of Ireland and in the rural England of the sixteenth century: "Fairy beliefs helped to reinforce some of the standards upon which the effective working of society depended." Houses were kept clean, children were carefully tended, neighbors were helped, borrowed property was promptly returned, and people looked out for each other, etc. These were reasons enough that fairy stories were well-loved among the people, for they made it certain that children learned early the importance of good social behavior. Moreover, fairy beliefs, like the later witchcraft beliefs, helped explain any otherwise inexplicable misfortune, which could then be combatted through the use of "supernatural" measures.[76]

The extent to which such fairy beliefs, as we find them in literature or in the trial documents, made their way into scholarly works was often purely a matter of chance. Not every inquisitor or judge had the distinctly literary ambitions of Rémy, who composed poems in his leisure time. And yet this is probably not the reason why the *benandanti*,[77] Zuanna delle Piatte, or Chonrad Stoeckhlin did not appear worthy of mention in the contemporary demonological literature. There were, rather, serious grounds for thinking that the game of the good society and the people of the night did not really fit the cultural grid of the demonologists. Fairy people or "good fellows" who worked miracles were not part of the worldview of Christian theologians. Miracles were, after all, a privilege of the "orthodox" church, which assumed that it alone had received a commission from God to administer His affairs on earth. The Jesuit Delrio wrote, "Miracula sunt Ecclesiae Catholicae & nulli dantur qui sit extra Ecclesiam Catholicam" (miracles belong to the Catholic Church and are not granted to anyone who is outside the Catholic Church).[78]

Demonologists wanted to write about diabolical gatherings, and therefore contradictory ideas had to be omitted or reinterpreted. Thus, demonologists usually only hinted at popular errors of the sort we are examining here. In addition, testimony about them was often mixed with references to heresy and witchcraft. And yet it is amazing to see that after the early examples from Milan in 1390 and Bressanone in 1457, fresh examples of ideas about fairies can be found over and over again. Suspected of witchcraft (*streghoneria*), a certain Benvegnuda Pinicella, from the Val Camonica, who admitted she had participated in dances on the Witch Mountain called Tonale, on the border with the Sulzberg Valley, confessed to the Venetian Inquisition, when they convened in Brescia in July of 1518, that she had gone traveling with the Mistress of the Game (la Signora del zuogo).[79] The *benandanti* of Friuli, whom the Venetian Inquisition turned into witches, testified around 1600 that, led by an angel, they traveled during the Ember nights to certain places in order to battle the *Malandanti* (evil-goers) or the *streghoni* (witches).[80] The Hessian fortune-teller Diel Breull (d. 1632) from Calbach claimed, to the contrary, that during the Ember days he would go up onto the Venusberg, where Lady Holt would show him the dead and their punishments. Breull, who called his travels the night journey (*Nachtfahr*), triggered off one of the largest Calvinist witch hunts of all time.[81]

The question naturally arises whether there is any common pattern to be found behind these ideas of a "good society," regardless of who referred to it or did not refer to it. The conception of a good people existing parallel to the dreary world of daily reality, especially ideas of music of unearthly beauty, played by the night people or by the *Säligen Lütt* (blessed, i.e., dead, people), carries with it possible traces of a peasant utopia. Stories about the "blessed" were well known not only in Central Switzerland but also in the Austrian Alpine region, and especially in the Tyrol (northern, eastern, and southern Tyrol) and in Carinthia. Synonyms for them were "the blessed women," "the noble maidens," "the blessed girls" or even the "holy people," or the "angelic people."[82] They were enchanted but peaceful people from the mountains who helped human beings, spoke with animals, rewarded the good and sometimes punished the bad, and they possessed the gift of flight.[83] Here is a legend from the Obervinschgau ("Val Venosta" in Italian) that people connected to a hill that is situated in the middle of the valley, a hill called *die Salge* (the blessed).

> In the old days the *Salg*-maidens used to live here. They dwelt under these blocks of stone in broad, magnificent chambers and were kindly disposed and friendly to people. They were usually cheerful, but now and again, and especially during bad weather, they fell into bad moods. Often, dressed in white, they sat of an evening on the "big stone" under the old larch tree and sang all sorts of songs. One evening as they were singing like this, a herdsman passed by and was so enchanted by the beautiful singing that he stopped, sat himself down on a rock, and listened deep into the night to the *Salg*-maidens, until they disappeared with the setting moon.[84]

A mournful tale from Lüsen in the South Tyrol contains another reference to the *Saligen* folk: "Back then was a happy time, for every place a *Saliges* dwelt enjoyed blessing and full plenty." Peasant utopias were connected to the existence of the *Saligen*. They helped in gathering berries and in spinning flax, and they gave advice about what should be planted and when the fields should be plowed or harvested. They spun threads that had no ends, baked bread that never got smaller, no matter how much one cut off; milk that increased when the *Saligen* drank of it. Whoever was permitted to dance with the *Saligen* could count himself lucky, and very lucky peasants were even allowed to take a *Salige* to wife.[85] The demonologists also knew of fairies who helped with the housework but they connected them with classical antecedents:

Some were called *penates, lares domestici*, spirits of the house, night ladies, white ladies, good ladies, who can be heard in the dark of night, and whoever hears them imagines that they are doing all the housework, going up and down stairs, opening and closing doors, lighting fires, drawing water, preparing food, and carrying wood into the kitchen, . . . washing the plates and platters from which one had eaten, putting them away in their places, and doing other jobs too. These spirits are called *Manes, Drulli, Cobold, Gutele*, etc.[86]

Such notions of fairies were widespread throughout much of Europe and had a close relationship to ideas of witchcraft, although they were usually starkly opposed to the witches.[87]

The most amazing aspect of the Lucerne records is the strength of the reports concerning the appearances of spirits, which the skeptic Cysat not only described and tried to interpret, but which he himself also experienced (in their demonic versions) when he climbed Mount Pilatus and Mount Rigi.

There are other spirits too up in these high and wild Alps. Some of them can be heard and seen only at night, sometimes riding horses and sometimes taking the shapes of real persons, whom one knows to be living. Sometimes they come up the mountain and through the forest near Lake Pilatus, riding and racing with a full charge of horses in such a mass as if they were several hundred horses, and with such a loud rushing and with such force that the whole mountain seems to be shaken by them, and it sounds like an earthquake, and as if many great cannons were being fired at once. And sometimes it roars around the dairy huts at night, making such a wind and such a shaking that it feels as if it is going to collapse, as I myself experienced in 1566 and again in 1572, when I was up there with my group on Alp Fronstafel, when we were staying overnight there. This I heard and experienced myself. Moreover, a large dog that was with us, after whining miserably for a long while, went crazy on the spot and scratched its own eyes out.[88]

Here it is not even the personal experiences with demonic armies of spirits that provide the truly sensational aspects of Cysat's reports, but his observations concerning the blessed people (*Säligen Lütt*), especially because of their spatial and temporal closeness to notions of the night phantoms (*Nachtschar*). As late as 1568, many claimed to have seen these spirits moving through the streets of Lucerne, "playing delightfully on stringed instruments." Many averred that they had been visited by the *Säligen Lütt* in their houses, where they cooked and feasted even though on the next day no one noticed any decrease in the food supplies. And here we find a motif that recurs regularly in witchcraft trials too: the "trip to the cellar," the nocturnal invasion of someone else's wine cellar, where quantities of wine are consumed. But on the next day there is no noticeable deficit in the wine supply, for the night people, using their supernatural powers, as with the miracle of the bones, replenished whatever losses they caused.

An acquaintance of Cysat's, who had been a servant to a Lucerne city counselor around 1530, gave another detailed personal account of just such an experience. The owners of the houses visited by the *Säligen Lütt* did not actually belong to their number, but after such a visit they were obviously highly regarded by any neighbors or acquaintances who knew about the honor bestowed upon such households.

> And living persons also considered it a considerable honor to offer them society and friendship. Sometimes they traveled with them, but at other times they were visited by them in their houses, as in the case of persons about whom I heard the following, as someone testified before me and before other honorable persons. This person was in his youth a servant of a very old city counselor here, back around 1530, a man who with his old wife had the reputation of being "in" that society of the *Säligen*, which he also saw and experienced. These old persons used to sleep at night during the winter in the living room, and one night they bade their servant to leave the room, but he hid himself behind the stove and heard a swarm as if from a crowd of people coming in the parlor door (which were none other than these spirits). In the moonlight he saw a great multitude of heads standing around the bed of the old people, and he heard them mumbling and whispering something in secret amongst themselves (which he could not understand). And then they went into the kitchen, where they prepared food, cooking, steaming, roasting, and feasting, although next morning one could not tell that they had taken any food or drink, or anything else, or that they had altered anything at all. This old married couple were therefore held in even higher regard throughout the whole city, and were thought themselves to have been "blessed" [*sälig*], and I myself can testify to having often heard this claim in the days of my youth.[89]

Here again we find the typical references to fairy beliefs from one's child-hood. But whenever Cysat allows his own experience to affect his story, as he repeatedly does, it means that at least as late as the 1560s notions of fairies were still alive in Switzerland, and that they were still believed. For example, according to folk beliefs, those who "traveled" with the good society sup-posedly received advantages from them. Cysat repeatedly emphasized that "the living who traveled with them [the society of the blessed people] were regarded as holy and blessed—unfortunately, I regret to say, the world was and still is in many places thoroughly blinded by these old superstitions."[90] The wife of one of Cysat's acquaintances from the local honorability main-tained that her soul often went on trips and therefore could reveal things "that no one in our fatherland knows of yet." Here we find ourselves again in the complex of prophecy, although in a rationalized form. When asked about it, the woman explained that she did not travel in the body, "for her body remained lying there in bed, and only her spirit or soul went traveling out in this way."[91]

We have seen this motif of the soul's journey in other contemporary sources. We find it repeatedly mentioned in witchcraft trials, for example in the witchcraft trial documents from Lucerne from 1499 and 1500, that is, three generations before the recorded observations of Cysat. Fortune-teller Hans Tscholi came from the valley of Entlebuch between Lucerne and Bern, a high alpine valley with a rebellious population and a tradition of regular political uprisings.[92] He testified that in his family there always had to be someone "who was ecstatic from time to time, and who had to travel among the dead, and now he was the one who had to undergo this." Tscholi's rap-tures were thus completely involuntary, and he did nothing to bring on this condition. The dead commanded him to take care of the surviving members of his family. In return, Tscholi requested information about who might be threatening his land with witchcraft. So Tscholi became a witch doctor, just like Zuanne delle Piatte, Chonrad Stoeckhlin, or Diel Breull. He discovered harmful sorceresses in Entlebuch and throughout the surrounding coun-tryside. Mostly he found women who caused storms, because as in all pre-industrial societies it was the weather that determined the harvest and therefore the welfare of both individuals and the whole community.[93] One of the most important tasks of a witch finder, therefore, was to detect those whose ill will was damaging their neighbors or the whole society.[94] Witnesses testified that Tscholi was known as a witch finder and that he was sought out by people in trouble. When the Krienbach River overflowed its banks after a storm on Mount Pilatus and when rumors circulated about who was responsible, people sought out Tscholi. He announced that the dead had informed him that four women, whose names he gave, had tried to destroy the little town by causing a storm and the flooding of the Krienbach.[95]

Tscholi thus knew how to employ his ecstasies as legitimation for his divinatory and magical practices. Was it just a conventional topos, or was it part of his defense when he claimed that his trips occurred involuntarily? Whatever the case, we find the same assertion in the stories told by our horse wrangler from the Allgäu, Chonrad Stoeckhlin. In the hearing held 15 November 1586, he tried again to convince his inquisitorial judges that his trips had nothing at all to do with magic: "He claimed that he needed no art for his journey, other than what he has already confessed, namely that he falls unconscious."[96] His participation was not voluntary. Just as with the Benandanti, Stoeckhlin was summoned to his flight by his angel. And although he obtained many advantages from traveling with his "good society," his night phantoms, he once complained that he "wished that someone could stop him from going off on these trips, for he did not feel good about them."

10.

Wuotas

IN THE ALLGÄU Stoeckhlin was an isolated figure with his ideas about the night phantoms. We cannot find this notion in any other texts from that specific region, not in contemporary chronicles or trial documents, and not in later collections of legends. Of course Stoeckhlin did belong geographically to the region of those eccentric references to the night people which spilled northward over from the valley of the Lesser Walser Valley into the Oberstdorf basin.[1] In the legends of the Allgäu a vague idea of "the journey" does crop up a few times, but it is clear enough that this meant the "wild journey," which along the northern edge of the alpine chain was just another name for the "wild hunt." The more usual name for this phenomenon in the Allgäu, however, was the "army of Muetes" or the "army of Wuetes," or simply "Muotas" or "Wuotas" for short.[2]

This idea is still alive today. Terrible thunderbolts in the midst of a storm, or for that matter all kinds of unexpected, loud noises, are referred to with this term. When children play too loudly, people still complain about the "hellish noise": "Hey, you're thundering like Wuotas!" And this detail is already a obvious sign that Wuotas was radically different from the people of the night. Not heavenly music but awful noise was its characteristic. In addition, Wuotas did not bring any good; instead, it caused frightful damage. And this was true from the earliest references onwards. All the later examples, such as those in Cysat or in the *Chronicle of the Counts of Zimmern* point in the same direction, and when nineteenth-century researchers collected legends of the "furious army," it was still the same. And now we have finally arrived at the "wild hunt," that legend under which the night people and the night phantoms are usually subsumed, even by contemporary reports. The women of Oberstdorf, and specifically Anna Enzensbergerin (1526–1586), whom Stoeckhlin accused as a witch, were convinced that Stoeckhlin had been traveling with "Wuetten's army."[3]

If we look throughout the whole Alemannic linguistic region, we do find some references to the furious army in the fifteenth and sixteenth centuries. In fact, the idea was so well-known that it could be deployed in political polemics. The pugnacious Hans Salat of Lucerne (1488–1561), for example, composed the following verses in his anti-Zwinglian satire of 1532, *The Triumph of the Swiss Hercules* ("Triumphus Herculis Helvetici"):

> And then from the rocks comes a horrible horde [*schar*]
> Emerging from the stone wall
> Mounted on horses and many other kinds of animals,
> Hideous in shape and gruesome in form,
> I thought the devil was attacking me.
> And yet things turned out better.
> They flew away from my hut
> Through bushes, up hill and down dale, over the meadow
> and through the woods.
> I thought this is indeed an odd prince,
> These are the people from Brattelematten.[4]

Brattelematten was a large alpine meadow near Lucerne, which was named as the place of the witches' dance in many of the witchcraft trials from Lucerne. So the army of Wütis (as it was called in Swiss sources) was associated here with witches, but in other cases with the people of the dead, which then carried connotations of the devil. The position taken by the Zurich theologian, Ludwig Lavater, is interesting for us, because he classified the army of Wütis under the general category of the dead and of the dance of death, and concluded with a statement that obviously did not draw on literary histories but was derived from what he had heard himself: these are beings "who sometimes seem to have accompanied people. No one can adequately describe each and every form in which these spirits appear, for the Evil One, who stages and produces these things, can transform himself into all forms, as the ancient poets say of Proteus." When souls appeared, they just had to be delusions of the devil because according to God's plan, "the souls of the faithful remain in heaven and those of the damned stay in hell until the Last Judgment, and so they don't wander anywhere."[5]

The furious army requires a separate examination here because with this topic we have a perfect example of the errors that have often been made in understanding old folk beliefs. Folklore scholars of the mid-nineteenth century developed a variety of theories about folktales without paying any attention to the actual testimony of persons who claimed (long before anyone collected folkloric reports of such legends) to have personally traveled with the night phantoms, or with the night people, or with the blessed people (the *säligen Lütt*). Research into ideas about the night people and the night phantoms was conducted within the framework of mythological studies, as we can see clearly in the case of Franz Josef Vonbun. This "father of Vorarlberg legend research" had heard of the night people from his great aunt, an old woman of Walser stock, when he was a child. This old lady, born two generations before the famous collector of fairy tales, that is, probably about 1760, had not told Vonbun any "fairy tales," however, for she maintained that she had experienced "it" herself.[6] But during his university studies in Innsbruck, Vonbun fell under the heavy influence of German romanticism. Stimulated by the Innsbruck professor of Germanic literature Ignaz Vinzenz Zingerle, who from 1842 onward had followed the lead of the Brothers Grimm in collecting the "Folk Legends of the Tyrol," Vonbun in turn published in 1847 a first little volume of "Folk Legends of Vorarlberg," containing thirty-six texts, three of which were legends of the night people drawn from the Greater Walser Valley.[7]

In the interpretations that he provided, as opposed to the texts of the legends themselves, it becomes clear that Vonbun was already deeply in debt to Jacob Grimm's (1785–1863) "German Mythology," which had appeared in 1835. And the night people, understood as a specific, regional variant of notions of the spirits, received separate treatment in a new chapter in the second, expanded edition of 1858. Grimm's mythology grew to seem increasingly obvious, however, and by the end of the century it became a simple dogma. In 1860, the Wild Huntsman or the furious army was placed at the very beginning of Zingerle's "Legends of the Tyrol."[8] And this, in turn, influenced the "Folk Legends of Vorarlberg," for the last edition, published under the editorship of Hermann Sander in 1889, adopted wholeheartedly the organizing principles of Grimm's mythological assumptions. The work was now divided into ten chapters (plus an eleventh chapter entitled "Miscellaneous"), which subsumed the night people under the category of the army of Wuotanes. Wuotanes was in turn associated with the late Teutonic king of the gods, Wotan, who therefore—on the analogy of the Ten Commandments—found a place of importance right at the beginning. Local conceptions such as Muotas, Wuotas, or even Guotas[9] were now simply reinterpreted and reshaped according to the precepts of mythological theory as synonyms for Wotan's Army.[10] It was now unavoidable that researchers into folk narratives, such as Karl Reiser from Oberstdorf, would also deploy the schema of Jacob Grimm to interpret the legends of Allgäu,[11] but the rise of this interpretive school, strongly accelerated as it was by nationalism, was by no means restricted to Germany. The paradigm was employed throughout the whole Germanophone area, as we see not only in the textual classification schemes of Zingerle and Vonbun, but in Swiss examples as well.[12]

In Switzerland, of course, such citations were not entirely misleading, because this was precisely the area in which the notion of the night phantoms was later to be found. It can be shown from early medieval sources that the late-Germanic cult of Wotan did establish a foothold here and that it was still flourishing in the early seventh century. In the biography of the most important missionary to this region, Saint Columban (543–615), we read

> Thereupon they came to their destination [i.e., Bregenz]. And when he had seen it, the Man of God [i.e., St. Columban] said that it did not look the way he had expected, but that he would remain there for some time nonetheless, in order to plant the faith in the hearts of the heathen. In that neighborhood lived the people called the Swabians [*Suevi*]. Now as he was sojourning there, living with the inhabitants of the town, he observed that they were preparing to make a heathen sacrifice. In the middle of the place they set up a large vessel, which they call a barrel [*quem vulgo cupam vocant*], large enough to hold twenty buckets, and filled it with beer. But the Man of God strode up to this barrel and asked what was going to be done with it.

They replied that they wanted to bring a sacrifice to their God Wodan [*Illi aiunt se Deo suo Vuodano nomine*], whom they also called Mercury, according to others. But when he heard of their corrupt intentions, he blew in wrath at the vessel, whereupon it exploded wondrously with a great noise and broke into pieces. And the beer flowed like a swift river out of it. From this it was clear that the devil had been hiding in the barrel in order to ensnare the souls of votants through their heathen sacrificial drink. But when the heathen saw this, they were amazed and concluded that the Man of God had a mighty breath, with which he could destroy even this strongly reinforced vessel; whereupon he scolded them with the words of the gospel, urging them to discontinue such sacrifices in the future and telling them to go home. Whether by his powers of persuasion or through the force of his teaching, many of them were thereupon converted to faith in Christ and received baptism.[13]

This Merovingian biography originated only a few years after the death of this Irish missionary, composed around 640 by the monk from the region of Turin, named Jonah, who wrote it in the Benedictine monastery of Bobbio. His sources were the testimony and reports of persons who had known the saint. They had told of a miracle of the sun, which had occurred at the birth of the saint and had made visible his election as a special man of God. Even if the story was not literally true, at least in the biography Saint Columban was catering to the needs of the heathen. A "miracle of the bear" proved that he was a "lord of the animals," and his strict asceticism finally brought him so far that an "angel of God" appeared to him (*angelus Domini per visum apparuit*), revealing to him the structure of the world (*mundi conpagem monstravit*) in order to show him his future path in life.[14]

Saint Columban was similar to the horse wrangler Stoeckhlin in at least a couple of ways. His angel, too, communicated unknown things to him: the hidden structure of the world and secrets of the future. These apparitions also proved his saintliness and granted him credibility in the eyes of his contemporaries. So what made the holy man different from the herdsman? At least this: Columban really did confront the cult of Wodan. In contrast, almost one thousand years later, Stoeckhlin and his fellow inhabitants of sixteenth-century Oberstdorf had as little knowledge of the late-Germanic god Wotan as they did of the Celtic horse-goddess Epona. Indeed, none of the legends collected in the nineteenth century actually spoke of "Wotan." Of course, the folklorists who came after Jacob Grimm did not really dispute this fact. But at the conclusion of his collection, along with stories about the night people, Vonbun also assembled legends of men with white horses or with broad-brimmed slouch hats, whom he simply identified with Wotan.[15]

The winding paths and wild goose chases of German mythologists, whose political influence peaked in the 1930s, do not concern us here in detail, but we have to sketch their basic approach because it demonstrates the ways in which seemingly harmless scholarly research can be misused, especially for political purposes.[16] In 1934, the Viennese specialist in Old Germanic Literature, Otto Höfler (1901–1987), published a work entitled *Kultische Geheimbünde der Germanen* (Secret ritual groups of the ancient germans). In this work he interpreted the myth of the wild hunter as a reflection of a supposedly ecstatic cult of Wotan in which secret teams of men eradicated the harmful elements from their society. It is clear enough that this fiction legitimized, and was intended to legitimize, the secret deeds of the Nazis who also used "teams" such as the *Schutzstaffel* (i.e., the SS) and the storm troopers. As early as the 1920s, Höfler was himself a member of the storm troopers, although they were still prohibited in Austria, and in the 1930s he became a coworker of the SS-*Ahnenerbe*. The Reichsführer of the Order with the Death's Head (the SS) intervened personally to guarantee the rapid success of Höfler's German academic career.[17]

The Viennese "school of ritualists," who absorbed the then-current ethnological literature and assumed that Teutonic myths were a reflection of actual rituals, found their most embittered opponents in the members of the so-called Viennese "school of mythologists."[18] Well before the *Anschluss* of Austria to Nazi Germany, the representatives of this school of interpretation were just as firm in their National Socialism as the ritualists, but they totally rejected the idea of ecstatic fighters drawn from the ranks of the blond, blue-eyed Teutons; instead they thought of ecstatics as "degenerate" (*Artfremd*). For them the wild hunt was a demonized vestige of the ancient Germanic "high religion,"[19] demonized by Christianity, which thus came in for the sharp criticism that was part of the Nazi *Kulturkampf*. During the Nazi period, both within Germany and without (as in Austria) this school of mythologists depended on Alfred Rosenberg, the Nazi minister for ideological questions. Take for example, Edmund Mudrak of Vienna. In 1938, together with other followers of Rosenberg, Mudrak demanded a systematic "folklore on racist foundations," which would study the "pure" beliefs of the ancient Teutons in order to set up a racially pure German faith over against the "degenerate" Christian ("Jewish-Roman") Church. [20]

In this context, research into the supposed army of Wotan was bound to seem politically highly useful to both of these antagonistic schools of Germanic studies. All too quickly and predictably, "tall men in slouch hats" showed up among the night people in the article on the night people published in 1936 in the *Handwörterbuch des deutschen Aberglaubens* (Encyclopedia of German superstitions).[21] And yet the topics "wild hunt" and "furious army" (*"wilde Jagd"* and *"Wütendes Heer"*) did not receive separate articles, even though there had been plenty of references to these notions in the earlier volumes of this multivolume lexicon, published between 1928 and 1941. The volume that would have contained them (*W-Z, with Supplements*) was finally published in 1941, but obviously by that point no one wanted to burn his fingers on a topic that had been so contaminated through direct exploitation by Rosenberg and the SS-Ahnenerbe.

This corruption and misuse of research results provoked open opposition even under the Nazi dictatorship.[22] And after 1945 these efforts at stitching together a spurious continuity were fundamentally repudiated, even though, astonishingly enough, almost all of these scholars survived the change of regime with no trouble.[23] Editors of legend collections also acknowledged the new zeitgeist, as if Wotan himself had been tried before the Nuremberg tribunal.

In a greatly enlarged new edition of Vonbun's legends of Vorarlberg, in 1950, Richard Beitl sensibly decided to organize the legends by their respective valleys and to provide a concordance with which one could find three differently arranged stories of the night people.[24] A short while later Beitl followed the same organizational principle of arranging things by their geographical origin when he published his own extensive collection of legends, including new legends from Vorarlberg.[25] In his interpretation, Wuotas and the night people now made up a subchapter within the complex "Forms and Motifs of the Legend in Vorarlberg," in which Wuotas was no longer connected to Wotan but instead to the furious army (*das Wütende Heer*); Beitl contents himself with simply pointing to a possible common etymological root for Wotan, Wuotas, and the furious army.[26] Beitl regarded the main differences between Wuotas, the night people, and the night phantoms (*Nachtschar*) as mainly their geographical distribution. While Wuotas is found mainly in the lowlands of Vorarlberg and in the Allgäu, and legends about the night people are spread mainly in Montafon and in the Walser Valley, the names "night phantoms" (*Nachtschar*) and "people of the dead" (*Totenvolk*) are limited to Graubünden and Rhaetia, that is, to eastern Switzerland.[27]

In the 1970s an *Atlas of Swiss Folklore* was published based on data collected between the years 1937 and 1942. It shows all too clearly the methodological nonsense of trying to interpret certain beliefs as coming truly from the "German race." The legends of the wild hunter or of the furious army can be found in French Switzerland (where they are known as the *haute chasse*, or the *chasseur maudit*) and in Italian Switzerland, too (*Cascia selvàdiga, Cascia salvàdiga*).[28] The ideas of nocturnal armies of the dead, moving about and fighting, the processions of subterranean divinities with their swarms of attendant spirits, have been well-known ever since classical antiquity. Herodotus and Pausanias, Pliny the Elder and Tacitus, Tertullian and Eusebius of Caesarea, all mention these spirit processions.[29] The medieval army of the dead, the devil's swarm (*des tiuveles geswarme*), as it is called in the version of the *Song of Roland* written by Pastor Konrad, was newly described for the first time as the "furious army" (*das wüetende her*) in the early thirteenth-century poem *Moriz von Craon*.[30] Around 1230 the poet known as Der Stricker equated the "devil's army" with the "furious army,"[31] while the *Night Blessing* (*Nachtsegen*) in a Munich manuscript (the "Codex latinus monacensis 615"), dating from roughly 1300, established the connection between "*trutan* and Wutan, Wutan's army and all his men."[32]

In his eighteenth Lenten sermon, "On the Furious Army," Geiler of Kaisersberg set down an unforgettable portrait of the horrible society of the dead made up of men and headless horses with missing members, their intestines hanging out, and with generally horrifying external appearances; he also included the hunter with his dogs and retinue, who soar through the winds at night with a hellish noise, threatening anyone who stood in their way. Obviously none of this has much to do with Stoeckhlin and his night phantoms. And yet Geiler also remarked

> You say, what do you mean by the furious army? I cannot tell you much about it; in fact, you know more about it than I do. Common people speak about it thus: It is composed of those who die prematurely, before the time God has ordained for them, such as mercenary soldiers or those who are stabbed, hanged, or drowned. They must roam about long after their death until the time comes which God ordained for them. And thus God uses them to achieve whatever His divine will decrees. And those who roam like this, they go about mostly in the Ember fasting times, and especially during the Ember days before Christmas, which is the holiest time. Each one roams about dressed in his own clothes, a peasant as a peasant, a knight as a knight, tied to a rope and holding before him some internal organ. Another carries his head in his hand and runs on ahead of them, screaming, "Get out of the way, so that God may give you life." This is how the common man talks about them.[33]

Here we have a clear description of the furious army as a popular belief or idea, one that could not be reconciled easily with orthodox Christian belief. Moreover, this "horrible, frightful furious army," as Hans Sachs (1494–1576) called it, this army that spread fear and terror as innumerable German texts of the sixteenth century affirm, including the full descriptions in the *Chronicle of the Counts of Zimmern*, appears to have had little to do with the fairy-like appearance of the night people.[34] Attempts to explain these legends, in which connections have been drawn to the wild hunt and to other similar phenomena, have mobilized highly divergent versions of these legends, emphasizing similarities to the "poor souls" (not yet in purgatory) or to the witches. The thorough researches of Guntern in the Upper Valais Valley even turned up a few old storytellers who produced a charming explanation: This army of spirits was simply "the evil society" (*böse Gesellschaft*).[35]

If we can reject the possibility that this phrase was just a euphemism, the idea that there was an "evil society" that stood in sharp contrast to "good people" or to the "good society" is immediately persuasive. We have seen

Wuotas

that the fairy appearance of the night people does not fit at all well with the demonic qualities of the furious army, and the same is true of the night phantoms in the version told by our herdsman of Oberstdorf, Chonrad Stoeckhlin. He did have a "leader" on his nocturnal travels, to be sure, but this was supposedly an angel, a brilliant figure, clad in white with a cross on his forehead and without the slouch hat or other horrible attributes. Moreover, this leader is a truly helpful spirit, who promises his adept progress in spirituality and a greater hope that he would attain a worthy place in the hereafter, the other world. His night phantoms, who led men and women peacefully to distant places, seem but a faint echo of better-known myths and legends. Perhaps one should not even raise the tangled question of where these ideas came from; instead, let us see how they functioned. What connection did the story of the night phantoms have to the real world in which Stoeckhlin lived?

11.

Healing and Prophecy

Because of their mobility and their independent lifestyle, herdsmen in many regions of Europe were seen as members of a social group to whom contemporaries attributed a special charisma. Emmanuel Le Roy Ladurie has given us perhaps the most impressive example of this special status in his famous book on the heretical village in southwestern France, Montaillou. There too it was herdsmen, moving back and forth across the French-Spanish border of the Pyrenees, who managed to keep the tradition of the Cathars alive even after the Inquisition began its persecutions. Once the persecutions began, Guilleaume Belibaste (d. 1321), who belonged to the highest caste of the *perfecti*, was able to disappear among the herdsmen along with many other Cathar missionaries.[1] In the case of the *perfecti*, this life of transhumance, of migrating with their herds, may have even strengthened what one finds in the nature of mountain herdsmen everywhere. The direct confrontation with the forces of nature, the camaraderie around the campfire, the freedom from feudal oppression, and perhaps also the monastic asceticism of their solitary hermitages, along with the leisure required for contemplation, and the necessity of depending on their own experience in borderline situations—all of this produced a breed of men who deeply impressed their contemporaries. Added to all of that were the professional qualifications that came from daily contact with animals. Herdsmen, like blacksmiths, belonged to those male occupational groups to whom folk medicine has often ascribed special magical powers.[2]

Chonrad Stoeckhlin was, among other things, also a "healer," an occupation that was more important before professional physicians became common.[3] At his first hearing he listed those clients he had helped, and from his list we see that Stoeckhlin was well known as a healer not only in his village but perhaps beyond his village as well. People used to gossip about him, and he, too, used to brag about his successes. He had moved in a milieu that recognized these abilities, and thus his reputation was enshrouded in a local "narrative tradition."[4] This fact prompts an interesting if unanswerable question: To what extent did all these stories influence Stoeckhlin's behavior and sense of self-worth? In theory it seems obvious that there must have been a real influence. And yet it would be conceivable, too, that the herdsman was pressured by rumors of his abilities, so that he no longer had any choice but to meet the demand for ever greater achievements. Perhaps he himself came increasingly to believe in his own powers, but at the very least it is obvious that stories about his participation in the trips of the night phantoms or with the Wuotas raised local expectations concerning him.

Our herdsman clearly did little to dampen these expectations, although he seems to have tried to control them. While magistrates at that time were uncertain about the status of charismatic healers, Stoeckhlin tried to provide a Christian interpretation of his abilities. It is understandable that he regarded his "art" as thoroughly beneficial and in harmony with the divine plan, as indeed most contemporary healers did: "He said he could, and indeed that he had, through the grace of God, helped people, horses and cattle, who had been injured by bad people; he would enjoin them to pray and to fast."[5] Here again we find that element of asceticism that had come to characterize Stoeckhlin's world of ideas, according to his own testimony, ever since he first had encountered the ghost of his deceased friend Jacob Walch. It is clear that this topos was drawn from contemporary sermon *exempla* from the realm of Christian hagiography. But it is also possible that this pious story was mainly intended to impress the high court and the episcopal counselors in far-off Dillingen. In his village they would hardly have believed such stories, because we get an entirely different picture of him from the circle of witnesses who knew him. According to them Walch and Stoeckhlin were often to be found in the tavern, and they had never turned down a drink. Walch himself was said to have been dead drunk on the night he had agreed to return from the dead. At our distance we can no longer determine how much of a negative impact Stoeckhlin's heavy drinking had on his reputation as a healer.

In any event, his recognized contacts with the supernatural led his neighbors to think of his abilities as a healer and oracle as concentrating in one area of special importance to folk culture in the sixteenth century. They began to connect Stoeckhlin's specialized powers of diagnosing and treating magical illnesses to special abilities of finding the guilty ones. In this way Stoeckhlin took on the role of charismatic healer, a role that was then widespread throughout all of Europe and can still be found today in the alpine region.[6] Such healers are used not only for natural illnesses but especially for supernatural illnesses. The ordinary practices that made up this craft were divination, various oracular techniques, and the arts of counter-magic, similar to those usages we find in non-European societies.[7] In the late Middle Ages, European society had two different legal traditions with which to interpret the activities of witch doctors: On the one hand, canon law condemned such practices severely and equated them theologically with harmful magic. This was the position of the *Malleus Maleficarum* (the so-called *Witches' Hammer* of 1487), which dealt thoroughly with the question "Is it allowed to cure bewitchments through the use of other bewitchments?" In this section the author complained that ordinary people often trusted witches more than they did their priests.[8] On the other hand, Roman law did not regard this kind of harmless "white magic" as a capital crime at all. In the course of the sixteenth century secular courts tended more and more to adopt the theological point of view.[9]

Our horse wrangler was active in detecting witches, and he knew how one could force witches ritually to take back or "reverse" their magic.[10] In the folk culture of broad areas of Europe, this was regarded as the most elegant way of dealing with bewitchings and enchantments. As a local oracle for these matters, Stoeckhlin thus occupied an important position as a specialist within his area's "magical folk culture." In the criminological categories of his day, he stood accused of divination, which was understood as depending on a previous secret or open pact with the devil.[11] It is, however, of great interest that, unlike many other fortune-tellers, Stoeckhlin did not claim to have learned his art, nor did he need any of the usual magical tools such as sieve, shears, mirror, or crystal. The wrangler did not need these aids because he derived his knowledge of the future or of secret connections from a different source entirely.

In one of his many interrogations Stoeckhlin explained the connection he saw between his prophecies and his trips with the night phantoms. Asked about the origins of his certitude that a woman in Oberstdorf by the name of Anna Enzensbergerin was the witch responsible for the sickness of his client, Chonrad Stoeckhlin told his interrogators that

> He knew in the following way that Enzensbergerin was a witch and that she had caused the tavern-keeper's wife to fall ill: When the taverness got sick, she had asked him as her blood relative for aid and counsel. And so, on one of his trips he had inquired about her of his guide, whom he supposed to be an angel, whereupon his guide answered that the Entzensbergerin had done it to her. And [to cure it] he should go to her, Anna, and ask for her help, three times in the name of God and the Last Judgment, and then she would be compelled to help. Which happened just as he had expected.[12]

Stoeckhlin did not want his guide on the trip to give him just the name of this presumed witch (and of several other women), for he also wanted to learn the ritual by which the witch could be forced to take back her magic. Of course this ritual was already well known throughout the region, and so this part of his testimony is not exactly credible.[13]

The actual status of healers and local fortune-tellers within sixteenth- and early-seventeenth-century society is not easy to determine. For a start, one must recognize that their services were in real demand and that people came in contact with them fairly often. Heinrich Kramer (known in Latin as Institoris), the author of the *Malleus Maleficarum,* complained: "There are very many such witches, for they are always to be found at intervals of one or two German miles [five to ten English miles], and these seem to be able to cure any who have been bewitched by another witch."[14] His estimate seems to have been remarkably accurate. Frequently these were socially marginal persons, who eked out their living by offering magical services. And yet at the other end of the social hierarchy we also find learned or supposedly learned magicians who used their arts to gain entry to the princely courts of the day: the Englishman John Dee at the Imperial Court of Prague,[15] the gold-maker

Healing and Prophecy

Marco Bragadino at the courts of Mantua and Munich (who was executed in 1591),[16] or the alchemist Leonhard Thurneysser zum Thurn (1530–1596), personal physician to the elector of Brandenburg and a man who among other things became famous for his spectacular marital woes.[17] Here we should also mention those learned magicians who advocated experiments that led in the direction of natural science: Girolamo Cardano (1501–1576) and Giambattista della Porta (1538–1615), men who both dealt theoretically with the question of persons who magically flew through the air.[18]

Of all these learned magicians, only Cardano appears to have had ecstatic experiences, which he recounted in his autobiography and in his dream book.[19] Concerning reports of such experiences, however, the major demonologists were unanimous. Jean Bodin (1530–1596) wrote in 1581 that "Girolamo Cardano of Milan, a distinguished philosopher of our age, has recorded in his 'Genesis' the fact that he was often taken through ecstasies in raptures out of his body, as he wanted, so that he became completely without corporal sensation. But I think that all who voluntarily and while waking undertake these raptures are magicians." The great Bodin thus did not hesitate to declare that Cardano had gone on a witches' flight, and for this purpose he unscrupulously attached to Cardano a famous quotation from the writings of another learned magician, Giambattista della Porta of Naples: "We have a new history of this in the Magia naturalis of a certain Neapolitan [i.e., della Porta], who writes that he has witnessed a test of a witch, who smeared her totally naked body with a witches' salve and then fell unconscious, and when she came to herself three hours later, she told strange stories of many lands that nonetheless turned out to be true."[20] This journey of the soul thus served to acquaint her with foreign lands, and her reports of them had been tested and found to be correct. So here we find another cliché of that time. There were of course intellectuals such as Michel de Montaigne (1533–1592), for example, who expressed their doubts about this path to the truth.[21] But these folk magicians were by no means alone in their hope that they might learn unknown things through flights of the soul.

For Stoeckhlin, the phantoms of the night came to occupy a central position in his self-consciousness as a healer and prophet. It was his participation in this myth that enabled him to take on a charismatic role in his community. As a member of the night phantoms, Stoeckhlin earned respect in his village and quite possibly well beyond it, and gained clients from a social level, too, who would otherwise never have turned for help to a common herdsman. From other parts of Europe, we recognize this phenomenon of well-known healers or fortune-tellers with clienteles who came from surprisingly large catchment areas. In Nuremberg in the 1530s, for example, the city council became agitated over a certain Kunigund the Shepherdess, known as the "sorceress of Dormitz," to whom subjects of the imperial city, "the peasants and also our own citizens" constantly went traipsing off in droves.[22] The female healer Els, from the village of Ettringen in the Bavarian signory of Schwabeck, was known throughout an area with a radius of sixty miles and was consulted because of her magical recipes, which she sold for two gulden apiece.[23] The magician Christoph Gostner, from the Puster Valley in the Tyrol, who worked as an innkeeper and coppersmith in the bishopric of Bressanone, had a recruitment area that even extended from Drauburg in East Tyrol to Bolzano and Merano in South Tyrol.[24] In 1609 the episcopal government in Dillingen got worked up over a magician and prophet named Nikolaus Lachenmayer in Obergermaringen, "who attracted masses of peasants from 'round about," and "even taught this kind of necromancy to his own sons." The little imperial city of Kaufbeuren, in whose jurisdiction Lachenmayer was living, did not take his case so seriously. An inquiry was begun, but the town council seemed satisfied with his explanation that he "helped people and cattle with blessings, roots, herbs, and with other natural means." The government in Dillingen was furious that the magistrates of Kaufbeuren (who were Protestant, of course) had not only accepted the excuses of the "magician" but had gone on to defend him. Most of these magicians, however, who possessed healing and oracular powers, or what was ordinarily called "the art," had learned their crafts and had not, like Stoeckhlin, had them "bestowed" through a mystical experience. In this respect Stoeckhlin clearly assumed a special place among the large number of "adepts" in the region.[25]

This is, however, not the case if we lift our gaze beyond southern Germany. From many parts of Europe and far beyond, we know of ecstatics who obtained special healing arts from their soul travels. The *benandanti* of Friuli, for example, did more than fight to protect the harvests, for they also possessed divinatory abilities, and in particular "the ability to heal the victims of sorcery and to recognize witches."[26] This is also roughly the case with the Hungarian Taltos. Investigations into the healers of Romania have shown that those illnesses which the popular imagination identifies as caused by fairies or witches can be cured only by healers (*descantatore*) whose souls travel out of their bodies and could have visited the other world.[27] According to popular Greek notions, supernatural illnesses can only be combatted by healers who have received their powers from supernatural beings, such as nereids.[28] It is the same in the traditions of Bulgaria and Dalmatia,[29] and the Hungarian historian Gábor Klaniczay has argued that this whole complex of ideas is related to shamanism.[30]

In the summer of 1586, of course, the problem in the bishopric of Augsburg did not seem like an ethnographic puzzle. A series of terrible storms had destroyed the harvest, and unknown diseases had broken out. Throughout the whole bishopric an obscure disease known as the "epidemic death" raged so severely that the cathedral chapter of Augsburg relocated south to Füssen for fear of the pestilence. Up in the mountains, too, in the district of Rettenberg, the "epidemic death" took hold.[31] It is quite possible that these conditions lent a special explosiveness to the current scandal surrounding Stoeckhlin: when consulted, he had named a sixty-year-old woman named Anna Enzensbergerin as a witch. And she, reacting in panic, had fled the village, a dramatic and sensational action because for her contemporaries fleeing to avoid prosecution was always taken as a half confession of guilt. Anna Enzensbergerin's escape seemed to confirm Stoeckhlin's powers as a witch doctor. In the eyes of his neighbors in Oberstdorf, he had fingered the right one. So when, after a time, the deeply suspect old woman came back to Oberstdorf, Stoeckhlin's diagnosis was not forgotten. On the basis of the herdsman's word, the "judges and jurymen of Oberstdorf" had her arrested. And then they reported this successful step to the bishop and his government in far-off Dillingen. The messengers of the court, who had no magical powers and had to move on the humble level of facts, usually took four days to make the journey of about a hundred miles (twenty-two German miles) from the northern edge of the Alps to the Danube River.

12.

Witches' Flight

Dramatic events, like these stories of people who returned from the dead and of angelic apparitions, stories that were deeply rooted in daily life, may not have enjoyed much credibility any more among the serious and responsible men of the capitals and major trading cities of the Renaissance, but in the alpine valleys and in the Allgäu of the sixteenth century they were not yet absolutely out of the ordinary. In 1583, for example, in the village of Hindelang, near Sonthofen (downstream from Oberstdorf), there was a sensational event. Barbara Wilhalmin, the wife of Petter Berung, had stood before her assembled fellow-churchmembers on Laetare Sunday (the fourth Sunday in Lent) and had spectacularly summoned a neighbor of hers to God's Tribunal in the "Valley of Jehoshaphat." After the church service she had climbed "up onto the roodscreen," which guaranteed the woman the attention of all in attendance,

> proclaiming openly and with a loud voice that Andreas Prell from the said Oberndorf, together with his wife Ursula Schmidin, should give her their reply before God's Tribunal in the Valley of Jehoshaphat, on the third or fourth day, or on some other day that year as it may please God, and for this they were summoned in the name of God the Father, the Son, and the Holy Spirit. Which order or summons she shouted and proclaimed once, twice, and a third time.[1]

The same court that investigated Stoeckhlin three years later asked her, "What had prompted her to issue such an unusual and terrifying summons. Who had suggested this or advised her to do this?" And she testified that Prell and his wife had cursed her as "an evil woman or 'witch.'" She had thus been accused of witchcraft and had wanted to defend herself against this dangerous accusation without involving the government. She told the court that "in a dream God and her holy angel" had told her how to behave.[2] Behind her outburst in church was the severe crippling that afflicted the seventeen-year-old Prell boy, for which they held her responsible. So, at the beginning, we find one of those typical conflicts among neighbors that so often led to witchcraft accusations.[3] The neighbors' son had been gathering pears under Wilhalmin's tree, and she had threatened him, "She said she would anoint the pears so that he would not gather too many more of them." So when, shortly thereafter the boy went lame in his hip, his parents saw her threat as the cause of his ailment and began to worry about witchcraft: "Prell had cursed her whenever he met her alone in the village or in the fields." It is also clear why the supposedly injured Prell family had not gone to the government with their complaint: they needed the witch alive, for only she could take back the magic.[4]

This summons to the Tribunal of God in the Valley of Jehoshaphat as a response to witchcraft accusations was still in use decades later despite the efforts of magistrates to combat it, and we find echoes of it even in the last century.[5] The custom has also been recognized in the local demonology, but always with the note: "One could adduce a great many of such examples, not just old ones but also new, not only foreign but also some that have occurred in our beloved fatherland."[6] For Barbara Wilhalmin, neither her angel nor the fact that she had had so little trust in the government got her into deep trouble. She was not even interrogated for witchcraft by the district court at Rettenberg. District judge Hans Sigmund von Freiberg, district governor Johann Huber, and county clerk Mang Rether were advised by the government in Dillingen to urge the two contending parties "to leave off harassing each other with extralegal means."[7]

So we can see that even dramatic events did not necessarily lead to witchcraft trials, let alone to witchcraft executions. The tolerance for unusual occurrences was astonishingly high. But it was otherwise in the case of our herdsman who flew with squadrons of the night phantoms. The woman he had accused in the spring of 1586 after a rash of injuries, sixty-year-old Anna Enzensbergerin, had not yielded to his suggestions that she reverse her harmful magic with the customary ritual, but had instead taken to her heels. So when she returned, the "Judges and Jurymen of Oberstdorf" arrested her. They trusted the authority of the herdsman. But who made up this group? As in financial matters, the commune of Oberstdorf also had wide-ranging rights to assist in judicial affairs. In the sixteenth century the council of the town was composed of a captain and eight committeemen or jurors, who met under the chairmanship of the district governor. According to the legal ordinance of 1518, the episcopal district governor passed judgment with the help of fourteen jurors from the commune. At the end of the sixteenth century the elected district governor was assisted by a district judge, but how they got along and who took precedence probably depended mostly on their personalities.[8]

The upper class in Oberstdorf thus followed Stoeckhlin's suspicions about Anna Enzensbergerin, which rested on absolutely no legally credible evidence. The bare testimony of the herdsman, which he supposedly based on what he had learned from his leader in the night phantoms, sufficed for her arrest and led finally to her being burned as a witch by the district judge's criminal court (*Pfleggericht*). Perhaps the men of Oberstdorf were proud of their ability, with the assistance of a local prophet, to turn a seriously suspect woman over to the episcopal government. The government, however, did not react exactly as the communal representatives of Oberstdorf had expected. The district judge (*Pflegrichter*) of the court of Sonthofen-Rettenberg, now the nobleman Alexander von Schwendi (together with the above-mentioned district governor Johann Huber and county clerk Mang Rether), sent an inquiry on 18 July 1586 to the government in Dillingen. There had been, they reported, several cases of injury suffered by men and beasts in the town, and an old woman had been accused of causing them by a certain Chonrad Stoeckhlin, the horse wrangler. The captains and jurymen of Oberstdorf had thereupon arrested her and put her in jail. On 23 July the high-ranking members of the Dillingen Ruling Council (*Hofrat*) took up the matter of "witches and sorcerers in Oberstdorf." In attendance were Bishop Marquard vom Berg and his counselors Wilhelm Schenck von Stauffenberg, Court Marshall Georg Wilhelm von Stadion, Erhart von Wösternach and Hans Jacob von Rietheim, all from the ranks of the knights; together with Dr. Johann Baur,

Dr. Thomas Vogl, Dr. Albrecht Faber, and Dr. Johann Retther, from the ranks of the learned jurists; and finally, Chancellor Thomas Seld. They ruled that the suspected witch, Anna Enzenspergerin, should be kept in jail but that Chonrad Stoeckhlin was to be interrogated as well. Moreover, inquiries were to be made to find an executioner who would know "how to torture these kinds of people."[9]

This intervention of the episcopal government brought our herdsman into danger for the first time. The arrest order from the central government was obviously understood by the local court as a hint, and so investigations into the uncanny horse wrangler, Chonrad Stoeckhlin, the hero of our story, whom they had previously trusted, now turned to his disadvantage. Presumably they had learned during his initial testimony on what basis he claimed to know that Anna Enzensbergerin was guilty. In any event, on or about 27 July 1586 he was arrested by officials of the bishop of Augsburg and taken from Oberstdorf to Fluhenstein Castle, near Sonthofen, about ten miles away, carried away, in all likelihood, on a wagon to which he was chained, as was normal with criminal suspects. The mighty castle near Sonthofen had been built in 1362 by Count Oswald von Heimenhofen and inherited by the bishop of Augsburg about a hundred years later: it was now the official residence of the episcopal district governor for the lordship of Rettenberg.[10] There on 29 July 1586 Stoeckhlin was interrogated, for the first time, by the district judge, district governor Johann Huber, and the county clerk, Mang Rether. And so began the fateful series of hearings from whose records we can extract almost all of what we know about the case of Chonrad Stoeckhlin.[11]

These inquisitors for the bishop of Augsburg were deeply suspicious of Stoeckhlin's nocturnal flights, his "supposed trips with the phantoms of the night,"[12] for they suspected him of being a male witch. To their questions, however, the herdsman developed a set of clear distinctions among three sorts of flight or "journeys," as they were called in the contemporary language:

> He indicates further that there are three sorts of journey, and that those with whom he travels are called the phantoms of the night (*Nachtschar*), while the second is called the "righteous journey" (*die Rechte Fahrt*), which is the one in which the dead are led to their places. The third kind of journey is the

witches' flight. They travel through the air, but about their flight he says he knows nothing. He claims he was never among them.[13]

This answer was bound to be unsatisfactory to the jurists, if for no other reason than that they had never heard of the night phantoms, and, indeed wanted to hear nothing about them. Here we can see clearly how seriously the intentions of the court influenced the outcome of the trials. Whereas the famous Spanish inquisitor to the Basques, Don Alonso Salazar y Frias, worked to exculpate suspects, including even those who maintained that they had indeed traveled to the Aquelarre (the witches' sabbath),[14] in the bishopric of Augsburg a judgment of guilty was programed from the very beginning.

The phantoms of the night in this way became the central object of interrogation. On the basis of the written reports from the first hearing, the episcopal councillors in Dillingen formulated an official questionnaire in autumn 1586, with no fewer than 146 questions, of which questions 15 through 69 dealt with "the journeys." The first of these questions doubted whether without the use of magic his soul could really separate from and leave behind his body. The questions reveal that these educated councillors suspected that Stoeckhlin had used a witches' salve, composed of bat blood, herbs, and the fat of his own unbaptized children who had died in infancy.[15] Stoeckhlin denied all of these questions in his hearing on 15 November 1586 and related no more details of his journeys with the phantoms of the night because the leading questions of the court seemed dedicated to proving him guilty of the crime of witchcraft. Questions 29 and 30 transformed Stoeckhlin's white leader with a red cross on his forehead into a black sex-devil. The councillors in Dillingen were of the firm opinion that the squadrons of the night were really the "phantoms of witches and sorcerers" (question 33).[16]

In the 1580s the bishop of Augsburg's jurists were taking their cue from the epoch-making work *De magorum daemonomania* by the French jurist Jean Bodin,[17] as translated into German by the Strasbourg jurist and writer Johann Fischart (1546–1590). We know this was the work that inspired them because they spoke of the "witches' imperial diet" (*Hexen Reichstag*), a term that occurs only in Bodin as translated by Fischart.[18] In his book, in the section on divination, Bodin distinguished various sorts of dreams, "visions," and the apparition of angels, and emphasized most strongly the distinction of whether the phenomenon in question was sent by God or the devil. The criteria by which one could make this distinction included, of course, the content of the special communication but, especially, the personal quality of those to whom the phenomenon appeared.[19] Bodin thought very little of "raptures" (Verzückungen) because, as far as he was concerned, it was easier for the devil to carry a person bodily through the air than first to separate the body from the soul and then "carry away" (verzücken) only the soul, if such a rapture was even possible.[20] Bodin represented the opinion of most demonologists of the sixteenth century when he asserted that witches could indeed be carried bodily through the air,[21] whereas opponents of witchcraft trials such as Johann Weyer (1515–1588) proposed that the flight of witches is "not entirely different from the ecstatics, who are so raptured that they lie there exactly as if they were stone dead."[22]

"Despite vehement urgings," as the hearing protocol reported, Stoeckhlin stubbornly stuck to his original story about his journeys with the phantoms of the night. "He claimed that he needed no artifice for his journey."[23] But with respect to the composition of the phantoms, which comprised many people, Stoeckhlin did add the following clarification: "Not only men travel as phantoms of the night, but women, too. And they approach, in his opinion, the entrance of hell, but there they neither dance nor do anything, neither do they produce anything. And there are no men or women there whom they worship." He claimed to travel only four times a year. His "journey overtakes him by day or by night; once it was about three or four o'clock, once about noon, and another time it was at vesper-tide; and when he went off during the day, he also came back during the day."[24] These statements of Stoeckhlin fitted well with the observations of the Reformed theologian of Zurich, Ludwig Lavater,[25] and those of Jean Bodin, who claimed that the spirits of darkness, "appear more during the night than the day, and much more often in the night between Friday and Saturday, than on other days."[26] On the other hand, Stoeckhlin made difficulties when he declared that "On his trips, when he saw the pains and joys of the dead, he did himself participate but was not himself affected at all."[27] Inquisitors ever since the days of the Malleus Maleficarum had found (and Bodin cited this fact, too) that in their raptures witches experienced the sabbath as reality.[28] As far as Stoeckhlin was concerned, his leader was an angel and not a devil. He also insisted that he had never traveled bodily. And while under way, he sensed nothing. He was not sure, however, which orifice his soul used to escape the body. "He thinks that if his journey overtakes him while he is sitting, then his body remains there sitting." But most often he lay down on his right side.[29]

Stoeckhlin explicitly denied the suggestion that he took part in dances or that he worshipped someone at the places to which he traveled with the night phantoms. Nonetheless, the princely councillors in Dillingen came to the fixed conclusion that Stoeckhlin was a male witch, basing this idea on the following points, which we can find in their questionnaire with its 146 questions:[30]

- No one could recognize witches unless he already belonged to their society (question 70);
- The phantoms of the night were really the witches' flight to the sabbath (questions 15–40, 95–104);
- His angel was really his sex-devil (questions 6–7, 117);
- The woman Stoeckhlin accused, Anna Enzensbergerin, claimed that she had learned her witchcraft from Stoeckhlin's deceased mother;
- Shortly thereafter, her step-sister Barbara Luzin, confirmed this accusation (questions 1–6);
- Several of Stoeckhlin's children had died early—perhaps he had sacrificed them to the devil or used their corpses for making witches' salves (questions 8–14).

The idea of the witches' flight had grown during the sixteenth century until it was the customary paradigm. Just as earlier the "Canon Episcopi" had been the model for interpreting night flights, so now all other possibilities of flight (except for technical achievements of various sorts) were subsumed within the idea of the witches' flight.[31] The attraction of this idea obviously lay in the fact that in it theological and popular ideas could come together. The Christian idea of demons fitted seamlessly together with the popular belief in malevolent spirits, even though a certain "surplus" of popular notions was left over, which stuck out beyond the tight contours of Christian theology just like the clothes that Charlie Chaplin tried to stuff into his suitcase. The church tried to trim away these "excesses" (these "super-stitions" in the literal sense of the word),[32] in order to preserve a basic faith in harmful demons.

A notion of harmful, flying creatures had existed already in Greco-Roman antiquity, as we find in the well-known idea of "Strigae,"[33] but many other cultures had such notions, too. In the so-called Germanic laws of the early Middle Ages, such as the *Lex Salica* or the *Pactus Alamannorum,* which were composed about the late sixth or the early seventh century, and applied also to the Allgäu, execution was the prescribed punishment for *strias.* In a noteworthy contrast, however, the *Law of the Saxons,* dating from A.D. 785, forbade the very belief that a man or a woman could be a "striga" (*verum aliquem aut feminam strigam esse*). Burning someone to death for this crime, therefore, (*et propter hoc ipsam incenderit*) was itself a capital crime (*capitis sententiam punietur*).[34] And yet from early court financial records, we find women from the South Tyrol who were executed as *strigae,* as early as the thirteenth century. In 1296 a judge from Zenoburg in the lowlands of Bolzano registered a payment for the execution of two *strigae* (*pro exustione duarum strigarum*).[35]

The term used by Burchard of Worms, *holda,* cropped up less and less as a synonym for night-flying persons, but probably throughout the German-speaking alpine region it was replaced by its literal opposite: *uneholdi,* a term we find for the first time in a glossary dating from the twelfth century. Ear-lier, for example, in the Gothic Bible translation or in the famous Saxon bap-tismal oath of the eighth century, the concept of *Unholden* had denoted Germanic gods, whom Christian missionaries had interpreted as demons. They were clearly not human but rather supernatural beings. In Old High German glosses the word *unaholda* simply meant *diabolus,* the devil.[36] But as the new concept of witchcraft (*Hexerei*) came into Germany from Switzer-land over the course of the fifteenth century, people translated it with the term *Unholderei,* whereas in certain Romance-speaking areas the older Latin concept was preserved. And so we find direct descendants of *striga* in the Rhaeto-Romantsch *striegen* as well as in the Italian *stregha* and the Romanian *strigoi.* The *strigoi,* by the way, were not simply "witches" (*Hexen*), because this Romanian concept included the popular idea that such persons' souls left their bodies on certain nights in order to fly to certain places, even to the ends of the earth, where they fought with one another.[37]

Even Heinrich Kramer (1430–1505), the Alsatian author of the *Malleus Maleficarum*, used the word *Unholden*. He wrote a letter to the city council of Nuremberg referring to what he called his *Unholden Hammer*, and not his *Hexenhammer*.[38] *Unhold* (in Latin texts usually rendered as *striga*) was thus the term used throughout southern Germany for those demonic beings which one thought of as flying through the air, and so *Unholdenfahrt*, the journey of the *Unholden*, would be the corresponding concept. Yet there were still other synonyms for flying women, terms that come closer to the night phantoms, such as the name, "the night travelers," *die Nachtfahrenden*. In the Lesser Walser Valley, too, in the first known witchcraft trial from that valley, they spoke not of witchcraft (*Hexerei*) but of *Unholden werkh*. In 1538 in Bregenz, Anna Mutterin from Mittelberg was interrogated under torture for *Unholden werk*. And Elsa, Hans Schmid's wife in Mittelberg, had also stood under suspicion at that time.[39] It took a hundred years before the new term *Hexerei* was accepted as an equivalent: In 1623 a certain Barbara Schneiderin from the Tannberg Valley (between the Greater and the Lesser Walser Valleys) came before officials in Bregenz together with her relatives. In a deposition she complained that a certain Osch Walch had "accused her of being not only a *hexe* and an *unholde*, but also a corrupter of children, and that he had thus wounded her honor."[40] It is perhaps no accident that this successor to Stoeckhlin, here in the immediate neighborhood of Oberstdorf, had the same last name as his deceased friend, the oxherd Jacob Walch.

We can see just how thoroughly the idea of human flight came to be demonized by examining an amazing autobiographical document. Thomas Platter (1499–1582), who was later a famous doctor, spent his childhood in the Valais as a goatherd, and he reported the following experience from that time:

> Once we two herdsmen were in the woods, conversing about childish things. Among other matters, we wished that we could fly, so that we could fly up over the mountain, out of this land and into Germany; for this is what the people of Valais called Switzerland. Then there came a huge, gruesome bird zooming at us so that we thought it was going to take one or both of

us away, and so we began to scream, and to defend ourselves with our shepherds' staffs, and to bless ourselves, until the bird flew away. We said to one another, 'We did wrong in wishing we could fly; God did not make us to fly but to go on foot.'[41]

Wanting to fly was so common a desire that it could be entertained even by shepherd boys in the farthest reaches of Valais. But according to Christian theology in the Middle Ages, the dream of flight defied God's order. The Christian "prohibition of flight," exemplified by Simon Magus, who fell to the ground at the command of Saint Peter in one of the apocryphal gospels, was obviously known even to small children. The attacking alpine vulture clearly had something demonic about it, and it could be driven off only through the use of "blessings," defensive blows in the form of apotropaic prayers.[42]

13.

Heuberg

STOECKHLIN CLAIMED to have gone with the night phantoms to places where he saw pain and joy. But this bloodless vision seemed credible neither to the court or the episcopal government in Dillingen, nor to the members of his commune in Oberstdorf either. Once torture was seriously employed, moreover, and as accusations spread, the Oberstdorf witchcraft trial began to take on a life of its own. In his detailed testimony of 29 July, 15 November, and 23 December 1586, the horse herdsman provoked ever more suspicions, until finally, in his last hearing, he confessed to everything the judges wanted to hear. Yet, already at his first hearing, when Stoeckhlin was still firmly convinced of his identity as a healer and witch finder, he deeply implicated two women, Anna Enzensbergerin and Barbara Luzin (1506–1587). Both of these women must have been arrested at the beginning of August, along with three or four other women, for the records contain a reference to Enzensbergerin, Luzin, "and the other now imprisoned witches." From later reports it is clear that these must have been Barbara Kapellerin (who died in jail sometime before 19 November 1586), her sister Catharina Kapellerin (who died in jail before 19 December 1586), and Anna Weberin (who confessed on 19 December 1586).[1]

Eighty-year-old Barbara Luzin, the stepsister of Stoeckhlin's mother, at first denied that she was a witch, but by 26 and 27 August she yielded up a lengthy confession.[2] Enzensbergerin, too, must have confessed under the pressure of torture because an undated interrogation plan intended for Chonrad Stoeckhlin refers to the fact that both she and Luzin had agreed in this confession that they had learned all of their witchcraft from Stoeckhlin's mother, Ursula Schedlerin, who had died in 1571. With these confessions, Stoeckhlin's own reputation was seriously damaged, for ever since the days of the *Malleus Maleficarum*, being related by blood to a witch had been regarded as the most damning evidence of witchcraft. Another witch doctor was also accused by the suspected witches.[3] This was Conrad Schmid, captain of Niderndorff, who was supposedly "a powerful magician because he had helped many persons and cattle." The puzzling fact that witches were not supposed to help but only to harm did not distract the court. Stoeckhlin was asked whether Schmid, too, had "journeyed" with his society.[4]

On the basis of the testimony of Enzensbergerin and Luzin, the government in Dillingen put together the lengthy interrogation questionnaire ("Interrogatorium") with 146 questions for Chonrad Stoeckhlin that we have already mentioned. In doing so, the government in Dillingen was proceeding on the assumption that Stoeckhlin was a witch doctor or witch finder, and they took it as axiomatic that no one could recognize someone as a witch unless he had, himself, traveled with the witches.[5] In this context Stoeckhlin's stories about his travels with the phantoms of the night were of special interest, and as we have already mentioned, the questionnaire devoted a large portion of its attention to them. Otherwise they asked him all the well-known and stereotypical questions, although they did deviate slightly from the standard canon drawn from the doctrines of witchcraft. They asked about the pact with the devil, sexual intercourse with the devil, the practice of harmful magic, the witches' flight, the witches' salve, the murder of children, the witches' sabbath (in which Stoeckhlin's dealings with "Queen Venus" drew special attention), his "rebaptism" by the devil, the devil's mark, and his supposed transformation into an animal (a cat or a wolf).

Shortly before Christmas 1586, the prosecutions reached a first climax. Several confessed "witches" had testified that they had seen horseherdsman Stoeckhlin many times up on the Heuberg [literally, Hay Mountain] at the witches' dance. In fact, one woman by the name of Anna Weberin told him this to his face when she confronted him in jail. Such confrontations with confessing defendants often created dramatic moments in the otherwise secret judicial procedures of the early modern period. When Anna Weberin confronted Bregenzer's Grethe on 19 December 1586, for example, each woman accused the other of taking part in the witches' dance on the Heuberg, a witches' sabbath with "dancing, hopping, feasting and drinking," details that may remind us more of a peasant wedding.[6]

What exactly did the Heuberg mean? In the consciousness of modern Germans, the most famous witch mountain is Brocken or Blocksberg in the Harz Mountains of central Germany, but this notion was totally unknown to sixteenth-century Germans. It was first created in the seventeenth century by the widely known publication of Johannes Prätorius (1630–1680),[7] and then, through the witches' sabbath scene in Goethe's *Faust*, it entered world literature. In the late Middle Ages and at the beginning of modern times, the Blocksberg was at most known only within its near surroundings. In the fifteenth and sixteenth centuries, the best-known supraregional meeting place for the witches was the Heuberg in southwestern Germany. This fact is easily explained. After all, the cumulative idea of witchcraft only came together in the course of the late Middle Ages in the area of the Duchy of Savoy, in a region that was then the center of western Christendom, for the pope was then residing not in Rome but in Avignon. Within the German language area the word *Hexereye* and the cumulative demonological concept of witchcraft appeared for the first time in Switzerland, mentioned for the first time in the year 1419, in Lucerne, and from there it spread into southwestern Germany. Here we find the earliest known witch trials in all of Germany, and it was here, too, that Heinrich Kramer obtained the experiences that provided the basis for his *Malleus Maleficarum*. Southwestern Germany was thus, so to speak, the sluice gate through which the powerful new idea of witchcraft flowed into Germany.[8]

In southwestern Germany these fantasies attached themselves to places that had already possessed a mythological meaning. It stood to reason that the witches' dance always took place in remote locations—on moors, in woods, or in the mountains. These ideas crystallized around prominent mountain plateaus, alpine foothills or even flat meadows, and did not focus on the highest mountain peaks, which were all too remote. It is still undecided to what extent these places were the same as those of prehistoric, heathen religious cults and whether, therefore, some cultic continuity might actually have played a role in identifying these spots with the witches' sabbath. It is noteworthy, however, that the Heuberg was recognized as the place where the goddess Venus had held her secret court. In fact, the Heuberg was also called "Venus Mountain." At the beginning of the fifteenth century, Heinrich von Wittenweiler, a poet from the Swiss Thurgau, included in his poem called the *Ring* a scene in which the witches (whom he already called *häxen*) fly to the *Höperg* (i.e., the Heuberg), where giants and heroes, including Dietrich von Bern (i.e., Theodoric the Great, king of the Ostrogoths), were found along with lords and dwarves.[9] Similar associations were later attached to the Blocksberg, at least in the minds of later demonologists. "In Spain, Germany, France and other European lands, mountains are also notorious for these assemblies: in Swabia the Heuberg; among the Lower Germans, in the Land of Brunswick, the Blocksberg (*Mons Bructerorum*), where the old heathen prophetess Maid Velleda had her home."[10] A good demonologist with a humanistic education would naturally invoke Tacitus.

Thus as early as the fifteenth century, the Heuberg was famous well beyond the region. For example, at the Council of Basel in 1435, Johannes Nider (ca. 1380/90–1438), the demonologist from Isny in the Allgäu, identified the Heuberg as the place where the *Unholden* assembled.[11] Or, to take another example, in 1520 a woman condemned to be burned to death for witchcraft declared that she had flown on her staff to the witches' dances on the Heuberg.[12] And the same location crops up again in later Swiss witch trials, as well as in those of Alsace. The whole Alemannic language area was agreed in seeing the Heuberg as the central place for the witches' dance.[13] During the sixteenth century, knowledge about the significance of the Heuberg was also spread in part by professional executioners, who were invited to come from just those places, even if far off, that had had early experience of witchcraft trials. And these expert executioners passed on their insider knowledge wherever they went. In the Oberstdorf witch trials, this was the role taken by an executioner from Biberach, sixty miles to the northwest. He had conducted large witchcraft trials in the Swabian region,[14] a master-torturer who brought with him information about Heuberg and its significance into the Augsburg episcopal jurisdiction of Rettenberg.[15]

After several months of denials, Chonrad Stoeckhlin finally confessed in December 1586 to all the crimes of which he was accused, listed as they were in the rhetorical questions of the court. He confessed, however, only after the most cruel torture, with procedures that we will not describe here in detail. In one hour-long procedure, burning brandy, gunpowder, and pitch were employed to "burn off his skin from his genitals up to his head," an excruciating experience from which Stoeckhlin almost died.[16] After such tortures had broken his every resistance, at the hearing on 23 December, Stoeckhlin even admitted that he had a sex devil, which the interrogating judges had been insinuating from the beginning. He now confessed that with his demon-lover and with his other playmates he had traveled to the Heuberg to the witches' dance, where they had danced, feasted, and copulated.

Stoeckhlin now also accepted the notion that his mother had played a central role. He admitted that she had taught him magic when he was sixteen and had also advised him that if he should ever be thrown in jail, he "should employ the excuse of the night phantoms." Of course his mother had died fifteen years earlier, and it is highly doubtful that there had been any talk at that time of Stoeckhlin's being a member of the night phantoms. In addition to his mother, Stoeckhlin now accused his dead friend Jacob Walch, who he said had dug up the corpse of a dead child to help his mother concoct a witch salve. But Stoeckhlin covered for his fellow herdsmen. He regarded the rest of them as "honest folk," none of whom had had any dealings with the devil.[17]

With the forced application of this learned interpretation and through the deployment of torture, Stoeckhlin's trips with the phantoms of the night were travestied as ridiculous. He now admitted that he had traveled to the Heuberg, "and every time on a goat," where he had supposedly seen the other witches: Barbara Berchtoldin and Bregenzer's Grethe, her brother Hans Raminger, Appolonia Erbin, her sister Barbara Erbin, Katarina Voglerin, Catharina Städerin, Barbara Schrautolffin, Barbara Kapellerin's daughter, her sister Elspeth Kapellerin, Michael Mayr's wife, and Michael Mathen, the son of an old Walser. It was his mother who had first taken him to the Heuberg.

About twenty-seven years ago his mother had taken him for the first time to the Heuberg and introduced him to the Evil Enemy. And had told him that he must renounce God and his saints. And then he had offered the great devil his hand and had pronounced his agreement. Afterward his mother had brought his sex devil to him, and he had practiced filthiness with her, and then he had drunk and eaten and rejoiced. And afterwards he had traveled home again.[18]

Even so, he insisted that he had made such journeys, now a witches' journey on the back of a goat, only four times a year: "always only at Easter, Whitsun, Saint John's Day in the summer, and at Christmas time."[19]

Interestingly, new contradictions now opened up in the testimony of the confessing witches, two of whom (Anna Enzensbergerin and Barbara Luzin, his step-aunt) insisted that Stoeckhlin had not traveled with the normal witches' flight but had journeyed instead "with the furious army." This firm testimony led the investigators to turn to Stoeckhlin again to find out "what sort of journey that is, and what the furious army is" (question 95), and whether it was not the same thing as the "great swarming of witches" (question 96).[20] Again and again the questions of the learned jurists in Dillingen reveal that they did not understand and did not want to understand such popular ideas as the phantoms of the night and the wild hunt, Wuetas and Muotas.[21] On the basis on Christian demonology they condemned notions that came from folklore. Their master in this was the great Jean Bodin, the man whom political and economic theorists usually celebrate as a protagonist of the modern. And yet Bodin was one of the worst demonologists of the sixteenth century, for it was he who invented the vision of a massive, supraregional witches' assembly that threatened all of Christendom. In Fischart's German translation this vision was called the Imperial Diet of the Witches (*Hexen Reichstag*).[22] Although Bodin's *Démonomanie* had been silent about where this imperial diet of the witches took place, there was no doubt on this point throughout the German Southwest, in the western parts of Austria, and in German-speaking Switzerland. They met at the Heuberg.[23]

14.

Witch Hunt

On 23 January 1587 Chonrad Stoeckhlin and Bregenzer's Grethe, the wife of Jacob Dösser, were condemned for the crime of witchcraft and burned to death by the notorious Master Hans of Biberach, an executioner who had learned to specialize in witch hunts. In the year of his death Chonrad was thirty-seven or thirty-eight years old.[1] We actually know very little about Grethe Raminger, the sister of the "witch man," Hans Raminger who had fled (Raminger's nickname was "Bregenzer," and his sister was therefore called "Bregenzer's Grethe"). And yet it seems likely that she was the woman who, during the course of the hearings and the testimony of witnesses, turned out to be the "chief witch" of the whole region. Witnesses generally reported rumors that were current because their testimony had to seem credible and had to be verifiable by other witnesses. Stoeckhlin's participation in the society of witches was obviously deduced from the notion that being a witch was inheritable, as the *Malleus Maleficarum* had asserted a hundred years earlier.[2] Stoeckhlin's long-dead mother Ursula Schedlerin was now labeled "the most notorious witch in Oberstdorf," and maybe the villagers really thought so. Denouncing her, however, could also have been an act of revenge, for the charge came from Anna Enzensbergerin, whom Stoeckhlin had branded a witch. Anna was probably also responsible for the arrest of Anna Luzin, a stepsister of Stoeckhlin's mother—his step-aunt.[3]

Anna Enzensbergerin fell victim to the witch hunt in 1586. She died in jail presumably as a result of being badly injured under torture. She was not alone in this fate: seven other women also died in jail as a result of torture. They were considered guilty, and their bodies were consigned to the flames.

The only reason so many defendants died before they could be executed was that the torture ordered by the episcopal court was completely inhuman. Altogether about twenty-five persons fell victim to the Oberstdorf witch hunt, including many with whom Stoeckhlin had dealt. Of course Chonrad's mother, Ursula Schedlerin, was long dead and could no longer be called to account, but her eighty-year-old stepsister could be. Barbara Luzin was arrested with the others in August 1586, after Stoeckhlin asserted that his guide to the night phantoms had indicated that she was a witch. According to her own testimony, Luzin had been twice married. Of her four children, three girls had died, and the son had gone off to war. In 1587 she was burned to death as a witch. A certain Barbara Berchtoldin, the unmarried daughter of one of the court flunkies, who was executed in July 1587, may have been a relative of Stoeckhlin's wife, Anna Berchtoldin. Similarly, a woman named Elspetha Schedlerin from Wolferthal, who was burned at the stake on 28 November 1587, may have been related to his mother, as may be the case for a certain Elspeth Luzin. This also holds for Barbara Erbin from Oberstdorf, who was identified as "the horse wrangler's near cousin's wife," and her sister Appollonia Erbin from Oberstdorf, Ulrich Huber's widow. Among Stoeckhlin's more distant relatives we may be right in identifying Ursula Huber, wife of Jacob Mutter, and with her we may have a connection to one of the earliest witch trials in all of Vorarlberg, namely the trial in 1528 of Anna Mutter from Mittelberg in the Lesser Walser Valley.[4] Another convicted witch, Catharina Voglerin, "wife of Hans Stöckhlin, who is also called Claus," from Reichenbach, was presumably one of Chonrad Stoeckhlin's in-laws. All of these women were executed in 1587. Of the other families, the Kappellers were hardest hit. They were another family who had immigrated from the Lesser Walser Valley.[5] The wife of Jörg Schrautolff, Barbara Kapeller of Oberstdorf, was one of those who died early while under arrest, in 1586. So did Catharina Kapeller. And in 1587 Elspeth Kapeller of Gerstruben, the unmarried sister of Barbara, was also executed. That year Barbara Kapeller, the daughter of the just-mentioned Barbara Kapeller, also died in jail.

The chronology of the witch hunt can be fairly well reconstructed for the year 1587 because the episcopal council records, owing to the importance of these events, were kept in far greater detail than usual. After the execution

of Chonrad Stoeckhlin and Bregenzer's Grethe, there must have been further executions before 6 February because on that date District Judge Alexander von Schwendi composed a report, stating that the executioner had been
paid "his expenses and salary for the seven persons he has burned." These
costs obviously included those who had died in jail and whose corpses had
been consigned to the flames; their jail expenses and the costs for their torture are also included in this reckoning. So this initial list surely included, in
addition to Chonrad Stoeckhlin and Bregenzer's Grethe, Anna Enzensbergerin, Stoeckhlin's step-aunt Barbara Lutzin, Anna Weberin, and the elder
Barbara Kappellerin. Three further suspects were released, however (including Walburga Ritterin and Ulmann's Barbara). At the time of Stoeckhlin's
execution, nine more men and women had been implicated by Stoeckhlin,
and shortly before his death he had reconfirmed these accusations. The trial
document fastidiously recorded their names in a separate list.

In a decree dated 13 February 1587, the councillors in Dillingen ordered
"that because of the testimony from the nine suspects, the three sisters Barbl,
Appel, and Katharina Stederin should be taken prisoner and should be interrogated using the old questionnaire, employing no torture at first, but
using torture if necessary, and their testimony should be sent here to Dillingen. You should suspend operations against the other suspects until you receive further instructions."[6] From the lists of denunciations forced out of
Chonrad Stoeckhlin on 23 December 1586 and 21 January 1587, in which these
nine persons were named, we also learn that the additional suspects were
Katharina Stederin and Appollonia and Barbara Erbin. It is clear that they
were now going after Stoeckhlin's relatives. On 7 April 1587 Barbara Erbin,
the "near cousin's wife" of the horse wrangler Stoeckhlin, produced a "confession with and without torture." She had been interrogated about points
that the court had extracted from the testimony of Stoeckhlin and Bregenzer's Grethe, but despite three hours of torture they were unable to force
her to confess. Three days later, however, she was again severely tortured,
and this time after one hour she asked to be let down from the "ladder," the
instrument of strappado, for she was now ready to confess everything.

In her confession, Barbara Erbin told a most interesting story in order to
explain why she had taken up a pact with the devil. Three years earlier she

had had a fight with her husband, who had, "as so often at Shrovetide, gone off to the tavern," without satisfying her complaints about their debts. So she concluded she would just have to give up on him, but as she sat alone, spinning in her little room, a handsome man came in the door and said to her, "My dear woman, you look sad; what's the problem?" And she replied that they had such heavy debts, "and yet my husband is always drinking wine and spending his time in the tavern." Then the handsome stranger said, "If you follow me and do my bidding, I will give you money enough." And Barbara Erbin then asked what she had to do, and the stranger said that she "should deny God and the saints."

On the third time she said that she went with the devil to the Heuberg where there were "quite a lot of people, and she had eaten, drunk, danced, and fornicated, and she had been happy." Along with a fairly skimpy description of what happened at the Heuberg, there was extensive interrogation about the harmful magic she had practiced. As fellow witches, she accused only women who had already been executed: her sister Appollonia Erbin, Barbara and Catarina Kappellerin, Anna Enzensbergerin, and Bregenzer's Grethe, but then also the captain, Conrad Schmid from Niderndorff. Later, however, she added the names of the younger Barbara Kapellerin and Elisabeth Kapellerin, and also Catharina Stederin, wife of Hans Raminger. The court now asked pointedly (at the order of the government) about the three women who had been let go: Walburga Ritterin, Jacob Geiser's wife, and "Ulmann's Barbara." She refused to implicate them, even though "the common man" regarded Ulmann's Barbara as deeply suspect. In this, her second round of testimony under torture, Barbara Erbin confessed to numerous cases of harmful magic, which the court tried to confirm locally over the next few days by questioning those who had been affected by the supposed magic. The results of these investigations are noted down in the margin. Take, for example, the one-year-old child of Hans Straub who had supposedly been murdered by witchcraft: "We find that he testifies merely that he never had any special suspicion of witchcraft."[7] At a third interrogation under torture, on Saturday 11 April 1587, in which holy water and consecrated candles were employed to drive away the devil, Barbara Erbin confessed that she had actually become a witch six years ago in Tokaj in Hungary. There, too, she had attended great assemblies like those on the Heuberg.[8]

On 13 April 1587 the district court of Rettenberg issued a detailed report "to the court on account of Appollonia and Barbara Erbin," noting that the order of the government, dated 13 February, had now been carried out. Hans Raminger had escaped, it was true, but Catharina Stederin, as well as Barbara and Appollonia Erbin, had been arrested and the latter two had both confessed in the week after Easter. Concerning the three women who had been released, there were no new reasons for suspicion. The executioner from Biberach was also apparently satisfied in his demands.[9] This letter arrived just four days later, on 17 April, in Dillingen, and on 22 April 1587 the government in Dillingen issued the execution order on the legal basis of Article 109 of the criminal code known as the Constitutio Criminalis Carolina (1532). And the government also ordered investigations to be begun on the basis of the accusations against Anna Nickhin, wife of a smith from Rubi, and Ursula Huberin, wife of Jacob Mutter. The following three persons now needed to be arrested: Catharina Voglerin, wife of Hans Stoeckhlin, called Claus; "the young Barbl Capellerin"; "and her cousin Elsbetha Kapellerin in Gerstruben," who had all been accused "in the previous confessions." They were all to be tortured, and further testimony from other witnesses was to be gathered. Furthermore, all reasons to suspect Jacob Schmid, the captain from Niderndorff, were to be gathered and turned over to the "officials of Königsegg."[10]

These suspicions directed against Conrad Schmid of Niderndorff are interesting, first because he was a man, but second because he was an official, and third because he belonged to a foreign jurisdiction, namely the County of Königsegg-Rothenfels. By spring 1587 at the very latest, therefore, they had begun to correspond with neighboring territories concerning the witch hunt. Of course, witch trials were never kept secret, and executions were among the most massively effective public spectacles of the early modern period. At the most sensational executions one could now and then expect crowds numbering in the tens of thousands who came from near and far,[11] and this was surely the case with the executions of Chonrad Stoeckhlin and Bregenzer's Grethe in January of 1587. In terms of propaganda, therefore,

the ground was well-prepared when the episcopal court of Rettenberg began
to transmit witchcraft accusations to the surrounding territories. Whether
they were successful in pursuing Michael Math, who belonged to the jurisdiction of Vorarlberg, can be seriously doubted because the government in
Bregenz was extremely restrained in dealing with witch trials and in addition
would have been risking real conflict with its own subjects.[12] But it was otherwise in the case of the lordship Königsegg-Rothenfels. We learn that the accused Schmid was immediately arrested and that witch hunts had begun in
the county. As early as 20 May 1587, we learn that the confession of Conrad
Schmid was expected to arrive from the town of Aulendorf, the county seat
of Königsegg. This would have been his final and official confession, because
that is what would have been important for the trials in Oberstdorf.[13] The
Math family, however, appears to have gotten tangled up in a witch hunt five
years later. There is an inventory, dated 26 June 1592, concerning the possessions of a certain Martin Math[ens] from Oy, whose wife was being held
in jail in Sonthofen. His possessions came to the sizable sum of 998 gulden,
of which his house was worth 300 gulden, his lands, including eight yoke
(ca. 300 acres) of plowland, were worth 320 gulden, and "horses and cattle"
to the value of 96 gulden were on hand. Math had lent out 150 gulden, while
he himself owed 636 gulden, making a net worth of something more than
310 gulden.[14]

In its answer to the order dated 22 April, the district court reported on 13
May that the sisters "had stubbornly maintained their denials," and so, on
8 May, their capital trial had been held, and they had been executed "by fire."
The three newly arrested women had also been interrogated already, and
Katharina Voglerin had finally "confessed after extensive torture." The Kapellerin had been "tortured on the ladder for more than three hours," but she
had admitted nothing. Because of such strong suspicions, they had recently
sent for the executioner of Tettnang, just south of Ravensburg near the Lake
of Constance. The court included with its report an inventory of the marital property of the arrested suspects.[15] In a seven-page reply to the report of
the district court, the episcopal government in Dillingen on 20 May made
detailed recommendations about how the trial should proceed. Following
up on the testimony of Voglerin, the court was urged to investigate "two

new ones," namely Catharina Ramingerin, wife of Poschen Henslein, and "Elsa, wife of the turner," who was also known as "the wife of the glazier from Rubi." On the other hand, further testimony from Voglerin should now rather be sought with the help of the *priest* rather than with the aid of torture, because she had become so inconsistent. But if she remained constant in her testimony against the Kapeller sisters, she should be executed by burning, for it was beyond doubt that "both of these Kapeller women" were "grossly infected devil's sorceresses," and if they would not confess to anything, the reason was "that they were impeded by the devil himself or that they had been bewitched by others of their ilk, or that they had secreted in their clothing or in their persons, such as in their private parts of their bodies little secret magical objects." The "Masters" (the executioners) had probably already shown how to get the truth out of them. The priests too were told to pray from the pulpit during Holy Mass for the opening of their hearts, and they were to petition God specifically for this, but without naming the two Kapeller sisters. Stubborn Els Kapellerin was to be asked why she wanted to be tortured so long, seeing that her sister Barbara had already confessed to everything.[16]

On 16 July 1587 it was decided that the body of Verena Remin from Oberstdorf, who had died in jail, was to be burned, while Barbara Berchtoldin was to be executed after being confronted one more time with Catharina Stederin. The pastor was told to admonish her not to commit any perjury against her. And now Catharina Ramingerin, Anna Hindelangin, and Hans Nickhin were to be arrested, too. The goods of Hans Raminger, who had fled, were to be confiscated. The inventory of the goods of the already executed witches Anna Enzenspergerin, Barbara Luzin, and Els Kappellerin came to a total of 125 gulden. However, Jörg Schrautolff and Hans Vogeler were to be allowed the use of their property until their deaths; it was to be confiscated only afterward.[17]

On 23 July came the response from the district governor (*Landammann*) of Rettenberg. Barbara Berchtoldin had now revoked her accusations directed against Catharina Stederin and Anna Nickhin, claiming that she had "committed a terrible injustice." And so she was interrogated again, using the threat of torture, and asked why she had accused these women.

To which she said that they should just do with her as they wanted, but she knew nothing ill of the two above-mentioned women, and that she had accused Catharina Stederin simply because she had thought that they had already arrested her and taken them both down to jail from Oberssdorff, and that that meant that she must be a witch also. But she swore on her life that she knew nothing evil about Stederin or about any witchcraft connected with the wife of the smith from Rubi [Anna Nickhin]. (And that because of her accusation and confession, she had felt great grief, sorrow, and remorse after she had accused them both).

Thereupon Barbara Berchtoldin's execution was set for Monday, 27 July 1587, but the trial against Stederin was temporarily suspended.[18]

The government of the bishopric of Augsburg, in its answer dated 31 July, approved the procedures of the district court [*Pfleggericht*] but insisted on a further interrogation of Anna Nickhin. So in her case the recantation of Berchtoldin was useless, for Nickhin had been denounced by many of the already executed witches, "such as by both Kappellerin women, both Erbin women, the Voglerin woman, and by Verena Remin." Berchtoldin was now to be "executed by fire." Stederin should be kept under arrest, while all of those who were still to be arrested should be asked about her complicity. Concerning the issue of confiscations, the government decided that not only the goods of the women but also the goods of their husbands should be seized. Half of their property should be confiscated, or, if there were children, just a quarter.[19] In a response to orders dated 17 and 25 August, the district court wrote on 1 September that that very day had seen the executions of Anna Hindelang of Oberstdorf, Elisabeth Seelos of Rubi, and Anna Nickhin. The next to be arrested were Engla Schrautolffin, Anna Freyin of Reichenbach, and Barbel, the wife of Michael Dossen.[20] On 5 October, Catharina Stederin ("wife of Poschen Heussler, the innkeeper of Oberstdorf") was finally released from jail, after she swore an oath not to take revenge and paid the expenses incurred on her behalf. Barbara "Engla" Kapellerin, who was also known as "Schrautolffin," was not so lucky. At the command of the government, and joined by Barbara Sträubin of Oberstdorf, she was burned as a witch in mid-October. As in other witchcraft trials, the limited space in the local jail dictated that in Sonthofen, too, only small groups of defendants could be tried at one time. This consideration comes out clearly from the order of the government to the "officials of Rettenberg," mandating the execution of this group of four women and saying that they should now "go after the most deeply suspect and proceed against them in the same manner they had with their predecessors."[21]

The detailed response of the district court, dated 17 October, survives in a copy filed with the formal report issued by the episcopal privy council, which is rare luck because normally such correspondence was only filed with the appropriate "office." At the beginning of the Oberstdorf witchcraft trials this was "the file of Retenberg," but as the seriousness of the trials became clear, they were filed in a separate "criminal drawer" (*Malefizlad*).[22] To understand the typical style of this expanding bureaucracy, let us examine this correspondence more closely. First, the reports of the officials from Rettenberg were summarized, noting that "from among the accused witchwomen," they had

> arrested Ulman's daughter Barbel, that in a few days Elspet Lutzin should also be in jail, and that they should be prosecuted just as the other witchpersons were. The officials also indicated that Hans Schwartz's wife of Buchberg had made herself deeply suspect, and they begged to know how they should proceed against her." Then the report summarizes the results of the meeting of the episcopal privy council, that is, the response that we have already seen: "And so they were ordered to take into custody the above-named woman. . . . and to interrogate her as they did the others, first using no torture [the so-called *gütliche Frage* or benevolent questioning] but then using torture [the so-called *peinliche Frage* or painful questioning], and they should send all her testimony down to us for our information. Dated 22 October [15]87.[23]

The next notice in the official record, an entry dated 6 November, reacting to the Sonthofen report of 31 October, reports that Anna Metzin, wife of Hans Schwarz from Burgberg, had died. Ulman's Barbara, Hans Schrauttolf's wife from Oberstdorf, who had recanted her confession, now had to be forced to confess all over again, for, on the basis of testimony from other witnesses, her recantation seemed untrustworthy. On the other hand, Anna Freyin was to be released because there was no further incriminating testimony against her. Death and execution had freed up two places in the jail, however, and so two new women could be arrested: Els Freybergerin and "Elsa, the sister of Engla Schrautolffin."[24] From the entry in the protocol of 27 November, responding to the report of 22 November, we learn that Elspetha Freybergerin had recanted. The privy council ordered that either the priest from Burgkh or the one from Sonthofen should be employed to bring her to repentance and to a renewal of her confession. And the same treatment should be given to Elsa Schedlerin.[25] These pastors were obviously successful because on 9 December the officials in Rettenberg were able to report that, on that very day, Elspetha Freybergerin had been burned to death, while Elspetha Schedlerin from Wolferthal had died in jail on 28 November. On 17 December the privy council therefore commanded that the next suspects be taken into custody.[26]

For the year 1588 all of the sources fail us. Even the privy council records are unusually thin. The reason for this failure is unknown. Even so, it is clear that the Oberstdorf witch trials came to an end in 1588 because the records from 1589 deal only with problems stemming from the inventories taken from the witches executed in 1587 in Rettenberg. But it appears that anger was still pervasive throughout the district of Rettenberg. On 6 February 1589 the district judge, Alexander von Schwendi, in a highly unusual gesture, resigned his office.[27] Because of missing records, a complete list of those executed as witches can no longer be reconstructed, and so the precise social position of the accused must remain unclear. Even so, we can say this much: that Stoeckhlin accused men as well as women, but that the court was readier to accept accusations directed against women;[28] moreover, men showed themselves readier to flee when they found themselves in such a dangerous situation. Altogether, therefore, of the roughly twenty-five persons executed, only one was a man, namely Stoeckhlin himself. To put it in other words, 95 percent of all the persons executed as witches in the Augsburg episcopal jurisdiction of Rettenberg were women. The persecution seems to have been especially hard on families who had immigrated, for we know this to be the case of the Walser families of Kapeller and Berchtold. Around 1600 Gerstruben had a reputation as a "pure village of Walsers," which would mean that several of the other witches (Elisabeth Seelos, Anna Nickhin, and Elsa

Nickin) were either Walser women, or married to Walser men, or perhaps both. And the Math family, who crop up over and over in Stoeckhlin's stories, were Walsers who had moved to Oberstdorf. In any event, the proportion of Walsers burned as witches was highly disproportionate.[29] And yet there was obviously no merely mechanical process by which every woman was immediately suspected of witchcraft or subject to later suspicion. Even among those severely accused, not all were executed. We know explicitly that at least seven women were let go in 1587: Anna Freyin of Reichenbach and Katharina Stederin in September 1587;[30] Michael Gösser's wife Bärbel; Jacob Gösser's wife; Walburga Riterin or Rülerin; Catharina Stederin, the wife of the innkeeper Hans Straub of Oberstdorf; and Barbara Ulman, the wife of Hans Schrautolff of Oberstdorf. And in nine more cases (which we have included in the total of twenty-five) the final disposition of the case is actually unclear.

The witchcraft trials triggered by Chonrad Stoeckhlin had the characteristics of a primary ignition, and they came at a time of extreme social tension throughout the region. Harvest failures and famine became common, and hitherto unknown diseases broke out as a result of malnutrition. The Oberstdorf trials were the spark in a powder keg. Already in 1586 we hear of witchcraft trials in neighboring lordship of Königsegg-Rothenfels, presumably in its district center of Immenstadt. Then in 1587 witchcraft trials broke out in the bishopric of Augsburg's administrative seat of Dillingen itself, in neighboring Wittislingen and the judicial districts of Lauingen and Höchstädt, belonging to the princely dynasty of Palatinate-Neuburg. The western Bavarian districts of Schongau and Rain on the Lech also began their first trials, as was also true of the imperial cities of Augsburg and Nördlingen and their neighbor Oettingen, the center of the county of Oettingen-Wallerstein.[31] In July 1587 the government in Dillingen tried for the first time to put the brakes on the rising witchcraft panic. Because "defamation of witches" now threatened to get out of control among the lower classes, and hoping to stop this fateful development, the government ordered its pastors "from their pulpits to forbid the accusation of witches."[32]

But the evil was not to be contained. Even though the trials in the district of Rettenberg obviously were brought to an end in 1587, the spark had already leaped over to others. In 1588 witchcraft trials began in the district of Oberdorf just to the north of the district of Rettenberg-Sonthofen; in 1589 they spread to the so-called District along the Road around Schwabmünchen, as well as in Wehringen, and Bobingen, while in 1590 the fire broke out throughout the whole bishopric and far beyond. In the western districts of the duchy of Bavaria, in Weilheim, Schongau, Rauhenlechsberg, Wolfratshausen, Tölz, Starnberg, Dachau, Erding, Pfaffenhofen, in its capital city of Munich, and in its university town of Ingolstadt, as well as along the Danube River down to Straubing; in all the districts of the bishopric of Freising, including the county of Werdenfels along with the district towns of Garmisch, Partenkirchen, and Mittenwald; in the Palatine-Neuburg towns of Lauingen and Höchstädt; in the county of Oettingen-Wallerstein, in the imperial cities of Nördlingen, Donauwörth, Augsburg, and Kaufbeuren, in the lordships belonging to the Fugger family, in the lordships of Osterzell, Erolzheim, Kellmünz, Nennslingen, and Pappenheim, in the county of Königsegg-Rothenfels, the county of Waldburg, as well as in the imperial abbeys of Kempten and Obermarchtal. But standing as a generator in the very center of this great wave of persecutions was the bishopric of Augsburg under Bishop Marquard vom Berg. And here the fires of persecution burned from the far south (the district of Rettenberg) to the extreme north (the jurisdiction of Wittislingen, northwest of Dillingen). The episcopal seat of Dillingen conducted trials continuously from 1587 onward, and the fires burned in the districts of Wittislingen, Dillingen, Zusmarshausen, Dinkelscherben, Bobingen, Wehringen, Göggingen, Grossaitingen, Kleinaitingen, Oberdorf, Helmishofen, Nesselwang, and Füssen. And in 1592 the flames of witch persecution sprang up again in the district of Rettenberg-Sonthofen, this time consuming nine persons, women from Haslach, Rettenberg, and Oy. It took the plague of that year to bring the witch trials to an end.[33]

With the trial against Chonrad Stoeckhlin, Bishop Marquard vom Berg had started not only the first wave of trials in this whole region of southern Germany, but in the district of Oberdorf (modern-day Marktoberdorf), where witchcraft trials took 68 lives, he began the single largest persecution to be found anywhere between the Danube River and the Alps. All told, in five years he must have presided over the execution of more than 150 persons as witches. And when one notes that over 95 percent of the executed were women, it seems ironic that the first victim—Chonrad Stoeckhlin— was a man. With an estimated population of 75,000 inhabitants, the executed made up roughly 0.2 percent of the inhabitants of the bishopric of Augsburg, but in some places, of course, the share was higher. In Oberstdorf with about 800 inhabitants and roughly 25 victims, the toll came to more than 3 percent; in Marktoberdorf with its ca. 700 inhabitants and 68 victims, the toll came to almost 10 percent.[34] Thus one can only agree with the contemporary poet who wrote in the Fugger Newsletter for 1590: "Marquard vom Berg . . . was an initiator of these things; having innumerable witches, he destroyed many of them with fire."[35]

15.

Peasant Rebellion

As we have seen, being related to a witch was enough to prompt the suspicion that one was a witch, according to both folk beliefs and the *Malleus Maleficarum*. And yet, astonishingly enough, the immediate family of Stoeckhlin did not get caught in the judicial net. His father, who was living in the Sonthofen spital, was not called before the court for questioning, nor was his wife or their two surviving children. In fact, the witch trials of 1586–87 and 1592 seem to have barely affected the solidity of their community. Perhaps this was because the bishop's judicial machinery served in surgical fashion to get rid of a few troublemakers, who had been disturbing the peace by making threats or in other ways. The village seems to have coped effectively with the episcopal government's sometimes excessive zeal for persecutions. But generally, the demand for trials coming from the bishop's government ran oddly parallel to a demand coming from the locality. In the beginning there is no doubt that the initiative for prosecuting witches came from the community, and we can see that even during the summer of 1587 the government in Dillingen worked mainly to dampen the wave of trials. Altogether there is no sign at all that the village of Oberstdorf was out of sympathy with the results of the witch hunt.

This is, however, an argument *ex silentio*. With its strong tradition of self-government, the village would have been fully capable of exerting itself forcefully against the bishop's government if it had wanted to do so. They could have done so by simply refusing to cooperate. A privy council report dated January 1586 complained that crimes the district justices were expected to prosecute, were "mostly denied by the subjects of this district and concealed from the district officers." If people clammed up, the government was powerless.[1] But villagers could also force the government into action. In July 1586 it was the local community that had arrested the suspected witch Anna Enzensbergerin, following Stoeckhlin's denunciation of her. In this way the episcopal government was faced with a virtual *fait accompli*. Obviously, at first no one planned that the shadowy horse wrangler would be swept up in the witch hunt. This was the government's doing, and the community then accepted this result even though Stoeckhlin had been its employee for years. To that extent the village clearly trusted the government. There is no surviving evidence for any kind of local protest.

In the country district of Rettenberg this was worth a great deal, for here, as in the whole Allgäu, in nearby Switzerland, and in the Vorarlberg,[2] there was a sturdy tradition of resistance. The political fighting for hegemony that characterized the power struggle of the fifteenth and sixteenth centuries generally ended indecisively. From 1400 on, the League of Peasants from Appenzell had stirred up latent discontents among the peasants of the Allgäu as well. In particular, peasants from the upper valley of the Iller and from the Lesser Walser Valley showed a lively sympathy for the antifeudal rebellions of the Swiss, who succeeded in freeing themselves from the overlordship of the monastery of St. Gall. A contemporary wrote that "they all want to be Appenzellers."[3] The lower classes of Allgäu were regularly insubordinate. In 1415 a peasant uprising shook the princely abbey of Kempten; in 1424 citizens of Augsburg destroyed numerous castles in Allgäu belonging to robber barons. Dependents and officials of the ruling dynasties in Allgäu lived in constant danger. In 1433 the Heimenhof officer Hans Schnaitter was killed by the Ernst brothers from Oberstdorf. And when knights Ulrich and Hans von Heimenhofen found the two outlaws, they tried at once to stab both of their captors. Knight Hans von Rechberg was shot in 1464 by a peasant. In 1470 the people of Oberstdorf rebelled and plundered the house of Knight Hans von Heimenhofen; in 1477 Hans Köberlin, an illegitimate son of that knight, was killed in Oberstdorf during a brawl.[4] In 1491 the peasants of the princely abbey of Kempten rose up again in a successful revolt, this time under the symbol of the *Bundschuh*.[5]

This tradition of rebellion continued into the sixteenth century. During the great Peasants' War of 1525, Allgäu was one of the major centers of the revolt. One of the three large peasant armies in Upper Swabia was called the "troops of Allgäu," who assembled in the region around Kempten.[6] On 12 February 1525 the subjects of the bishop of Augsburg, those of the prince-abbot of Kempten, and those of the noble lordships in Sonthofen assembled, and pledging to support one another against their lords, they swore to live according to "godly law" and no longer according to feudal law. Their pragmatic demands included the abolition of serfdom, the end to certain taxes, and the freedom to hunt and fish. Three days later the peasants from the district of Rettenberg formally added their demands to the list: among other things they insisted on the abolition of ecclesiastical control over capital punishment (Article 6), a demand aimed directly at their judicial lord, the bishop of Augsburg.[7] After negotiations in Oberdorf with the bishop broke down, this band of peasants formed themselves into a continuing "Christian Association for the region of Allgäu." When these peasants heard that the knights were about to attack them, they assembled near Leubas and organized themselves militarily. And they informed the government that they had founded an alliance, "a clear sign that they intended to be taken seriously as a political force."[8]

Composed in Memmingen, the famous Twelve Articles were a manifesto summarizing the demands of the peasants, among them the right to choose their own pastors, the return of common woods to them, and the abolition of arbitrary punishments by the courts. This was not a program for revolution but an attempt on peasant principles to establish the basis for a flourishing life of cooperation. The Twelve Articles from Allgäu quickly became the program of the whole Peasants' War, undergoing twenty-five printings in just two months, with an estimated total print run of some twenty-five thousand copies, an enormous number by the day's standards.[9] Even cities the size of Kempten and Memmingen were forced to join the huge rebellion. One of the leaders of the Allgäu troops was the peasant Walther Bach, from Oy in the district of Oberstdorf; his name is recorded in the "Territorial Constitution [*Landesordnung*] of the Upper Swabian Peasants."[10] Even after the defeat of the great uprising, it is clear that in the long run these "subjects" did not really sink into subjection. In particular, in the very region where the great witch trials later took place, new disturbances cropped up. In 1577 peasants from near Durach stabbed Prince-Truchsess Hans von Waldburg; in 1580 there was an uprising among the weavers of Isny; in 1596 the peasants of the lordship Königsegg-Rothenfels rose in rebellion around Immenstadt; in 1598, led by Ulrich Vogler from Fischen, the peasants from the upper parishes, including Tiefenbach near Oberstdorf, marched eight hundred-strong to the district seat of Immenstadt. And in 1597 and 1598, the weavers of Isny burst out in protest again.[11]

Finally, in 1605, roughly fifteen years after the great witch hunt, the villages of the district of Rettenberg arose in a general rebellion. This revolt displayed an undiminished self-confidence, as the subjects, meeting in "open communal assemblies" swore oaths of resistance to the bishop. This uprising was directed against a religious edict, dated 10 March 1603, issued by Bishop Heinrich V von Knoeringen (r. 1599–1646), an edict that threatened anyone with exile and loss of inheritance rights if he maintained contact with Protestant places, such as the imperial cities of Kempten, Memmingen, Wangen, Isny, Leutkirch, and Lindau, or the Swiss canton of Graubünden. The edict also contained prohibitions against dancing, magical charms, "indecent" speech or behavior, and other spiteful provisions. Tax increases, including consumption taxes on wine, and restrictions on such communal rights as the right to choose judges (who would now be appointed by the bishop) piled up grievances to the breaking point.[12]

The spark of rebellion was ignited by one of the richest peasants of the district, Hans Rid, son of a former judge from Wertach. Together with several other like-minded men from the neighboring community of Hindelang, Rid put together a "directory" and contacted the upper district, the village of Oberstdorf. Under the leadership of the radical spokesman Hans Hueber, several wealthy Oberstdorf peasants, including Hans Brack, Konrad Brack, and Thoma Gerstlin, came together and quickly pushed aside the more moderate peasants from the lowlands. At the end of March 1605 the peasants assembled in the open on a hill at the foot of Grünten Mountain between Agathazell and Burgberg, within full view of the episcopal judge, a symbolic challenge that he well understood. On 2 April 1605, with the Swiss Confederation as their model, the peasants joined together on a rise that is even today called Rebels' Hill and formed an alliance. They called their assembly a "rural commune," a *Landsgemeinde*. Among the demands of these rebels can be found complaints about judicial expenses that went all the way back to the witch trials in the district of Rettenberg. Just the half-year's trial against Chonrad Stoeckhlin and Bregenzer's Grethe had cost the incredible sum of 750 gulden, expenses that had been run up by the appearance of the famous executioners, Hans of Biberach and Hans of Tettnang, along with their assistants, who had all been quartered with the innkeeper Georg Möss-mang of Sonthofen. Confiscating the estates of those executed had not come even close to covering the costs of the trial. Even the episcopal governor had criticized the extent of these charges, but the local community still had to pay them.[13] The heirs of the executed were still being dunned to pay these now almost twenty-year-old bills, and, naturally, discontent was brewing throughout the district over such old debts. District governor Alexander Straub was accused, moreover, of wasting money from the district account.

The rebellious rural commune of the district of Rettenberg elected a committee of thirty-two deputies, who were delegated to meet with episcopal officials and negotiate the implementation of their specific demands. Peasants thought of as too moderate were to be brought to reason by the use of sanctions, while those regarded as too friendly to the bishop's government were prohibited from using common lands and other communal equipment such as the forge or the baking oven. They even set a price of 20 gulden on the head of one old peasant, who had sought to remind his fellows of the consequences of the Peasants' War of 1525. At the same time, however, they tried to firm up their legal position by employing the Kempten jurist, Dr. David Megerlin, who composed a manifesto in the name of the peasants. This document was approved by a newly called "rural assembly," who sent it on to the government in Dillingen, where it arrived on 19 April 1605. One month later the episcopal chancellor, Dr. Leonhard Götz at Castle Fluhen-stein, received the elected delegation of deputies from the district, while an unruly mass of peasants waited outside the castle. Konrad Vogler from Oberstdorf expressed their conviction that written documents would prove that they should not be subject to serfdom.[14] Indeed, one of the most important of the peasant demands was immediately granted: they were allowed to view all the documents that bore on their rights as well as their district's financial accounts. Then the documents, which did not in fact confirm their hoped-for rights and freedoms, were shown to the waiting crowd outside the castle gate. Afterward the government demanded that the peasants calm down and wait for further decisions of the bishop concerning their demands. The peasants took the rest of the day discussing this proposal, and then rejected it. In a written protest called the "First Sonthofen Agreement" (*Rezess*), they proclaimed that they would insist on their "old rights." The episcopal councillors had to go home with the dispute still unsettled.[15]

Meanwhile, district governor Straub suffered a panic attack. He feared the inspection of the village accounts by the "rural assembly," and he fled. At another meeting on "Rebels' Hill," several peasants, including Captain Hans Bach of Stephansrettenberg, were forced to join the rebels; in the process, Bach's house door was smashed in. In times of peace such an act was a serious trespass, but under these circumstances it was an expression of the executive powers claimed by the rural assembly. Amidst great tumult, the judicial officer Brutscher of Sonthofen was finally forced by rebel leader Thoma Gerstlin from Oberstdorf to hand over the key to the district coffers. The bishop of Augsburg, who felt helpless in the face of this revolt, sought support from the Emperor Rudolf II. In August 1605, an imperial commission read out a mandate in his name, calling for an investigation of claims and complaints on both sides and requiring the peasants to pay their taxes and to obey their territorial lord. Innkeeper Jörg Erb of Oberstdorf then cried out to the crowd gathered before the castle that "Anyone who had taken the oath to the rural assembly and wished to stick with it should follow him." Immediately, and under the gaze of the imperial commissioners, the gathered mass stormed out to the open field and "using rebellious ceremonies," took the decision to disobey the imperial penal mandate.[16]

The prince abbot of Kempten and the official representatives of Archduke Maximilian of Austria, the barons Georg Fugger zu Kirchberg and Maximilian Schenk zu Stauffenberg, the city captain of Konstanz, along with several of their counselors, then met to negotiate with the chosen deputies of the peasants and their attorney. On 10 October 1605 they drew up the "Second Sonthofen Agreement," which required that the peasants give up their rural assembly and forbade them to use force but made concessions to their demands to examine the legal documents containing their rights and the financial accounts. They would not be punished for their tax strike but were required to resume paying their taxes. The peasant committees accepted this agreement, but it would soon become clear that they still retained executive powers. Over the next few months, they declared sanctions on their own authority, refused taxes, freed prisoners, and forced district officials to negotiate. They were especially angry about the imprisonment of three peasants (together with an obligatory oath that they would renounce vengeance). Their "crime" was that they had had sexual relations with their wives before their weddings. These new Counter-Reformation moral standards were not accepted, and the still-rebellious peasants demanded the annulment of the abjurations of vengeance. On 11 December 1605, Hans Hueber of Oberstdorf sounded the alarm bell because another apparently unjust arrest had been committed by the bishop's judge. Together with a second peasant captain, Hueber stirred up the villages and hamlets of the parish to assault the castle at Burgberg. The inhabitants of Sonthofen joined them in this attempt. Frightened by the approaching crowd of dissident subjects, the episcopal judge caved in and saved his skin by releasing his prisoners.

In certain matters these "subjects" began regularly to ignore their rulers and came to exclude anyone who sided with the bishop. In Sonthofen they founded a new school because the old schoolmaster had dissociated himself from the rural assembly. In September 1606, members of another imperial commission were received with derision. Peasant committees now took control of tax collection.[17] Meanwhile, both sides began to arm themselves. The bishop assembled professional soldiers in Füssen and in Nesselwang in order to reinforce his castles at Burgberg and Fluhenstein. For their part, the peasants began going to distant markets, where they were seen buying halberds and other military hardware, or so they said in Kempten. Of course, we should not take the term "peasants" too literally. Among the members of the Sonthofen committee were several artisans: bakers, coopers, millers, and the innkeeper Hans Seuter. According to the bishop's spies, Seuter was in fact the ringleader. In Oberstdorf the spokesman was the baker Hans Hueber.

The rural assemblies of 2 February and 12 May 1607 reached the decision that the administration of the district needed "to be set on an entirely new foundation," that is, they wanted a thoroughgoing political reform. They now refused all payments to the bishop, deposed all of the "authorized" officials, captains, and judicial personnel, disempowered the bishop's court, and replaced episcopal officers with representatives chosen by the people. The prohibition on fishing the Iller River was lifted; the official district record books were now declared to belong to the local community on the grounds that they had paid the bookbinding costs; orders coming from the bishop's judge were now ignored with the argument that any summons or subpoena only kept them, as peasants, from doing their field work. Practically speaking, the rural assembly had taken over the lordship, and now they began to take up their own foreign policy, too. Peasants from the neighboring lordship of Königsegg-Rothenfels (to the west of the district of Rettenberg) were invited to participate in the Rettenberg rural assembly. When an imperial commissioner on 31 July 1607 threatened the peasants with the imperial ban, they just laughed at him and replied that the peasants of Königsegg would supply them with wine and grain, while they themselves would "catch, slaughter, and dine on the fattest cattle in all the Alps."[18]

At the beginning of September 1607 on the occasion of the Sonthofen "Magnus" market these tensions finally erupted in a dangerous confrontation between the judge and the rebels. At Seuter's inn Karl von Hornstein and bailiff Brutscher were surrounded by two hundred peasants and publicly forced to inform them all when the government would recognize their elections and appoint impartial judges to the courts, and in addition when former district governor (*Landammann*) Straub, whom the bishop had meanwhile appointed to the post of financial comptroller in Augsburg, would return to render his accounts. Observers of this incident, including "several noblemen," were amazed at the eloquence and the seriousness of these peasants in confronting their "superiors." But there was as yet no real clash. On 16 October 1607, under the leadership of the Oberstdorf barber Hans Hueber, the rebels marched again to Castle Fluhenstein, encircled the walls and with shovels cut off the water supply to the castle. Surrendering without a fight to the superior force of the peasants, the castle defenders were immediately disarmed and roughed up. Then the peasants seized Castle Burgberg and took the episcopal district judge prisoner, but they quickly released him in exchange for his promise not to flee. All of the bishop's agents were now either flown or under arrest. Anyone who sympathized with the government, including for example Rettenberg's captain, Hans Bach, found his oxen, cows, sheep, and horses driven from their stalls. The house of the Sonthofen judge, Brutscher, was stormed and plundered. His wine cellar was drunk dry, and all his provisions and supplies were consumed on the spot.[19]

For a long time the bishop did not know how to cope with his rebellious subjects. After his castles were captured he saw no alternative to inviting the military intervention of the mighty Duke Maximilian I of Bavaria (r. 1594/98–1651), who was just then mobilizing in the name of the empire to seize the Protestant imperial city of Donauwörth. A company of his cavalry succeeded in recapturing Castle Fluhenstein before the onset of winter, although Burgberg had to be left in the hands of the peasants. Under the hardships of a severe winter, however, and with the threat of serious Bavarian intervention, the rebels lost their nerve. They gave up their open resistance,[20] and scattered to their villages, just as they had done eighty-two years earlier. In mid-December they offered the bishop their formal submission. He was smart enough to dispense with wholesale judicial punishments, demanding instead only the symbolic prostration of forty subjects, ten from each district-court. The peasants had to recognize the government's complete legitimacy and accept the abolition of their local district organizations. Moreover they had to pay the military costs of subduing their rebellion, costs that were set at 40,000 gulden, of which finally 8,000 gulden were forgiven and 12,000 set down as debts to be paid later. But the subjects had to pay the rest in one down payment and four annual subsidies. On 15 January the peasants of the district of Oberstdorf had to show up in Sonthofen to swear an oath of fidelity before the bishop's councillors and Judge Karl von Hornstein.[21] The barber Hans Hueber of Oberstdorf had to agree to serve ten years in the army fighting the Turks in Hungary. Following the suppression of the uprising, innkeeper Jörg Erb and Thoma Gerstlin were sent into permanent exile, but in 1614 they were pardoned and allowed to return, though under tough restrictions, including a prohibition on frequenting taverns and on carrying any weapon.[22]

Peasant Rebellion

Among the twenty-five peasants who were punished as leaders of the peasant rebellion, there were disproportionately many from Oberstdorf. Just from their names we can see that the family members of the women who had been burned as witches were still members of the community. The executed witches Ursula Huber, Jacob Mutter's wife, and Appollonia Erbin, known as "the miller Ulrich Huber's widow," may well have been related by blood or marriage to the ringleaders of the rebellion. Among the fomenters of the Rettenberg revolt were also such Oberstdorfers as Rudolf Steder, Georg Erb, Andreas Hindelang, Hans Walch, Hans Hueber, Conradt Vogler, Matheuss Erb, and Hans Schraudolph, all names that we recognize from the witch hunt even if we cannot say exactly how they were related to the women burned as witches.[23] A glance at a recent telephone book for Oberstdorf, including the suburbs Faistenoy and Ruby, suffices to prove that the names of Berchtold, Huber, Kapeller, Math, and Schraudolf have survived in the village, and in above-average numbers down to today. Only the name of Stoeckhlin can no longer be found in the upper valley of the Iller.

16.

Folk Beliefs

FEASTING ON OXEN and drinking wine cellars dry were thus not just motifs associated with the myth of the night people, for we have seen them also at those moments during the Peasants' War that came close to realizing the peasant utopia. The music of their peasant dances may even have resounded more sweetly at the time of the great uprising than it ever had before. But this time of carnival, this "world turned upside down," when peasants took control of the government, this time when the more they ate and drank, the more food and drink there seemed to be, and when even the oxen came back to life, reconstituted from their remaining hides and bones, this time of carnival was coming to an end. A wave of Counter-Reformation zeal washed over peasant villages even up in the mountains, bringing a time of Lenten restraint and cultural fasting. State building and moral severity worked hand in hand in this process. In the wake of the great witch hunt, Bishop Marquard vom Berg abolished concubinage among the priests of his territory. In 1590 he published a special "Alpine and Herdsmen's Ordinance" for the district of Rettenberg, and in the following year he issued a mandate against the decay of morals throughout the bishopric.[1] It was just then that witch hunts throughout his bishopric reached their high point, and almost all his district courts reported the arrest of "witches." The witch hunts in the districts of Markt Oberndorf and Schwabmünchen surpassed in size the previous hunts in Oberstdorf.[2] And the controversial Religious Mandate of the Augsburg Bishop Heinrich V von Knöringen (r. 1598–1650) also contained a paragraph condemning "Superstitious Blessings as well as magic and fortune telling, to which the subjects all too often resort instead of using natural and

God-ordained means."[3] In 1610 there followed a mandate against the "wicked, fraudulent, self-deceived and highly forbidden, superstitious healers" (*Segensprecher*), whose "blessings" and spells bewitched both men and cattle. In 1608 ducal advisors in neighboring Bavaria were already hard at work on the great *Mandate against Superstition and Witchcraft*, which was finally printed in 1611.[4]

In spite of these efforts on the part of the government to regulate the life and morals of mountain peasants, however, popular magic and apparently archaic customs survived up in the Alpine valleys or were newly reconstituted. For Alpine herdsmen the "weather forecast" was a lifesaver, whereas knowledge about the physical and psychic health of beast and man, as well as the uses of various plants, was always more than just a matter of the simple, natural observation of nature.[5] Of course we know next to nothing about what actually went on up on the alpine meadows. It was an oral culture, and even for conditions down in the valleys we have precious little information. It is hard to tell how old any particular custom is, such as the Oberstdorf "Wild-Man's-Dance,"[6] which reminds us of the legend (widespread throughout Allgäu) of "wild men" and of "ghostly, blessed *Säligen* maidens," who helped out with work, gave good advice, or appeared as the Lord of the Animals.[7] Sometimes they worked mischief during the rough roundups of Saint Nicholas's Day (6 December), when they appeared at the "wild Saint Nick's" in cowhides or in deerskins, with antlers or horns, and ornamented with bells and chains.[8] We are also reminded of the masked pranks of Fasching, especially on Hopping Thursday (*Gumpige Donnerstag*, the Thursday before Shrovetide) or on Shrove Tuesday or even on Fire Sunday (*Funkensonntag*, the first Sunday in Lent), which are documented as early as 1571, when the people from Bregenz, during that year of extreme cold and famine, wanted to "set up bonfires" on frozen Lake Constance.[9] Up in the alpine valleys of the Vorarlberg, burning a *Häx* (witch) in effigy on Fire Sunday was a matter of course. "Who would want it any other way?" as they sang in a so-called "Fire Song" from Montafon in Vorarlberg.[10]

The great witch hunt left its traces everywhere and imprinted itself on all sorts of traditional materials, from legends to popular customs. But this whole area from western Switzerland over to the Allgäu, the exact area where the myth of the night people spread, did have not only extremely severe witch hunts but also some of the earliest witch trials in all of Europe. In the Simmenthal, up in the Bernese Uplands, a high Alpine valley with an economy of cattle and grazing (where "the inhabitants are herdsmen"),[11] there were trials as early as around 1400 in which the fully developed image of the witch appeared. Johannes Nider (1380/90–1438), the Dominican friar from Isny in the Allgäu and official theologian at the Council of Basel, passed on this image in his famous *Formicarius*, which he wrote about 1435.[12] In the nearby Valais from the decades around 1400 we find the very first large-scale witch hunts, which were described and interpreted by the Lucerne court clerk and chronicler, Johannes Fründ (1400–1469). This source also makes it clear exactly when these persecutions jumped over from the Romance-speaking valleys to the German-speaking valleys. Scholars today are pretty much agreed in thinking that the complete and cumulative concept of the witches' sabbath arose in the last decades of the fourteenth century in the valleys of Savoy, Dauphiné, Vaud, and the Valais.[13]

Nider characterized the new kind of witchcraft in his *Formicarius* as a specifically Alpine vice, which he thought had arisen about sixty years earlier, that is, in about 1375. Completely independent testimony, written down a bit later in the Dauphiné, dates the rise of witchcraft to the same decade. And apparently Bernard of Como drew a similar conclusion on the basis of his inquisitorial archive.[14] Recently, the well-known medievalist Arno Borst has reinforced the conclusion of older research, connecting the first witch hunts with the persecution of Waldensians, a late medieval sect condemned as heretics by the Catholics. On the basis of confessions from the convicted Vaudoises (Waldensians) up in the most remote valleys to which they had retreated, the old theological fantasy of night-time flights and secret assemblies was transformed. In Pinerolo, high in the Savoyard Alps, a region that has been the center of an active Waldensian congregation since the fourteenth century, an Inquisitor "discovered" in 1387–88 that these heretics celebrated wild orgies and drank magical liquids provided by a Mistress of Ceremonies! Briançon, up in the French Alps, also harbored a Waldensian community, where a first witchcraft trial was held in 1428. It was not far from either place to the Lower Valais, which at that point still belonged to Savoy, and where witches were discovered in 1430—not far either to the Savoyard Val d'Aosta, where the first documented witchcraft trial took place in 1434. It was the same distance to Fribourg (in the Swiss Jura), and there, in 1438, witchcraft was explicitly called "Voudessie," or "Waldensianism."[15] In 1449 in the Val d'Aosta we note a trial against a healing-woman named Catherine de Chynal (1400-after 1449), who had grown up in the Valais. She had been denounced by a man who was then burned as a heretic, and she too was accused of being a heretic and of taking part in secret assemblies, which the documents call "Synagogues." This sorceress was convicted and required to abjure the "new heresy." She had to leave the diocese of Aosta forever and was required to wear a red cross on her chest and on her back to prevent the devil from ever approaching her again.[16]

Inquisitors in these Alpine valleys picked up the popular belief in nocturnal assemblies. One of the earliest witchcraft treatises, written about 1436 by Claude Tholosan, the chief prosecutor of Waldensians in Dauphiné, which included not only the Briançonnais but also the high valleys of Piedmont, begins with a quotation from Saint Augustine's *City of God* ("Ut magorum et maleficorum errores . . . " i.e., "May the false doctrines of the magicians and sorcerers be made clear to the ignorant"). In Tholosan's book we find certain passages that remind us more of the people of the night than of a witches' sabbath: "Moreover they waved their deceptive images before them in their dreams so that they believed that they went wandering about at night, in their bodies. . . . and that they ate and drank. . . . and sometimes danced a jig to the sound of an instrument. . . . And these faithless persons imagine that they eat and drink even though the food is not at all consumed."[17] But in contrast to his literary models, the inquisitor Bernardo Gui and Nicolaus Eymericus (authors of widely influential inquisitorial manuals), Tholosan no longer distinguished between dreams and harmful magic. For him these nocturnal flights and assemblies were real.[18]

In about 1435, as theologians gathered for the Council of Basel, where they could exchange opinions as if at a European trade fair, they heard not only reports of the trial of Joan of Arc, but also got the first public view of the new image of the witches' sabbath, an idea that had been invented in the region around Lake Geneva. Nider's *Formicarius* and other treatises came out of this context and were written for a learned readership. But then the new art of printing helped these early demonologists to achieve an unexpectedly widespread impact. Historian Walter Rummel has been able to show that reading Nider about sixty years later sometimes led to dramatic conversion experiences. Theologians who had earlier subscribed to the dream theory of the *Canon Episcopi* now freely took up the ideas of the witches' sabbath contained in the *Formicarius* or in the *Malleus Maleficarum*.[19] Along with this development there grew up a distinctly local, oral tradition, spurred on by the early witchcraft trials in the multinational region around Lake Geneva, a zone where languages and cultures have always mixed. As Joseph Hansen proved almost a century ago, here was the earliest center of witch hunting in all of Europe.[20]

The large region around Lake Geneva, specifically the Swiss cantons of Valais and Vaud, remained one of the major centers of European witch hunting down to the third decade of the seventeenth century.[21] In the valleys of Graubünden the hunts did not begin so early as in western Switzerland, but as late as the second half of the seventeenth century their self-governed peasant communes were still displaying an unusually virulent addiction to this gruesome kind of burnt sacrifice. Unlike the Vorarlberg or the Tyrol, which were governed by the Habsburgs, and unlike the principality of Bavaria, Graubünden had no central authority that could call a halt to these hunts.[22] It is one of the ironies of history that the very presence of centralized spiritual inquisitions, as they existed in the lands of southern Europe (Milan, Venice, Rome, Spain, Portugal) regularly led to restrictions on witch hunting in the seventeenth century or even earlier.[23]

In Oberstdorf and Sonthofen it was the witch hunt of 1586–1592 that clearly shaped local folk customs, for there has never been another event like this either before or after. Take for example the so-called "Egga-game," in Burgberg, near Sonthofen, which takes place the Sunday before Lent. In this "game," peasant activities are disturbed by a witch, who is finally captured and condemned to be burned.[24] Or take the practice (widespread throughout Allgäu, in all of the Vorarlberg, and in the Vintschgau of the southern Tyrol) of burning a witch doll on the first Sunday in Lent, which seems to be a version of the struggle between winter and summer or between life and

death.[25] These customs probably took root about the same time as they appear in art. In the wake of the great Oberstdorf witch hunt, in the neighboring episcopal town of Füssen around 1600, painter Jacob Hiebler
(ca. 1565–1620) was commissioned by Abbot Mathias Schober of St. Mang
(reg. 1579–1604) to produce a large cycle of the dance of death. This was probably the first cycle of this genre to be produced after famous pictures associated with the great epidemics of the fourteenth century, and Hiebler's
paintings were in effect a series of illustrated penitential sermons.[26] But this
one contains a dialogue between death and a witch. Death orders, "Jump up,
you ugly camel-beast, for now you really have to sweat in the fire; your pitch-
fork-riding has come to an end, for I am come to take you away from the
Heuberg immediately."[27] The accompanying picture shows the witch with
her goat—just as the judges in the Oberstdorf witch hunt had imagined
them.[28] In imitation of this model in Füssen, Oberstdorf got its own picture of a witch as part of a dance of death. In the Chapel of the Fourteen
Helpers in Need, built in 1635, painter Gabriel Neckher (1611–1687) of Füssen
copied Hiebler's picture from Füssen in about 1640. It is noteworthy that this
chapel was popularly known as the Witches' Chapel because of this part of
the picture.[29] This example of adopting a witch into the pictorial program
of a church suggests that we should remain alert to the possibility of gov-
ernmental influences in the invention of "timeless" fire rituals or in supposedly "popular" customs.

The Oberstdorf witch hunt, triggered by the testimony of Chonrad
Stoeckhlin, marks the prelude to the great regional witch hunt during the
years 1587–1592, when, in just five years, more people were executed between
the Alps and the Danube River than ever before or since. This South German
wave of persecution is significant in part because ideas about witchcraft became deeply embedded in the region. From the example of the trial that
started them all, we can see how Christian demonologists took up existing
popular ideas and transformed them in a process that we can also find in
other parts of Europe.[30] Intense, premodern ideas about the fairy folk may
well be significant here since it cannot escape notice that far more intensive
witch hunts were conducted well into the seventeenth century throughout
the whole region wherever the myth of the night people existed. Of course,

there were other factors as well that played a major role, such as the behavior of the government. Historian Manfred Tschaikner has shown specifically that the Austrian authorities in Bregenz and Innsbruck did everything they could to counteract popular desires for persecution.[31] It was just after the Prättigau gained its independence from Austrian overlordship (1649/52) and attached itself to Graubünden that horrific witch trials broke out in the three judicial districts of that valley, trials in which more than a hundred persons lost their lives. The Prättigau even produced its own home-grown Swiss-Reformed demonologist in the second half of the seventeenth century: Bartholomäus Anhorn (1616–1700), whose writings are of special interest for our story.[32] Further examples may be found in the County of Vaduz (today the principality of Liechtenstein) in the Upper Rhine Valley, where witch trials were carried out between 1648 and 1680 that cost over three hundred persons their lives, amounting to fully 10 percent of the population. This ongoing horror was derailed only by getting rid of the imperial count of Hohenems and replacing him with the princely house of Liechtenstein.[33] In the German, Rhaetian, and even in the Italian valleys of Graubünden, however, witchcraft trials continued into the eighteenth century. So, for example, in 1753 more than 128 persons stood trial for witchcraft in Poschiavo (Puschlav), and one woman was executed for the crime. As late as 1779 in the Rhaeto-Romantsch village of Oberhalbstein, Ursula Padrutt was tortured because of suspected witchcraft, just a few years before the last legal execution in all of western Europe, which took place in 1782, in the Reformed Swiss canton of Glarus.[34] In the view of the Milanese reforming bishop Carlo Borromeo (1538–1584), the whole region of Graubünden, as well as Valais, the Valle Mesolcina (*Misox*) in the canton of Ticino, and the north Italian Alpine valleys such as Val Tellina (*Veltlin*), were "infected with heretics and witches."[35]

In the confessions of the Vorarlbergers executed as witches, we find certain deviations from the usual depictions of the witches' sabbath, which show that here ideas of the phantoms of the night or of the night people had filtered in. As in the corresponding trials in Graubünden or Lucerne, the sabbaths were exceptionally merry: they "lived well with eating, drinking, and dancing," as Dorothea Sutter explained in her 1560 testimony in Lucerne.

They "drank wine several times, and often meat, cheese, butter, cakes, and the like," as the woman nicknamed "Bützenweberin" testified in Sursee.[36] These tales of dancing and jumping to drums and pipes, eating and drinking, make a livelier impression than the usual sabbath stories from other regions. The myth of the night people obviously formed a substrate of the confessions about the witches' dance throughout this region. Thus in 1597 Elsa Dünserin from the lordship of Sonnenberg in the Rhine valley, who was executed as a witch in Bregenz, confessed that at the witches' dance up on the Heuberg they had consumed a whole ox.[37] And we find the familiar pattern that an involuntary visitor to the dance was suddenly able to play for the dance even though he had never before held a violin in his hands. The miracle of the bones was integrated into this witch assembly, but in a way that made no sense at all, for witches were supposed to be harmful, not benevolent.[38] Urschla Tönzi from Davos (in Graubünden) makes an unusually confused impression with her confession concerning a society that danced at night. Caught up in the toils of a witch hunt in Schanfigg in 1659, she was asked who had invited her to the merry dances with the "'society' in Liechert's house at Klosters;" she replied that "she didn't know, because they didn't say."[39] As usual the witches' flights took place mainly during the quarterly Ember days, and usually we find the customary detail that only the soul traveled forth, leaving the body behind, as if dead in bed.[40]

Until our times few have remarked on the far-reaching effects of this forcible process of transformation. Although popular descriptions of witch dances have left obvious residues in the full-fledged demonologies,[41] it is also true that in popular stories the night people or the phantoms of the night, with their positive features, were immediately subordinated to the more powerful myth of witchcraft. But that is not all. Now the healer who cured a child became a "witch master;" the Muotas in Sonthofen became a host of witches; and even the "Rumplklausen" were transformed into devils.[42] Revenants and wild men are still found in the treasury of Allgäu legends but are now detached from all historical events.[43] One of these legends in which the myth of the night people with their wonderful music plays a role was recently republished in a collection of legends under the title "Die Hexenversammlung bei Oberstdorf" (The witches' assembly at Oberstdorf). This legend, collected by Karl Reiser, is affixed to a concrete location: "Outside of Oberstdorf, over against the Faltenbach, where there was long ago a solitary little house, long since fallen down, so that today one can hardly tell the place where it stood."[44] This is how a description of Chonrad Stoeckhlin's very own house might have begun. The houses belonging to executed witches were sometimes torn down so that nothing more would remain to remind one of their existence. And, in fact, it was not only the houses that were demolished, since popular ideas of witchcraft, too, were eradicated.

If in the legends of the Allgäu and Vorarlberg herdsmen are said to have special contact with superterrestrial beings,[45] as is true in other parts of Europe,[46] and if horse wranglers are said to have special contacts with the extrasensory realm, and if horses have long played a special role in folk belief, in folk medicine, and also in folk mythology, then these ideas must have contributed to the buildup of legends surrounding our horse wrangler, Chonrad Stoeckhlin. The role of the horse in the realm of magic and of the customs concerning the dead, and its participation in the nocturnal processions of the wild hunt, may have contributed, too.[47] But with the stories about the night people it is clear enough that throughout the Allemannic-speaking region of Germany the wild hunt had competition from a totally different sort of "night travel," a difference that is visible in the verbal contrast drawn between the army of Wuoten and the army of Guoten, about which Renward Cysat complained, since for him both were just expressions of demonic phantoms or popular superstition.[48] And Cysat also clearly hoped that both myths were dying out. He reported that ever since 1574, when the Jesuits arrived in Lucerne, no one told such stories anymore because these "deeply learned and worthy spiritual fathers" had set themselves the goal of "extinguishing and extirpating these and other superstitious and forbidden things (of which the world is full) from people's heads."[49]

With the Stoeckhlin trial we can observe the actual process by which ideas were eradicated and extirpated from people's heads throughout the bishopric of Augsburg, where the Counter Reformation had gained a foothold just twenty years earlier.[50] As we have seen, university-trained jurists showed absolutely no understanding for popular myths and ideas like Wuotas or the *Nachtschar*, and most clerics, especially the younger ones, would probably have been just as uncomprehending. It is also quite possible that an intensification of preaching and pastoral care had led to a transformation of certain folk beliefs into the somewhat Christianized shape that we find them in Stoeckhlin's idea of the *Nachtschar*. If we compare his testimony with stories of the night people or of *Säligen Lütt* [i.e., of wandering ghosts], we find the accent shifting away from the common nighttime banquet with dancing and music toward Christian notions of purgatory. It is also worth comparing Stoeckhlin's Nachtschar with the findings of Maja Boskovič-Stulli, whose fieldwork in Istria and along the Dalmatian coast has collected myths concerning the Krsniki[51] and with Carlo Ginzburg's Benandanti, which he discovered in the archives of the Venetian Inquisition. Such a comparison prompts us to recognize a striking lack of "functionality" in our horse wrangler's night flights. Stoeckhlin did not fly off to nighttime battles that might determine the success or failure of the local harvest; instead, he just flew to places where one could see "joy and sorrow." In contrast to the Benandanti or Krsniki, Stoeckhlin's ideas about night flying were lacking in contingency, that is, nothing else depended on them. Of course recently the question has been raised of just how "contingent" Ginzburg's Benandanti-myth actually was and of how much Ginzburg himself may have helped to create the meanings that he claimed to uncover.[52] In a sharp critique of Ginzburg's "pot-pourri research," Dutch folklorist Willem de Blécourt has concluded that the Benandanti were first and foremost healers and specialists in undoing magical spells. They either confirmed local suspicions concerning bewitchments or gave voice to such suspicions, and stories about their night battles may have been just a way of legitimizing this ability.[53]

We must make allowances for the likelihood that under interrogation Stoeckhlin would have given a Catholic or Christian slant to his description of the *Nachtschar*. He certainly would have tried to suppress details that were too reminiscent of the witches' sabbath.[54] Even so, if we hope to avoid pure speculation, his explanations of the purpose of his night flights apparently are strong proof that he had learned and then modified a great many Christian doctrines. And so we can only partially agree with Carlo Ginzburg, who after reading an earlier antiquarian account on the Stoeckhlin trial[55] concluded that our horse-herdsman was the one example "that evinces the most exact parallels to the *Benandanti*."[56] This is only true if we tone down somewhat Ginzburg's exaggerated claims to have discovered a mythic essence that supposedly survived over centuries or even across millennia without losing any of its vital force. Even if certain mythic fragments might actually be thousands of years old and might crop up again as motifs in various versions, we should bear in mind that they would then function in dramatically different contexts. In Vorarlberg we have just seen this sort of reformulation. The mythologem containing the miracle of the bones, which was an essential component for identifying the night people, was transferred to the witches during the witch hunts. Up on the high meadow of the Gelbrüfi in Vorarlberg, witches supposedly brought together the hide and bones of a cow they had eaten and then brought her back to life—this does not sound like a normal example of the sort of harmful magic performed by witches.[57]

We should, moreover, not underestimate the Counter-Reformation theologians' nose for non-Christian beliefs. Contemporary demonologists, such as Peter Binsfeld, insisted that sorcerers obviously used Christian concepts, prayers, and sacraments, but not in order to call upon God. Instead they were trying to compel God. Under the Christian dispensation, magic always implied a form of theurgy, that is, forcing the gods, even if it was only the apparently harmless blessing of horses.[58] Stoeckhlin functioned in his community not only as a healer but also as a soothsayer. And he explained his most remarkable soothsaying ability—being able to identify witches—by claiming that he had traveled with the *Nachtschar*. There is a parallel instance of exactly this connection in a second witch trial conducted in the bishopric of Augsburg. Just two years after Stoeckhlin was burned to death as a witch, a fourteen-year-old boy named Bernhard Vischer, from the district of Bobingen, aroused general excitement with his claim that he could identify witches. When he was asked where he had got this valuable skill, he announced that it came to him because he traveled with his cousin Hans "to strange destinations and locations to a great wild fire."[59] Following the precedent set with Stoeckhlin, the bishop's government in Dillingen again demanded a large inquisition, and this case of ecstatically tinged sooth-saying led once again to a huge witch hunt. In this case, too, as with Stoeckhlin, the clairvoyant boy had named the "right" women, that is, those who were already generally suspected of being witches.[60]

It is interesting to compare the fate of various popular myths and beliefs that were recorded over the past centuries in the course of criminal trials or in other ways. There is certainly now a whole school of folklore studies in Germany that regards any kind of cultic continuity with the utmost skepticism,[61] and yet as international historical research investigates the expression of folk beliefs at various levels, we repeatedly discover just such continuities, even when we use the most stringent and careful methods.[62] Jean-Claude Schmitt, for example, has found evidence of a strange cult surrounding a dog-like saint who healed children, a cult dating back to the thirteenth century (the so-called "adoratio Guinefortis canis," i.e., the adoration of Saint Guinefort the Dog). Schmitt proves that his shrine in a sacred grove was venerated until the first decades of the twentieth century. Excavations there have brought to light coins and children's shoes donated by pilgrims.[63] So here again we find that an insistence on "strict methods" actually disguises a taboo rooted in a panicky flight from the "Wotan-tainted" past of German folklore studies, a discipline that used to present itself as the nationalist form of Germanic scholarship.

If we compare a variety of popular beliefs surrounding the *Nachtschar* myth, we uncover a multilayered picture. The notion found by Carlo Ginzburg in the archives of the Venetian inquisition dealing with the Benandanti of Friuli, who went out to fight against *streghe* (witches), disappeared without a trace around the middle of the seventeenth century. Along the Dalmatian coast, however, the structurally and substantially identical belief in Kresniki survived until the 1950s. These were people who did battle with the *strigas* and were first described in detail by a seventeenth-century Italian writer. The Croatian ethnologist, Maja Boskovič-Stulli spoke personally with people who were still regarded as "Krsniki" in their own village. And there were still villagers who believed in the myth of ecstatics with special abilities, whose souls left their bodies behind at certain times in order to defend the harvest by fighting off the witch. It was only natural that these Krsniki, both men and women, were thought to possess divinatory and healing powers. This notion of the Krsniki survived in the Dalmatian islands right down to the time of mass tourism, but how old is it really and where did it come from? Because there are no sources earlier than the seventeenth century, one can only speculate about such questions. Unexpectedly,

Boskovič-Stulli maintains that they are neither Celtic nor Germanic in origin, but that they go back to an ancient Slavic myth that was possibly taken over by the neighboring Italians (as Benandanti).[64]

Just to complete the picture, let us note that Hungarian researchers maintain that the abilities of the "Tàltos" to go traveling as disembodied souls, to predict the future and to heal sickness, abilities that can be documented no earlier than the year 1584 (that is, almost exactly at the same time as Stoeckhlin's *Nachtschar*), are part of an ancient Hungarian myth, whose origins stretch back to the most distant Eurasian past, and are actually a descended from Siberian shamanism.[65] The history of ideas concerning the *Nachtschar* and the night people appears to lie in the middle-range between extinction and fully intact survival, just as with ideas concerning the *Saligen* (the spirit-dead) in Carinthia, the fairies of Scotland,[66] and the *donne di Fuori* of Sicily, those "ladies from outside,"[67] or the fairy-legends from Europe generally. All of these myths were contaminated by notions of witchcraft and survived in legends and fairy tales but without the idea that certain persons might still be identified today as real participants.

Gábor Klaniczay has recently pointed out that witchcraft beliefs provided a niche in which a shamanistic figure could fit:

> the role of the fortune-teller, the "knower," the healer, the professional magician, who brought his or her counter-magic to bear against the magical aggression of supposed witches and thus healed the bewitched and freed them from a curse. . . . The nature of the powers claimed by such healers, the sort of magic they used in their battle with the witches, the ecstatic techniques they employed to eliminate witches, their casting of spells or their foretelling the future, and the fact that their vocation often rested upon hallucinations, all of these characteristics merit the close attention of experts on shamanism or at the very least of historians of religion.[68]

The remarkable link that tied miraculous healing to witch finding survived even after the execution of Stoeckhlin and despite occasional periods of intense persecution. The most amazing example of this survival can probably be found in the Vorarlberg priest, Johann Joseph Gassner (1727–1779), the prophet of Catholic reaction against the Enlightenment, who, in the last

Folk Beliefs

quarter of the eighteenth century, declared that all sicknesses had their origin in bewitchment and with his astonishing exorcisms excited all of southern Germany until his phantasms were forbidden by Emperor Joseph II.[69]
History again showed its irony: just as in the Yucatan of the conquistadors,
where the Maya goddess Ixchel crept into the form of the Mother of God,
so here the popular notion of witch finder reemerged in the shape of a
Catholic priest. Gassner was, moreover, closely related to one of the two dis-
putants in one of the very last witch investigations held in Vorarlberg, an
inquiry that almost resulted in a witch trial.[70]

Finally, let us take note of a few other continuities of this sort. At about
the same time as Chonrad Stoeckhlin, the healer and folk-blesser Peter
Schoder from Vandans in Montafon (in the Vorarlberg) came to public attention as a central representative of "magical popular culture." He was active as a witch finder, triggering off witchcraft trials, and was much called on
by localities as far away as the Tyrol.[71] In his family a tradition of healing survived unbroken, as we see in the figure of Johann Josef Schoder of Vandans
(1818–1884), who became a medical doctor in 1848 and was celebrated in 1850
in a publication by a grateful patient, who described Schoder as "one of those
men to whom God grants special healing powers." Schoder was soon sought
out by numerous patients suffering from unusual diseases, which he treated
by means of "magnetism," or "simply by breathing on them or by mag-
netic stroking." Pains disappeared "as if by magic." In the *Viennese Medical
Weekly*, which had just been founded in 1851, Schoder was soon the object
of vehement attacks, which culminated in the conclusion: "We are amazed
at the credulity of our so-called human understanding. *Mundus vult decipi,
ergo—decipitur* [the world wants to be deceived, and so it is deceived]." In the
following years the so-called Viennese Doctors' Controversy flared up, in
which academic physicians squared off against the Vorarlberg charlatan, and
in which Schoder was defended by his patients. Under the heading of
"Schoderiana," 220 cases of miraculous cures were published.[72] And just a
few years ago a researcher found that belief in fortune telling and in "witch
doctors" is still strong in the Allgäu, and not just among peasants.[73]

17.

Shamanism

THE CONNECTIONS BETWEEN ecstasy, soul travel, fortune-telling, and powers of healing, which we find here united but still only in fragmentary form, have been brought together in other cultures into a type of religious expertise called shamanism. This concept was first used among the Tungus of Siberia,[1] but since the middle of our century it has been applied by students of comparative religion to cultures outside Asia. In the analysis by Russian anthropologist Vladimir Basilov, shamanism is a cult, "in whose spiritual center lies the belief that certain individuals, if chosen by the spirits, can go into a trance in which they encounter these spirits and take on the function of mediating between the world of the spirits and that of their own society."[2] Taking this description, we must acknowledge that it fits perfectly for Chonrad Stoeckhlin, too. And all the more so if we notice the complex of experience that Mircea Eliade (1907–1986) regarded as the "specific element," or the very heart of shamanism: ecstasy and "travel to heaven and the underworld."[3]

In Stoeckhlin's vocabulary these were paradise and the gates of hell. That Stoeckhlin's mythic world had become saturated with Christian ideas is not surprising since he did live, after all, in a Christian culture, and under a spiritual lord, the bishop of Augsburg. Basilov's research into shamanistic practices in Turkmenistan, a region that has been dominated by the high religion of Islam for more than a thousand years, has also shown that the shamans there see themselves as true Muslims: in their rites they pray to Allah and to Muslim saints. Conversely, in many Islamic saints, and especially in Sufism, the traits of great shamans reappear,[4] and Gábor Klaniczay has recently shown that the same is true of Christian saints who can understand the language of animals, command the elements, heal illness, and fly through the air.[5] This conceptual definition does not mean that we are committed to some ahistorical or timeless notion of a basic substrate within human imagination. Quite the contrary: as early as the work of Sergei M. Shirokogoroff (1887–1939), we find the attempt to prove that the religious ideas of the Tungus were deeply influenced by Buddhism and Lamaism, whose arrival can be dated with relative certainty. From then on, older animist ideas were inseparably mixed with influences from these high religions.[6]

Without following Ginzburg in his effort to demonstrate the continuity of secret cults back into Eurasian prehistory,[7] we can still recognize that the mythic world of many early modern Europeans provided fertile soil not just for magic but also for shamanistic ideas. After all, health care was rudimentary and poorly developed, their subsistence economy was plagued by scarcity and shortages, the official religious ideology only partially accommodated the needs of the population, and a non-Christian mythic repertoire was constantly available in the background. Together these conditions would have been quite likely to produce phenomena that students of comparative religion have classified as shamanism.

The separation of the soul from its body and its trip to certain places is the constitutive element for any great shaman. "Siberian, North American, and Eskimo shamans all fly."[8] Their ability to "fly magically" makes them similar to the spirits with whom they are in contact, and in many cultures these religious specialists also possess the gift of metamorphosis, of transforming themselves into animals. The contacts shamans have with the "other world" are made possible by their growing beyond the normal human condition, by this temporary death, by ecstasy and the departure of the soul from the body.[9] Such a flight of the soul was rightly envied by Christian demonologists, for anyone who had these powers might stand as a serious competitor to the Christian priest, especially since the latter was restrained in his abilities by the official doctrines of his high religion. An orthodox priest could never claim a direct line to the hereafter and found himself relegated to the "servants' staircase" of the ecclesiastical hierarchy; he was not allowed to foretell the future and did not normally work as a healer, although in this respect his blessings and exorcisms brought him closer to the work of the magician. Probably the most irritating aspect for the church lay in the fact that folk magicians pretended to lead the very life reserved only for the most extraordinary saints of the high religion.

Shamanistic ecstasies can be found in Europe from the early Middle Ages down to today. Let us mention here only the so-called legend of Gunthram in the "History of the Lombards," where the soul exits as a little animal from the mouth of the sleeping person.[10] There are parallel examples in folk tradition, such as in southern France of the fourteenth century, where in Pamiers the servant Arnaud Gélis had experienced an initiation in 1312 that was similar to Stoeckhlin's. From that day of initiation on, his soul went traveling with the good ladies or with the souls of the dead (*cum bonis dominabus seu animabus defunctorum*) to special places, to the most beautiful and cleanest houses. Like his cousin before him, Gélis functioned as a messenger from the beyond, whose services were required by numerous customers. The reports taken down by Bishop Jacques Fournier (1285–1382), the later Pope Benedict XII, were unusually detailed, but in broad outline they reveal what we can also find in Iceland in the sixteenth century, in Sicily in the seventeenth century, in Hungary in the seventeenth and eighteenth centuries, and in Croatia and Slovenia as late as the nineteenth and twentieth centuries, just to name a few examples.[11] In each of these examples, there are problems of transmission, as in the case of the Sicilian ladies from outside. They loved children and harmed no one, except perhaps when they defended themselves. Luck smiled on those whom they visited. Anyone who went "traveling" with them, by having souls that left their bodies on certain nights, obtained the capacity to heal and to foretell the future. Their assemblies were enlivened by wonderful music and frolicsome dancing, and wherever they went there was plenty of food and drink. Sometimes they even helped people with their work. The historian Giuseppe Bonomo knew of these *donni de fori* almost exclusively from the manual of the priest Giovanni Vasalli, composed around 1460, which threatened punishment for those who believed in such nocturnal flights.[12] This seemed to prove that this book was only a localized translation of the famous goddess Diana from the *Canon*

Episcopi. But Gustav Henningsen's examination of the records of the Spanish inquisition in Palermo has now shown that between 1579 and 1651 there were 65 actual cases that dealt with this notion of fairies. These *donne di fuori* or *douas de fuore* were labeled *brujas* (witches) by the inquisitors and their leader, La Señora Grazia, Reina de las Hadas (queen of the fairies), or La Señora Griega (the Greek lady), etc., was immediately identified by the theologians as a demon.[13]

The remarkable point about these examples is that although they present motifs that also show up in literature, here they appear in a preliterary stage. Stoeckhlin did more than just talk about the *Nachtschar*. He traveled with it. And the same is true of the Sicilian *donne di fuori*, the Friulian Benandanti, the Hungarian Táltos, the Dalmatian Krsniki, and of the Swiss *Säligen Lütt*. To a certain extent this is even true of some witches of the fifteenth and early sixteenth century in the southern Tyrol and in Alsace, where women also said that their souls left their bodies at night and traveled to specific places. And to that extent we now have to place all the stories of witches' flight in a different context from the usual one. They were not just the product of Christian demonology or of torture, for behind such stories, including even testimony given in official hearings, at least in many regions of Europe, there may possibly lurk experiences of ecstasy.

And yet we can only partially accept the thesis of the Russian folklorist, Vladimir Propp, who believed in the historical *survival* of a shamanistic substrate in magical fairy tales.[14] It is fairly clear that no pre-Christian cults survived the thousand years of Christian acculturation. The Celtic, Germanic, Slavic, and Roman mythic repertoire was broken up, dissolved, and partially extinguished, just as with the Turkmenic mythic repertoire after the introduction of Islam.[15] Even so, the surviving fragments of myth, these vestigial mythologems, were powerful enough to generate new myths over and over again.

18.

Bricolage

To what extent, then, were the stories of the *Nachtschar*, as Stoeckhlin told them and as they led him to the stake, an echo of distant times? Such speculations, such games with the mythic treasures and the mosaic stones of historical tradition are surely amusing, as we can see from the works of Ginzburg and from the discussions he has provoked. And they should be permitted, too, as long as we remain aware of their methodological limitations. And yet, for our interpretation, the question of origins is of almost no significance. At least among scholars and theorists, notions of cultural diffusion and the search for origins have lost their attraction these days for the simple reason that hunting for origins becomes an exercise in anachronism, requiring one to evoke an earlier time period that lies completely beyond the later actors' world of experience.[1] Instead it is crucial to see that stories like those of the *Nachtschar*, independent of their derivation or origin, were a lived contemporary reality, "a knowledge of practice" that came to life: the stuff of legends and a report of real, lived experience at the same time.[2] Here we do not need to discuss again the function of the story of the *Nachtschar* (see chapter 11); let us rather consider the mental structures, the ways and means by which stories were construed.[3]

As David Sabean showed several years ago, using the example of a soothsayer at the time of the Thirty Years' War, a peasant prophet to whom an angel appeared in 1648, clad in white and wearing a red cross on his chest, one can sometimes prove in specific cases that such visions were cobbled together out of contemporary materials. Vintner Hans Keil (ca. 1618-?), who lived in Gerlingen in the Württemberg district of Leonberg, had for many

Bricolage

years collected the so-called "New Tidings," primitive newspapers and single-sheet broadsides, dealing with angelic apparitions, raptures, heavenly signs, monstrous births, bloody rainfalls, etc. His own visions were an amalgamation of the ideas in the printed materials found when his house was searched. Like Stoeckhlin, Keil operated with the Christian catalog of sins and vices, but his visions also had an antigovernment tendency, and he was accused of calling the common people together for disturbances that verged on rebellion, and so this winegrower was forced to recant by the government. And after recanting he had to explain how he had invented his supposed visions.[4] Visits with the local pastor gave Keil the means to justify his visions by using the angelic vision of Cornelius, described in Acts 10:1–8, which he then connected with material from the pamphlets found in his room. Sabean shows that this Württemberg peasant stitched his visions together from separate fragments in a kind of bricolage, a procedure that French anthropologist Claude Lévi-Strauss describes as typical for so-called primitive cultures. The *bricoleur* pulls together the most various mythic fragments and components in a new way, using "a kind of intellectual bricolage," a process of cobbling received materials together that serves his current purposes.[5]

With this example of the vinedresser Keil, we can see on the level of popular culture just how written materials could enlarge the repertoire of a still largely oral culture.[6] The technique of bricolage remains essentially identical, however, in the case of another illiterate peasant prophet, who came to attention at about the same time, in a nearby region, and with a message that was also sharply critical of society. From his parish in the Electoral Palatine town of Mosbach, the theologian Bartholomäus Anhorn reported the case of a cowherd, who in 1659 had thrown his community into turmoil with an angelic apparition: "When he was up on the hill, near to the Schrekhof, tending his cattle, an angel appeared to him a second time and commanded him to go to the church inspector for the district of Mosbach, and to tell him what he had seen and heard. So he came to me, the author of this little book, while I was a pastor in Mosbach and inspector of the neighboring churches." But the cowherd had made a serious mistake in turning to the cleric. Pastor Anhorn reported in his chapter "On Visions" that he had threatened the peasant with hellfire and brimstone, admonishing him "most earnestly . . . to turn away from these devilish seductions and to stop deceiving other people with this phony vision." When the herdsman refused to give up his revelation, the pastor preached publicly against him from his pulpit and visited him at home in the company of another minister, warning the "visionary" about "God's inevitable punishment." Threatening his soul in this manner proved effective, and Anhorn reported triumphantly that the cowherd then confessed his fraud:

> Actually, no one had appeared to him, he had seen no angel nor any other vision; instead, because he was tending the cows and was alone in the fields almost all day, he had often meditated deeply upon, and with heartfelt groans had lamented, the sad condition of the common people; then one day he remembered that he had heard tell of angelic apparitions, which were highly regarded by everyone in all places. And so he undertook to invent some such thing, but with the best of intentions and with this purpose: in order that the district officials might be terrified, those men who treated their underlings harshly, and sucked the very marrow from their bones, but doing so mainly without the knowledge of our gracious prince. And in order that these officials would treat them more graciously, etc.

Anhorn prided himself that he had brought this phantasm to a quick end, for he shuddered to think of the consequences for the authority of both church and state if "wild" prophets should arise. How many superstitious people had believed the cowherd? How far had his fame spread? "As soon as these visionaries and new prophets gain just a little fame, they become at once proud, puffed up, and presumptuous: they boast of their own perfection and believe that neither Peter nor Paul, nor any of the other apostles, was their equal."[7] In the view of theologians it was only godless souls and remorseless rogues, simpletons, or poor unlucky people who found compensation in such visions. And Anhorn's socially reforming cowherd made it clear enough where he had obtained the material for his story. As with others, this *bricoleur* had used the available means, the materials he found ready to hand or in his immediate neighborhood.[8]

So where had Stoeckhlin, the horse wrangler from Allgäu, found his material? There were of course no printed writings at his house, and he was not asked where his ideas came from because the court did not care. And yet we find a few implicit indications. The ritual by which witches could be forced to take back their magic was known in that region. And, just a little earlier, angelic visions had been successfully employed as a means of self-legitimation in the neighboring village of Hindelang. Stoeckhlin's testimony also provides a few hints. Notably he claimed that his deceased mother had advised him to ask the *Nachtschar* for forgiveness if he were to be caught, a notion that, because of the amount of time that had passed, does not seem entirely credible. When he was asked whom he recognized on his trips, Stoeckhlin had answered that he did not know anyone traveling with him "except for Michael Mathens, the son of the Walser, who lives over in the Walser Valley."[9] In addition to his marriage to the Walser woman Barbara Berchtoldin and his friendship with the Walser oxherd, Jacob Walch, this hint of Stoeckhlin's more extensive connections to the Lesser Walser Valley is suggestive, for we have seen that ideas about the night people and the night phantoms were especially marked among the Walsers of Vorarlberg.[10]

From this vantage point the prospect spreads out before us to include that whole geographic region in which the fairy-like notion of the night people had its home. In contrast to the view set forth by Ilg,[11] just paging superficially through the older collections of legends from the Valais brings similar motifs to light; but in addition, perhaps because the miracles of the bones took place on remote mountain meadows, these were stories that especially appealed to herdsmen.[12] The myth of the night people could be found throughout the whole Walser region, from the Rhone Valley across the Upper Rhine with its side valleys, over into the Lesser Walser Valley in the uplands above Oberstdorf. One could of course suggest (without any real hope of solid proof) that there were Celtic roots to all of these fairy notions, for the Rhine and Rhone Valleys with their side valleys were, of course, part of the old area settled by the Celts, and the Rhaeto-Romans were themselves a mixed population made up of Romanized Rhaetians, Celts, and others who moved in from the Roman provinces. As against the optimism of Alfred Weitnauer,[13] however, there is no very convincing evidence for a continuity of myths and ideas here, but also no serious counter evidence. We have already mentioned the fact that ideas of fairies are regularly discussed in the literature in connection with a supposed "Celtic inheritance."[14] But one way or another the Walsers took up these ideas. It is plausible, perhaps, that their settlement patterns, living as mountain peasants on marginal soils, on steep hillsides of the side valleys and in the primeval forests of the highest valleys, places they had had to occupy as late immigrants, enabled them to preserve archaic myths and legends for an unusually long time.[15] We could perhaps see the spread of the cult of Saint Theodul as parallel to the distribution of the myth of the night people. Wherever the Walsers wandered, whether to Upper Italy, to eastern Switzerland or to western Austria, they carried with them, without any pressure from the authorities, a religious veneration for this legendary first bishop of the Land of Valais.[16] The most northerly spurs of this movement took the cult to Allgäu, as we can see, for example, in the parish church of Tiefenbach near Oberstdorf, or in the church of neighboring Hindelang, where Saint Theodul was venerated as a sort of patron saint of rustic fertility and as a protector against weather magic.[17]

Through his contacts with Walser culture, Stoeckhlin was thus familiar with a myth that was otherwise unknown north of the Alps. And he endeavored to employ its concepts for his own purposes. In these ideas he clearly found a metaphysical legitimation for his activities as prophet, healer, and witch finder. According to Lévi-Strauss the *bricoleur* is limited in the possible combinations he can choose only by the fact that the "constitutive units of a myth" are taken from a context in which they already have a meaning.[18] In the case of Chonrad Stoeckhlin this simply meant that he took the positive connotations of the night phantoms and the night people—similar to the attributes of the *benandanti* of Friuli or the *donne di fuori* of Sicily—and tried to make them useful for his own purposes by combining them with such elements as believers would find acceptable, notions like doing penance, in order to legitimate his role within a magical folk culture. Into his own story he could insert appropriate pieces, such as the well-known meaning of the Ember days or other times of the year for regular fasting. It was not only Ginzburg's *benandanti* who went forth at these times; other legends also depend on the idea that only children born during the Ember days can hear the music of the night people.[19] And a book of Valaisian recollections from the

Bricolage

1960s constantly emphasizes the meaning of the Ember days. For example, 72-year-old Josef Eyer from Naters (Upper Valais) said: "My father was born during the Ember days. His whole life long he could see more than the rest of us, and he knew more. And during the Ember times he was not his normal self, he was so strange." Eighty-five-year-old Genowefa Zenklusen from Simplon remembered: "My mother was a child of the Ember days. She saw much and always told us to pray for the souls of the dead. . . . During the Ember days my mother used to say, 'Today the souls of the dead are giving me no peace.'"[20]

Stoeckhlin's ascetic impulses, even though they are typical for ecstatics in many cultures, were also perfectly adapted to the major trend of the waning sixteenth century, pushed by all the major religious movements and especially by the Roman Catholic Church, filled with the spirit of the Counter Reformation. Stoeckhlin's saintly behavior made him a sort of trailblazer for the Counter Reformation because the ecclesiastical princes of that time, themselves, often fell far short of the demands of the new morality. Bishop Marquard vom Berg and such prince-abbots of Kempten as Albrecht von Hohenegg (r. 1584–1587) and Johann Erhart Blarer von Wartensee (r. 1587–1594) all had concubines and several children. They led a life "that was almost more worldly than spiritual," as the chronicles of the Protestant imperial cities remarked.[21] It is even possible that when this horse herdsman behaved more religiously than his spiritual shepherds, they took this as a provocation or even as a travesty. In any event, Stoeckhlin's extremely personal interpretation of the myth of the night phantoms was bound up with his activity as a healer and prophet. From his point of view, subjectively, the night phantoms were crucial to his role, because his special abilities rested on acts of initiation and incorporation. His skillful bricolage and his use of centrally important legends of folk tradition, regardless of whether he actually believed in them, demonstrate that he was indeed a "virtuoso representative and performer of popular culture."[22]

19.

Private Revelations

Sᴛᴏᴇᴄᴋʜʟɪɴ's "sʜᴀᴍᴀɴɪsᴛɪᴄ ᴀʙɪʟɪᴛɪᴇs," his swoons and journeys, cannot just be functionalistically explained away. Even if he played with the narrative material and popular beliefs that he found ready to hand, that does not prove that his stories must descend from supposedly "ancient" traditions. Mircea Eliade maintained that the experience of ecstasy is an "original phenomenon," one that is not dependent on any specific historical epoch or any specific culture or form of civilization.[1] On the other hand, the contents of any set of beliefs are naturally bound up with a particular "religious-historical milieu." As a religion Christianity was founded on divine revelation, and at the same time Christians continued to believe that God could at any moment intrude on the world. So why should God not continue to work miracles or allow angels to appear in order to reveal himself afresh? And even if some parts of the academic world or the world of business increasingly laughed at such stories, popular culture nonetheless remained widely receptive to them. "The common herd always believed such things," the official consistory reported concerning the visions of Hans Keil.[2]

Private revelations represented, therefore, a real struggle between popular culture and the culture of the upper classes, as we can see from the statistics of the Spanish Inquisition. After being founded in the late fifteenth century, it first mainly prosecuted those who had been forcibly converted to Christianity: the Jews (Conversos) and Muslims (Moriscos). By the mid-sixteenth century it was concerned with the new heresies of the Protestants. But then increasingly it was crimes of magic that came under fire, and finally, from the 1580s onward, persons who had experienced private revelations, including even some visionaries whom the Roman Catholic Church later beatified or canonized: these persons were more or less archaic ecstatics, who held that they had come directly into contact with the beyond and thus challenged the authority of ecclesiastical officials.[3] Viewed from the perspective of social history or the history of mentalities, the causes of this growing phenomenon are not yet clear, but we may suppose that they were prompted by increasingly intense Catholic missionary activity, the growing pressure for moral discipline, and possibly also by the rise of social tensions in the late sixteenth century. It was certainly no accident that at about the same time, in 1576, Teresa of Ávila (1515–1582) in her *Relaciones* formulated for the first time within the Roman Catholic Church a sort of theory of ecstasy that distinguished three stages: simple ecstasy, rapture, and the flight of the spirit.[4] Let us also note that it was not only spirits who flew. Even Saint Teresa claimed that she had levitated, and with Saint Joseph Desa of Cupertino (1603–1663) we find a saint who appeared on the stage of a Counter Reformation theater, claiming that he had actually flown through the air. In his case the church packed the willful Franciscan off to a remote monastery, but in 1767 he was canonized. During the Second World War he was venerated by American Catholic pilots as their patron saint.[5]

Private revelations were regarded as possible by the Roman Catholic Church, and they still are. And yet there was always the problem of "discerning the spirits," that is, the ability mentioned in First Corinthians (I Cor. 12:10) of differentiating between godly and demonic inspirations.[6] The apostle John in his first Epistle (I John 4:1) urged "Beloved, believe not every spirit, but try the spirits whether they are of God." Although the apostles regarded the "discernment of spirits" as a special gift of grace, at the end of the sixteenth century the jurists of the bishop of Augsburg acted in the full confidence that they had it. They had Jean Bodin's *Démonomanie* on their bookshelf, a book that discussed the "discrimination of spirits" at the very beginning.[7] In their heads they had their own ideas, while their ears rang with the sermons of Counter-Reformation theologians, especially those of the Jesuits of Dillingen. Both Roman Catholic and Protestant theologians agreed that one should not simply place one's faith in visionary dreams. With the peasant prophets of the Reformed Palatinate or of Lutheran Württemberg, Protestant church consistories exercised a "discernment of spirits" just as scrupulously as they did in Catholic Allgäu.[8]

In the seventeenth century in many regions of Europe, the upper classes were not themselves yet very far removed from magical thinking or the belief in revelations. A "witch doctor" like Stoeckhlin was actually able to trigger off a huge witch hunt with his soothsaying only because the jurists and theologians of the bishop of Augsburg were ready to grant his "revelations" a certain level of credibility. Spectacular prophecies and oracular visions also played a major role in the witch hunts conducted in the County of Werdenfels governed by the bishop of Freising in 1589, in the district court of Schwabmünchen under the jurisdiction of the bishop of Augsburg in 1589, and in the Bavarian lordship of Schongau, also in 1589.[9] It was only after this procedure was recognized as dangerous that the University of Ingolstadt issued a decree in 1591 formally condemning the belief in "fortune-tellers or black magicians who use black and devilish arts to accuse witches."[10]

Among the various kinds of private revelation, the most distinguished was "rapture," in which the recipient of the message was personally removed to another world. It is hardly surprising, therefore, that theologians regarded precisely this form of private revelation with special distrust. Bartholomäus Anhorn echoed Bodin in placing the question of private revelation at the very beginning of his demonology and spent a whole chapter on "Ecstasies and Raptures." Here he provided a tidy description of the physical concomitants of ecstasy, which combined "simultaneously a movement of the mind from its natural location with a suspension of all the outward senses of the person, so that he either sees, hears, and feels nothing or very little. Yea, often it appears that there is no more life in him. In such a rapture the mind or the memory works alone." Anhorn also distinguished raptures that were natural from those that were artificial, the godly and spiritual from those that were devilish, and he gave examples of each. In devilish raptures the devil took special pains to deceive, "as if in these pretended raptures the souls of the enraptured leave their bodies behind and travel in the world, through the air to heaven and hell, where they diligently look at everything, and when they return to their bodies, they report to everyone what they have seen."[11]

Private Revelations

This Reformed theologian from eastern Switzerland here described with fair accuracy just what Chonrad Stoeckhlin had experienced. His soul had traveled out of his body. Leaving the bodily husk behind, he had flown through the air and had seen Paradise and the gates of hell. On his return, he had announced what he had seen. Anhorn pointed to the great harm such ecstatics did to the church, and he cited as modern examples the Anabaptists, Thomas Müntzer, David Joris, Jan van Leiden, and the English Quakers. But then he turned his special attention to the "devilish raptures . . . of the sorceresses and witches, who often suppose that they have attended happy parties even though their bodies remain lying in some corner, immovable and insensate, until they return to themselves again." Referring to Saint Augustine, Anhorn then described which powers the devil, as the "ape of God," possessed and which ones he did not. Naturally, he could not perform real miracles, but with the permission of God he could send people into a deep sleep so that they seemed dead, and then later he could pretend to "resurrect them from the dead."

Displaying his unusual knack for ethnography, Anhorn noticed a similar phenomenon:

> This is where the Satanic raptures of the Laplanders belong, along with the midnight peoples who are devoted to the devil's service, as described by Olaus Magnus, when he writes, "If a stranger wants to know how things are back at home, they can tell him within twenty-four hours even if it is three hundred miles away or more, and this they do in the following manner: After the magician has performed certain ceremonies and has addressed his hellish gods with certain words, he falls to the ground, like a corpse, from which the soul has gone. And it seems that there is neither movement nor life in him."

But when he awakens from his rapture, he can give information about matters far away, just as if he had seen them himself.[12] In urgent tones Anhorn warned against still believing in such raptures "in our times," for ever since the Revelation provided by Scripture, such miracles have no longer been necessary; "the supposed raptures of today . . . are not godly but are partially invented, and partially Satanic raptures, . . . and whoever boasts of his rap-

tures gives an infallible sign that they were either invented or that such raptures come from the devil himself or from having a pact with him."[13] In
this battle against private revelations, we can find one final connection to the
inquisitions of southern Europe. The horse wrangler from Allgäu, Chonrad
Stoeckhlin, appears at first to have been unique and all alone, but he can now
be seen to fit into a broader panorama, the Europe-wide struggle between
popular culture and elite culture at the end of the sixteenth century. This
struggle can be understood from various perspectives. Lévi-Strauss would
probably see the contrast between different ways of thinking, the contrast
between the tinkerer and the engineer, or between mythic and conceptual
thinking. Peter Burke would stress the fight between popular and learned
culture, between the culture of Carnival and that of Lent.[14] The Danish cultural historian Gustav Henningsen would see a "diabolizing" of the "popular dream world, which represented a dangerous rival to the joyless society
of Christendom."[15] No matter which model one prefers, the confessional
regulation of thinking that the churches aimed at left no room for mythol-
ogizing charismatics. The time of the night phantoms was past. The process
of eradicating such stories from the heads of people had begun, an eradica-
tion accomplished by the "highly learned and worthy spiritual fathers," as
Renward Cysat called the Jesuits when they arrived in Lucerne.[16]

20.

The End of the Dreamtime

Specialists who study folk religion have often expressed amazement at the sudden change in mood and mentality that came over their respective regions when religious reforms were introduced. What had earlier seemed obvious was no longer obvious; this breakdown in consensus rested, in turn, on a shift in consciousness or mentality.[1] In the early modern period one such revolution in *Weltanschauung* took place, and in Oberstdorf as in the whole bishopric of Augsburg, this revolution was connected to a huge witch hunt. No longer could midwives use birth magic, nor could herdsmen bless their animals any more; priests now had to give up their concubines. Soothsaying was obviously condemned by the First Commandment and now served as proof that one had direct contact with the devil. And yet, in comparison with the wild stories told by Chonrad Stoeckhlin, these were mere bagatelles. What was one to think of a man who was led by angels or fairies to unknown places and who then returned in possession of the truth, knowing how to heal and foretell the future, thus calling the authority of both church and state into question?

Herdsman Stoeckhlin had failed to recognize that in this bishopric there was a superior shepherd, Bishop Marquard von Berg, who felt that he had to prove his competence in competition with other upwardly struggling territorial powers in the modern theater of force. By the end of the sixteenth century, ordinary people could no longer practice grassroots politics. Even peasant revolts served only to solidify the political structures of Central Europe. The very same Jean Bodin who had composed one of the most horrifying demonologies, the *Démonomanie* that was used against Chonrad

Stoeckhlin by the zealous and well-read episcopal jurists, this Bodin had also reformulated the watchword of the hour: *Princeps legibus solutus*, that is, "the prince is not bound by the laws," a doctrine that meant in practice that a prince could deride and disregard his subjects and lesser magistrates. The form of government called "absolutism," a term coined by Bodin,[2] would now no longer even permit its more "extravagant" subjects to live.

In this way yet another step was taken toward eradicating popular beliefs and myths. During the early medieval phase of Christian missions, the old gods had been deprived of their powers. The *Canon Episcopi* stands fully in this tradition, which denied to demons any major force or power. During the high Middle Ages belief in the old gods disappeared, but the teleological worldview of Christianity had not yet fully prevailed. And with the beginning of the great heretical movements, on through the work of the Inquisition, theologians discovered a "Dreamtime" among the denizens of the Alps.[3] In the course of countless trials they became persuaded that through the power of the devil and with the permission of God, human flight through the air to secret places was actually possible. From Thomas Aquinas (1225–1274) onward, this process of increasing acceptance led directly to the *Malleus Maleficarum* and to the other great demonologies. Thomas became the great doctor of the church, accepted as an authority in the catechetical literature of the fourteenth and fifteenth centuries. It was there that Nikolaus of Dinkelsbühl, Stephan of Landskron, and Marquard of Lindau derived their conviction that even revelations in dreams had a devilish character and could be evidence of *pacta tacita et expressa*, of tacit and explicit pacts with the devil. One of these devilish notions was the belief "that the people of the night go on journeys."[4]

Real conventicles of heretics, as well as surviving notions of fairies (in both cases, groups who were known as "good people") thus provided a conceptual basis for the witches' dance.[5] Although this thesis has been criticized and the old idea that the sabbath was invented by the Inquisition has even been revived,[6] there is much evidence in favor of the view that popular beliefs played an important role in the construction of the idea of the witches' dance. The Swiss idea of the night people or of the night phantoms is found in exactly those places where, in the late Middle Ages, the idea of the witches' sabbath took on substance in the forced dialogue between inquisitors and suspects. Here was where the *bona societas* was transformed into the society of witches. When physical force was deployed against folk magic and when lived folk beliefs and myths were demonized, another stage in their suppression was begun. The people of the night were pushed underground and the fairies took leave of history.

With his phantoms of the night, Stoeckhlin was looking for a personal compromise that would reconcile the stresses of myth, Tridentine Catholicism, and popular needs, but he was unable to find one. When push came to shove, not even his own neighbors were able to understand their "virtuoso representative of popular culture" any more. The witch hunt replaced the witch finder, the state replaced magic. The church became part of state administration, and these myths were transformed into the stuff of legends and fairy tales, falling into unconsciousness until, in the nineteenth century, their souls once again left their bodies. The Romantics, however, did not really discover them anew, but instead invented something entirely new out of them. Compared with the dangerous cerebral monstrosities of Jacob Grimm and the subsequent mythologists in his retinue, the stories of Chonrad Stoeckhlin were harmless. And the Romantics in turn have been shoved into the shadows by the *bricoleurs* of our century. But there we go again, speaking of high intellectuals and politicians, while Chonrad Stoeckhlin was only a herdsman who went traveling with the phantoms of the night.

Notes

Abbreviations

DSVBL   Franz Josef Vonbun, ed., *Die Sagen Vorarlbergs mit Beiträgen aus Liechtenstein. Aufgrund der Ausgabe von Hermann Sander* (1889), ed. Richard Beitl (Feldkirch, 1950)

DSWH   Karl Meisen, *Die Sagen vom Wütenden Heer und vom Wilden Jäger* (Münster, 1935)

DTF   Wolfgang Behringer and Constance Ott-Koptschalijski, *Der Traum vom Fliegen. Zwischen Mythos und Technik* (Frankfurt a.M., 1991)

GMO1-1978   Heinrich Bernhard Zirkel, *Geschichte des Marktes Oberstdorf: Einschliesslich der jetzigen Gemeindegebiete Schöllang und Tiefenbach*, part 1, *Bis zum Ausgang des 15. Jarhhunderts* (1st ed. 1937), 2d. ed. by Thaddaus Steiner (Oberstdorf, 1978)

GMO2-1974   Heinrich Bernhard Zirkel, *Geschichte des Marktes Oberstdorf: Einschliesslich der jetzigen Gemeindegebiete Schollang und Tiefenbach*, part 2, *Bis zum Beginn des Dreissigjährigen Krieges* (1st. ed. 1937), 2d ed. by Werner Grundmann (Oberstdorf, 1974)

GMO3-1976   Heinrich Bernhard Zirkel, *Geschichte des Marktes Oberstdorf: Einschliesslich der jetzigen Gemeindegebiete Schöllang und T'efenbach*, part 3, *17. und 18. Jahrhundert bis zum Anschluß an Bayern*, ed. Werner Grundmann (Oberstdorf, 1976)

HB   Wolfgang Behringer, *Hexenverfolgung in Bayern: Volksmagie, Glaubenseifer und Staatsräson in der Frühen Neuzeit* (Munich 1987)

HDA   *Handwörterbuch des deutschen Aberglaubens*, ed. Hanns Bächtold-Stäubli and Eduard Hoffmahn-Krayer, 10 vols. (Berlin, 1929–42)

HStAM   Bavarian State Archive, Munich

MFLT   Wolfgang Behringer, *Mit dem Feuer vom Leben zum Tod: Hexengesetzgebung in Bayern* (:Munich, 1988)

PA   Prozeßakte

StA   State Archive

VP   Verhörprotokolle

Translator's Preface

1. Carlo Ginzburg, *The Night Battles: Witchcraft and Agrarian Cults in the Sixteenth and Seventeenth Centuries,* trans. John Tedeschi and Anne Tedeschi (Baltimore, 1983).

2. *HB.* See also Behringer's remarkable study of Bavarian criminal jurisprudence, *Mit dem Feuer vom Leben zum Tod: Hexengesetzgebung in Bayern.*

1. Herdsmen

1. The basic source for this history is the trial record, *Prozeßakte* (PA), of Chonrad Stoeckhlin, now held in the State Archive (StA) of Augsburg; formerly preserved in the Bavarian State Archive in Munich (HStAM); Hochstift Augsburg, Neuburger file, doc. 6737. Here I depend heavily on the transcripts of the hearings called the *Verhörprotokolle* (VP).

2. Franz Ludwig Baumann, *Geschichte des Allgäus,* 3 vols. (Kempten 1883–94); Joseph Rottenkolber, *Geschichte des Allgäus* (Kempten 1951); Alfred Weitnauer, *Allgäuer Chronik,* 5 vols. (Kempten, 2d ed.: vol. 1, 1981; vol 2, 1984).

3. For the Bishopric of Augsburg, see Gerhard Kobler, *Historisches Lexikon der deutschen Länder. Die deutschen Territorien vom Mittelalter bis zur Gegenwart* (Munich, 1989, 2d improved ed.), 22 f.; Adolf Layer, "Geistliche Herrschaftsbereiche," in Max Spindler, ed., *Handbuch der bayrischen Geschichte,* vol. 3, (Munich, 1979, 2d improved ed.), §111 Hochstift und Domkapitel Augsburg, 949–62.

4. Friedrich Zöpfl, *Das Bistum Augsburg und seine Bischöfe* (Augsburg, 1956); Otto Bucher, "Bischof Marquard vom Berg 1575–1591," *Zeitschrift für Bayerische Landesgeschichte* 20 (1957): 1–52; Romuald Bauerreiss, *Kirchengeschichte Bayerns,* vol. 6, *Das sechzehnte Jahrhundert* (Augsburg 1965), 226 f.

5. *Tr. note:* The names of these mountains are evocative: Ruby Peak, Fog Peak, Heaven's Peak, the Great Wild One, the Raw Corner, Toad Peak, the Maiden's Fork, the Wild Man, Beaver's Head, Hammerhead, Fleecy Point.

6. *GMO* 1-1978, 106, 109, 142.

7. Richard Hipper and Aegidius Kolb, *Sonthofen im Wandel der Geschichte* (Kempten 1978), 234 (inhabitants), 379 (markets).

8. *GMO* 3-131 f. The figures are for the year 1650.

9. Karl Bosl, ed., *Bayern (Handbuch der Historischen Stätten Deutschlands,* vol. 7), (3d ed. Stuttgart, 1961), 554 f.

10. Karl Siegfried Bader, *Dorfgenossenschaft und Dorfgemeinde (Studien zur Rechtsgeschichte des mittelalterlichen Dorfes,* vol. 2), (Weimar, 1962), 318 f.

11. Frank Robert Vivelo, *Handbuch der Kulturanthropologie. Eine grundlegende Ein-*

führung, ed. Justin Stagl (Stuttgart 1981), 125, a German translation by Erika Stagl of Vivelo's *Cultural Anthropology Handbook: A Basic Introduction*, (New York, 1978).

12. Erich Keyser and Heinz Stoob, eds., *Bayerisches Städtebuch*, part 2 (Stuttgart, 1974), 501–4.

13. Hans Haushofer, "Von edler Roßzucht im Allgew," *Die 7 Schwaben* 10 (1960): 61–64; Adolf Layer, "Die Landwirtschaft," in *Handbuch der bayrischen Geschichte*, ed. Max Spindler vol. 3 (Munich, 1979, 2d ed.), 1067–73, at 1069.

14. *Tr. note: Ross* means horse in German.

15. GMO 3-1976, 72–74 (for the Alpine economy and horse breeding), 24–51 (for the Alps in the jurisdiction of the Oberstdorf community).

16. Wilhelm Abel, *Massenarmut und Hungerkrisen im vorindustriellen Deutschland* (Göttingen, 1972).

17. Irmingard Schwendiger, *Der Große Widderstein erzählt. Historisches, Glaubwürdiges und Merkwürdiges aus dem Kleinwalsertal* (Kempten, 1983), 89 f., following Alfons Köberle, *Volksgenealogie des Kleinen Walsertals*, published by the Heimatmuseum Riezlern. For "Berchtold" as an old Walser name, see the *Montafoner Heimatbuch* (Schruns, 1980), 158 f. For the Walsers, see pp. 37–42, 54, 165, 214–16.

18. PA, VP, Konrad Stoecklhin, 23 Dec. 1586, answer 27.

19. Sebastian Münster, *Cosmographia* (1st ed., Basel, 1544), (Basel, 1628), 964 f.

20. GMO 2-1974, 274 ff., and 300 (ill. 39), 306 (description).

21. GMO 1-1978, 254.

22. GMO 3-1976, 13–74 (Alpine economy), 17 f. (herdsmen), 24–51 (the Alps in the community jurisdiction of Oberstdorf).

23. StA Augsburg: Hochstift Augsburg, Neuburger file, doc. 7488. For a more detailed account, see *MFLT*, 193.

2. Shrovetide Conversations

1. Christian Pfister, *Klimageschichte der Schweiz 1525–1860. Das Klima der Schweiz von 1525–1860 und seine Bedeutung in der Geschichte von Bevölkerung und Landwirtschaft* (Bern, 1988, 3d ed.), 145.

2. Hermann Grotefend, *Taschenbuch der Zeitrechnung* (Hannover, 1991, 13th ed.), 160.

3. PA, VP, 29 July 1586, answer 4.

4. PA, VP, Chonrad Stoecklhin, 23 Dec. 1586, answer 27.

5. Peter Burke, *Popular Culture in Early Modern Europe* (London, 1978).

6. Paul Sartori, "Funkensonntag," in *HDA* 3 (1930), cols. 211–15; Richard Beitl, *Wörterbuch der deutschen Volkskunde* (Stuttgart, 1974, 3d ed.), 244 f.

7. Paul Sartori, "Fastnacht," in *HDA* 3 (1930), cols. 1246–61, at cols. 1251 f.

8. Paul Geiger, "Der Totenzug," *Schweizer Archiv für Volkskunde* 47 (1951): 71–76, with map; Anton Gattlen, "Die Totensagen des alemannischen Wallis" (Naters-Brig, 1948) (Ph.D. dissertation, Fribourg, 1948).

9. Claude Lecouteux, *Geschichte der Gespenster und Wiedergänger im Mittelalter* (Cologne, 1987), 37–65.

10. Richard Kieckhefer, *Magic in the Middle Ages* (New York, 1989), 151–75.

11. Johann Hartlieb, *Das Buch aller verbotenen Künste* (1456), ed. and trans. Frank Fürbeth (Frankfurt a.M. 1989), 42.

12. PA, VP, Konrad Stoeckhlin, 29 July 1586, fols. 1–1^v.

13. PA, VP, Konrad Stoeckhlin, 15 Nov. 1586, question 26.

3. The Specter's Message

1. PA, VP, Konrad Stoeckhlin, 23 Dec. 1586, answer 27.

2. Beitl, *Wörterbuch der deutschen Volkskunde*, 39.

3. PA, VP, Konrad Stoeckhlin, 29 July 1586, fols. 1^v–2.

4. *Lexikon für Theologie und Kirche*, vol. 6 (Freiburg 1961), cols. 806 ff.

5. Anti Aarne and Stith Thompson, *The Types of the Folktale* (FFC no. 184) (Helsinki 1961); cf. Leander Petzoldt, ed., "AT 470: Friends in Life and Death. Zur Psychologie und Geschichte einer Wundererzählung," *Rheinisches Jahrbuch für Volkskunde* 19 (1968): 101–61; Leander Petzoldt, "Die Botschaft aus der Anderswelt. Psychologie und Geschichte einer Wundererzählung," in *Märchen, Mythos, Sage. Beiträge zur Literatur und Volksdichtung* (Marburg, 1989), 101–44.

6. Ingeborg Müller and Lutz Röhrich, "Deutscher Sagenkatalog. X. Der Tod und die Toten," *Deutsches Jahrbuch für Volkskunde* 13 (1967): 346–97, motif F 29.

7. Joseph Klapper, ed., *Erzählungen des Mittelalters. In deutscher Übersetzung und lateinischem Urtext* (Breslau, 1914; reprinted Hildesheim, 1978), item no. 136:137 f., 338, following a manuscript in the Breslau Dominican Cloister.

8. *Die Jesuiten in Bayern: 1549–1773. Ausstellung des Bayerischen Hauptstaatsarchivs und der Oberdeutschen Provinz der Gesellschaft Jesu* (Weißenhorn 1991), 143 ff.

9. Francesco Guazzo, *Compendium Maleficarum* (Milan, 1626; English trans., 1988), 58–73 (chap. 17, "Whether the Spirits of the Dead can Appear to People"), 58–61.

10. Norbert Schindler, *Widerspenstige Leute. Studien zur Volkskultur in der frühen Neuzeit* (Frankfurt a.M., 1992), 154 ff.

11. Leander Petzoldt, ed., *Deutsche Volkssagen. 690 Sagen geschmückt mit alten Holzschnitten* (Munich, 1978), 374.

12. Erasmus Francisci, *Der höllische Proteus* (Nuremberg, 1690), 11–16.

13. On the further distribution of this story, see Klapper, *Erzählungen des Mittelalters* (1914/1978), 251.

14. Hartlieb, *Das Buch aller verbotenen Künste* (1456; 1989), 54 f.

15. Josef Guntern, *Volkserzählungen aus dem Oberwallis. Sagen, Legenden, Märchen, Anekdoten aus dem deutschsprachigen Wallis* (Basel, 1978), 500–503.

16. Mathias Maierbrugger, "Sagen aus dem Glödnitztal," in Gotbert Moro, ed., *Aus Kärntens Volksüberlieferung* (Klagenfurt, 1957), 59.

17. Markus Lutz, *Vollständige Beschreibung des Schweizerlandes* (Aarau, 1827, 2d ed.), vol. 1, 55 f.

18. Johannes Jegerlehner, *Sagen und Märchen aus dem Oberwallis. Aus dem Volksmunde gesamelt* (Basel, 1913), 208; Johannes Jegerlehner, *Sagen aus dem Unterwallis* (Basel, 1909), 169.

4. An Angel Appears

1. Arnold van Gennep, *Les rites de passage* (Paris, 1909); trans. Monika B. Vizedom and Gabrielle L. Caffe, intro. Solon T. Kimball, *The Rites of Passage* (Chicago, 1960).

2. J. Michl, "Schutzengel," in *Lexikon für Theologie und Kirche*, vol. 9 (1964), cols. 522–24.

3. Luke 2.8–20.

4. Jean Bodin, *De magorum daemonomania. Vom ausgelasnen Wütigen Teufelsheer, allerhand Zauberern/Hexen und Hexenmeistern/Unholden/Teuffelsbeschwerern/Warsagern* (Strasbourg, 1591), 17–35 [1st ed. in French, 1580; 1st German tr. by Johann Fischart, Strasbourg, 1586. I cite the expanded ed. of 1591].

5. Knud Rasmussen, *Grönlandsagen* (Berlin, 1922), 257.

6. Mircea Eliade, *Schamanismus und archaische Ekstasetechnik* (Frankfurt a.M., 1975; 1st ed. Paris, 1951).

7. M. Landau, *Hölle und Fegfeuer in Volksglaube, Dichtung und Kirchenlehre*, 1909; E. Bauer, *Die Armen Seelen und Fegfeuervorstellungen in der altdeutschen Mystik*, Ph.D. dissertation, Würzburg, 1960; Jacques Le Goff, *The Birth of Purgatory*, trans. Arthur Goldhammer (Chicago, 1984); orig. publ. as *La Naissance du Purgatoire* (Paris, 1981); Peter Jezler, ed., *Himmel, Hölle, Fegefeuer. Das Jenseits im Mittelalter. Katalog des Schweizer Landesmuseums* (Zurich, 1994).

8. Ph. M. Halm, "Ikonographische Studien zum Armen-Seelen-Kultus," *Münchner Jahrbuch der Bildenden Kunst* 12 (1922): 1–12; Wolfgang Braunfels, "Fegfeuer—Ikonographisch," *Lexikon für Theologie und Kirche*, vol. 4 (1960), col. 55.

9. Michael Petzet, *Die Kunstdenkmäler von Schwaben VIII. Landkreis Sonthofen* (Munich, 1964), 178, 284, 365, 390, 433, 479, 586, 647, 653, 674, 723, 847, 923, 986.

10. Le Goff, *The Birth of Purgatory*.

11. PA, VP, Konrad Stoeckhlin, 29 July 1586, fols. 2–2v.

12. *Tr. note:* A *Seelenführer* or "psychopomp" was the conductor of souls to the place of the dead.

5. The Phantoms of the Night

1. Richard Beitl, *Im Sagenwald. Neue Sagen aus Vorarlberg* (Bregenz, 1953), 351 f.

2. Grotefend, *Taschenbuch der Zeitrechnung*, 200 f.

3. PA, VP, Konrad Stoeckhlin, 29 July 1586, fol. 3r–3v.

4. Vivelo, *Handbuch der Kulturanthropologie. Eine grundlegende Einführung*, 164 ff.

5. C. Simonett, *Geschichte der Stadt Chur*, part 1, *Von den Anfängen bis 1400* (Chur, 1976).

6. *Tr. note:* Behringer refers not to Germans in general but to the Alemannic invasions that brought the Germanic dialect and culture from the Upper Valais into the Upper Rhine, Graubünden, and Vorarlberg.

7. Martin Schmid and Ferdinand Sprecher, "Zur Geschichte der Hexenverfolgung in Graubünden mit besonderer Berücksichtigung des Heinzenberges, der Gruob, des Schanfiggs und des Prättigaus," *Jahresbericht der Historisch-Antiquarischen Gesellschaft von Graubünden* 48 (1918): 73–252; Simon Leonhard Lötscher, "Volkskundliches aus dem Schanfigg und Prättigau," *Schweizerisches Archiv für Volkskunde* 18 (1928): 9–13.

8. Klaus Beitl, "Die Sage vom Nachtvolk. Untersuchung eines alpinen Sagentypus (Mit Verbreitungskarte)," in 4. *International Congress of Folk Narrative Research in Athens (1.9.–6.9. 1964). Lectures and Reports*, Georgios A. Megas ed. (Athens, 1965), Laographia no. 22, 14–21, esp. 15–18.

9. *Atlas der schweizerischen Volkskunde—Atlas de Folklore suisse*, founded by Paul Geiger and Richard Weiss. Continued by Walter Escher, Elsbeth Liebl, Arnold Niederer. *Kommentar* part 2, section 7 (Basel, 1971), 753–67, maps 258–59.

10. Aleida Assmann, Jan Assmann, and Christof Hardmeier, eds., *Schrift und Gedächtnis. Beiträge zur Archäologie der Kommunikation* (Munich, 1983), afterword by A. Assman and J. Assmann, 265–84.

11. Georg Luck, ed., *Rätische Alpensagen. Gestalten und Bilder aus der Sagenwelt Graubündens* (Chur, 1935; 2d ed.), 26.

6. The People of the Night

1. Lincke, "Nachtvolk (-schar)," in *HDA* 6 (1934), cols. 805–9; Beitl, *Wörterbuch der deutschen Volkskunde*, 586.

2. Beitl, "Die Sage vom Nachtvolk," 14–21. I am grateful to Klaus Beitl for giving me a photograph of his map.

3. Melchior Sooder, *Zelleni us em Hasital. Märchen, Sagen und Schwänke der Hasler, aus mündlicher Überlieferung aufgezeichnet* (Basel, 1943), 43; cf. Elsbeth Liebl, in *Atlas der schweizerischen Volkskunde* (1971), 753.

4. Lutz, *Vollständige Beschreibung des Schweizerlandes* (1827), vol. 1, 194 f.

5. Franz Joseph Vonbun, ed., *Die Sagen Vorarlbergs* (Innsbruck, 1858); Franz Joseph Vonbun, "Wuotan—Wuotan's heer," in *Beiträge zur deutschen Mythologie. Gesammelt in Churrätien* (Chur, 1862), 1–16.

6. Eduard Hengartner, "Alois Lütolf," in *Sagenerzähler und Sagensammler der Schweiz. Studien zur Produktion volkstümlicher Geschichte und Geschichten vom 16. bis zum frühen 20.Jahrhundert*, ed. Rudolf Schenda (Bern, 1988), 307–31.

7. Arnold Büchli, *Mythologische Landeskunde von Graubünden. Ein Bergvolk erzählt,* vol. 1, *Fünf Dörfer, Herrschaft, Prättigau, Davos, Schanfigg, Chur,* 2d ed. with introd. by Ursula Brunold-Bigler (Disentis, 1989); vol. 2, *Die Täler am Vorderrhein. Imboden,* 3d ed. with afterword by Ursula Brunold-Bigler (Disentis, 1989); see also the review by Barbara Kindermann-Bieri in *Fabula* 31 (1990): 327–31.

8. Marianne Preibisch, "Johannes Jegerlehner," in *Sagenerzähler und Sagensammler der Schweiz,* ed. Schenda 461–80; Hans ten Doornkaat, "Arnold Büchli," in *Sagenerzähler und Sagensammler der Schweiz,* ed. Schenda 521–98.

9. Karl Reiser, ed., *Sagen, Gebräuche und Sprichwörter des Allgäus,* 2 vols. (Kempten, 1897–1902).

10. Elsbeth Liebl, "Totenzug" and "Geisterheere und ähnliche Erscheinungen," in *Atlas der schweizerischen Volkskunde* (1971), 753–67 and 768–84.

11. Lucie Varga, "Ein Tal in Vorarlberg—zwischen Vorgestern und Heute," in Lucie Varga, *Zeitenwende. Mentalitätshistorische Studien 1936–1939,* ed. Peter Schöttler (Frankfurt a.M., 1991), 146–69; orig. publ. as "Dans une vallée du Vorarlberg: d'avant-hier à aujourd'hui," in *Annales d'histoire économique et sociale* 8 (1936): 1–20.

12. Luck, *Rätischc Alpensagen. Gestalten und Bilder aus der Sagenwelt Graubündens,* 26 f.

13. Karl Ilg, *Die Walser in Vorarlberg,* 2 parts (Dornbirn, 1956), part 2, 62 ff. *Tr. note:* The Walsers are the Alemannic descendants of the Germanic migrants who came over into the Upper Rhine from the Valais during the Middle Ages.

14. *Montafoner Heimatbuch* (Schruns, 1980), 259.

15. Christoph Daxelmüller, foreword to *HDA* 1, cols. v–xl, at cols. x f.

16. Lincke, "Nachtvolk (-schar)," in *HDA* 6 (1934), cols. 805–9; Beitl, *Wörterbuch der deutschen Volkskunde,* 586.

17. Jacob Endter, *Die Sage vom wilden Jäger und von der wilden Jagd,* Ph.D. dissertation, Frankfurt a.M., 1932.

18. Lincke, "Nachtvolk (-schar)," in *HDA* 6 (1934), cols. 805 f.

19. Arnold Büchli, "Wilde Jagd und Nachtvolk," *Schweizer Volkskunde* 37 (1947): 65–69.

20. Beitl, "Die Sage vom Nachtvolk," 15.

21. Liebl, "Totenzug," 759.

22. Georg Luck, ed., "Totenvolk und Nachtschar," in *Rätische Alpensagen. Gestalten und Bilder aus der Sagenwelt Graubündens* (Chur, 1935; 2d ed.), 26–31.

23. Arnold Büchli, *Mythologische Landeskunde von Graubünden*, vol. 2, *Das Gebiet des Rheins vom Badus bis zum Calanda* (Aarau, 1966), 464–84.

24. Beitl, "Die Sage vom Nachtvolk," 19 f. *Tr. note:* The German name of this valley is Kleines Walsertal.

25. Ibid., 19.

26. *Geschichte der Schweiz* (Munich, 1991), a summary of the articles dealing with Switzerland in Theodor Schieder, ed., *Handbuch der Europäischen Geschichte* (Stuttgart, 1968–87); *Handbuch der Schweizer Geschichte*, 2 vols. (Zurich 1972–77), see esp. vol. 1, Peter von Muralt, *Renaissance und Reformation*, 389–570; Peter Stadler, *Das Zeitalter der Gegenreformation*, 571–670. See also Benedikt Bilgeri, *Geschichte Vorarlbergs*, vols. 1–3, (Vienna, 1971–77).

27. Emil Vogt, "Urgeschichte," in *Handbuch der Schweizer Geschichte* (Zurich, 1972), vol. 1, 1–52, at 47 ff.

28. Rainer Christlein, *Die Alamannen* (Stuttgart, 1978).

29. *DSWH.*

30. R. Wenskus, "Über die Möglichkeit eines allgemeinen interdisziplinären Germanenbegriffs," in *Germanenprobleme in heutiger Sicht*, ed. H. Beck. (Berlin, 1986), 1 ff.; Herwig Wolfram, *Die Geburt Mitteleuropas. Geschichte Österreichs vor seiner Entstehung 378–907* (Berlin, 1987), 309–76.

31. Walter Torbrügge, "Vorzeit bis zum Ende der Keltenreiche," in *Handbuch der bayrischen Geschichte*, ed. Max Spindler, vol. 1 (2d ed., Munich, 1981), 1–64, at 52 f.; Volker Dotterweich et al., eds., *Geschichte der Stadt Kempten* (Kempten, 1989); Jürgen Untermann, "Sprachliche Zeugnisse der Kelten in Süddeutschland," in *Das keltische Jahrtausend*, ed. Hermann Dannheimer and Rupert Gerhard (Mainz, 1993), 23–28.

32. Ludwig Pauli, *Die Alpen in Frühzeit und Mittelalter. Die archäologische Entdeckung einer Kulturlandschaft* (2d ed., Munich, 1981), 181 ff.

33. Pauli, *Alpen* (1981), 160; following Gudrun Schneider-Schnekenburger, *Churrätien im Frühmittelalter auf Grund der archäologischen Funde* (Munich, 1980); Ludwig Pauli, "Heidnisches und Christliches im frühmittelalterlichen Bayern," *Bayerische Vorgeschichtsblätter* 43 (1978), 147–57. Fundamental for the debate concerning continuity: Hermann Bausinger and Wolfgang Brückner, eds., *Kontinuität? Geschichtlichkeit und Dauer als volkskundliches Problem* (Berlin, 1969).

34. Pauli, *Die Alpen*, (1981), 164.

35. Franz J. Bauer, "Von Tod und Bestattung in alter und neuer Zeit," in *Historische Zeitschrift* 254 (1992): 1–31.

36. Liebl, "Totenzug," 753.

37. *Tr. note:* The German for cemetery is *Befriedung* or *Friedhof,* both of which imply peace and pacification.

38. Otto Gerhard Oexle, "Die Gegenwart der Toten," in *Death in the Middle Ages,* Harman Braet and Werner Verbeke, eds. (Louvain, 1983), 19–77.

39. Aaron J. Gurjewitsch, "Probleme der Volkskultur und der Religiosität im Mittelalter," in *Das Weltbild des mittelalterlichen Menschen* (Munich, 1982) (orig. pub. Moscow, 1972), 352–400; Peter Dinzelbacher, *Visionen und Visionsliteratur im Mittelalter* (Stuttgart, 1981).

40. Will-Erich Peuckert, "Der wilde Jäger und das Wuotesheer," in *Deutscher Volksglaube des Spätmittelalters* (Stuttgart, 1942), 86–96, at 95. One finds the same point in Jacob Wecker, *Vel Goetia vel Theurgia. Wahre und eigentliche Entdeckung oder Erklärung der fürnehmsten Articul von der Zauberey* (Leipzig, 1631), 133.

41. Büchli, "Wilde Jagd und Nachtvolk," 66.

42. Ibid., 68; Liebl, "Totenzug," 755.

43. Guntern, *Volkserzählungen aus dem Oberwallis* (1978), 504 ff.

44. Josef Guntern, "Gratzug und Totenprozession," in *Volkserzählungen aus dem Oberwallis* (1978), 504–79, at 504, n.1.

45. Carlo Ginzburg, *Ecstasies: Deciphering the Witches' Sabbath,* translated by Raymond Rosenthal (New York, 1991), 80, orig. publ. as *Storia notturna. Una decifrazione del sabba* (Turin, 1989).

46. Andreas Blauert, *Frühe Hexenverfolgungen. Ketzer-, Zauberei- und Hexenprozesse des 15. Jahrhunderts* (Hamburg, 1989), 67 ff.; the texts can be found in *Quellen und Untersuchungen zur Geschichte des Hexenwahns und der Hexenverfolgung im Mittelalter,* ed. Joseph Hansen, (Bonn, 1901; repr. Hildesheim, 1963), 532–39.

47. Lutz, *Vollständige Beschreibung des Schweizerlandes* (1827), vol. 1, 139 (Hérens); vol. 2, 252 ff. (Sitten).

48. Joseph Hansen, *Zauberwahn, Inquisition und Hexenprozeß im Mittelalter* (Munich, 1900), 448; Hansen, *Quellen* (1901), 189, 460, 535; Richard Kieckhefer, *European Witch-Trials. Their Foundations in Popular and Learned Culture, 1300–1500* (London, 1976), 17.

49. Stuart Clark, "Le sabbat comme système symbolique: significations stables et instables," in *Le Sabbat des Sorciers,* Nicole Jacques-Chaquin and Maxime Preaud, eds. (Grenoble, 1993), 63–74.

7. Music of Unearthly Beauty

1. *DSVBL,* 29: "Die Verschmausung der Kuh."

2. Ibid., 30 f.

3. Ibid., 28.

4. Luck, "Totenvolk und Nachtschar," in *Rätische Alpensagen. Gestalten und Bilder aus der Sagenwelt Graubündens* (Chur, 1935; 2d ed.), 26–31.

5. Lutz, *Vollständige Beschreibung des Schweizerlandes* (1827), vol. 2, 345.

6. Jegerlehner, *Sagen und Märchen aus dem Oberwallis* (1913), 18.

7. Sooder, *Zelleni us em Hasital. Märchen, Sagen und Schwänke der Hasler* (1943), 43; see more stories of the night people on 25, 43–46.

8. Lutz, *Vollständige Beschreibung des Schweizerlandes* (1827), vol. 1, 123 f.

9. Luck, "Totenvolk und Nachtschar," 27.

10. *DSVBL*, 31 ff.; *Montafoner Heimatbuch* (2d ed., Schruns, 1980).

11. Beitl, "Sage vom Nachtvolk," 17 f.

12. Reinhold Hammerstein, *Tanz und Musik des Todes. Die Mittelalterlichen Totentänze und ihr Nachleben* (Bern, 1980).

13. Reinhold Hammerstein, *Diabolus in musica. Studien zur Ikonographie der Musik im Mittelalter* (Bern, 1974).

8. The Miracle of the Bones

1. Beitl calls "the music of unearthly beauty and the eating of the cow" the two chief characteristics of the legend-type of the night people, "Sage vom Nachtvolk," 19.

2. Ilg, *Walser in Vorarlberg*, 54 f.

3. Eduard Renner, *Goldener Ring über Uri. Ein Buch vom Erleben und Denken unserer Bergler, von Magie und Geistern und von den ersten und letzten Dingen* (4th ed., Zurich, 1991; orig. ed. 1936), 1–19.

4. Luck, "Totenvolk und Nachtschar," 26–31.

5. Reiser, *Sagen, Gebräuche und Sprichwörter des Allgäus,* vol. 1 (1895), 55 f.

6. Frederik Hetmann, ed., *Dämonengeschichten aus den Alpen* (Frankfurt a.M., 1977), 104 f. ("Das nächtliche Mahl"), following Jegerlehner, *Sagen aus dem Unterwallis* (1909). Another example from the Walliser Sanetschtal is found in M. Tscheinen and P. J. Ruppen, eds., *Walliser Sagen* (Sitten, 1871), 247 f.

7. Beitl, "Sage vom Nachtvolk," 18.

8. *DSVBL*, 29.

9. Ignaz Vinzenz Zingerle, ed., *Sagen aus Tirol* (Innsbruck, 1891), 14 ("The Banquet," from the Val d'Ultimo).

10. Luisa Muraro, *La signora del gioco. Episodi della caccia alle streghe* (Milan, 1976), 240–45.

11. Zingerle, *Sagen aus Tirol* (1891), 15 f.

12. *Tr. note:* Frau Hulda was the early medieval name given to the pagan goddess worshipped by the earliest versions of the witches, who were often called *Unholden.*

13. Zingerle, *Sagen aus Tirol* (1891), 16.

14. Maurizio Bertolotti, "Le ossa e la pelle dei buoi. Un mito populare tra agio-grafia e stregoneria," *Quaderni storici* 41 (May–August 1979): 477 ff.

15. M. Coens, "Pharaildis," in *Lexikon für Theologie und Kirche,* vol. 8 (Freiburg, 1963), col. 437; E. Hautcoer, *Actes de Ste. Pharailde* (Lille, 1882).

16. Thomas of Cantimpré, *Miraculorum et exemplorum memorabilium sui temporis libri duo* (Douay, 1597), 201 f.

17. Fundamental for this argument are the essays collected in Dieter Harmening, *Zauberei im Abendland. Vom Anteil der Gelehrten am Wahn der Leute. Skizzen zur Geschichte des Aberglaubens* (Würzburg, 1991).

18. Burchard of Worms, *Decretum,* in Jacques Paul Migne, ed., *Patrologia Latina,* vol. 140, 537–1058, at 973 CD; Hansen, *Quellen* (1901), 40; following H. J. Schmitz, *Die Bussbücher und das kanonische Bußverfahren,* vol. 2, 1898, 425 ff.; and now see Valerie J. Flint, *The Rise of Magic in Early Medieval Europe* (Oxford, 1991), 123 f.

19. Heide Dienst, "Zur Rolle von Frauen in magischen Vorstellungen und Prak-tiken—nach ausgewählten mittelalterlichen Texten," in Werner Affeldt, ed., *Frauen in Spätantike und Mittelalter. Lebensbedingungen—Lebensnormen—Lebensformen* (Sig-maringen, 1990), 173–94; e.g., 186, 191 ff.

20. *DTF,* 160 ff.

21. Michael Richter, "Die Kelten im Mittelalter," *Historische Zeitschrift* 246 (1988): 265–95, at 292 f.

22. J. Henninger, "Neuere Forschungen zum Verbot des Knochenzerbrechens," *Studia Ethnographica et Folkloristica in Honorem Bela Gunda* (Debrecen, 1971), 673–702.

23. A. Dirr, "Der kaukasische Wild- und Jagdgott," *Anthropos* 20 (1925): 139–47.

24. Uno Holmberg, "Über die Jagdriten der nördlichen Völker Asiens und Eu-ropas," *Journal de la Societé Finno-Ougrienne* 41 (1925): 34 ff.; Adolf Friedrich, "Knochen und Skelett in der Vorstellungswelt Nordasiens," *Wiener Beiträge zur Kulturgeschichte und Linguistik* 5 (1943): 189–247.

25. Leo Frobenius, *Kulturgeschichte Afrikas* (Berlin, 1933), 183 ff.

26. Mircea Eliade, *Le chamanisme et les techniques archaïques de l'extase* (Paris, 1951), *Schamanismus und archaische Ekstasetechnik,* trans. Inge Köck (Frankfurt, 1975), 159–65.

27. Waldemar Linngmann, *Traditionswanderungen: Euphrat-Rhein,* 2 vols. (Helsinki, 1937–38), vol. 2, 1978 ff.; Bertolotti "Le ossa e la pelle dei buoi," (1979), 470–99.

28. Hans Naumann, *Grundzüge der deutschen Volkskunde* (Leipzig, 1922); and also Gottfried Korff, "Kultur," in Hermann Bausinger et al., *Grundzüge der Volkskunde* (Darmstadt, 1978), 17–80, at 34 f.

29. Ginzburg, *Ecstasies,* 133–36.

30. Ibid., 141.

31. Henninger, "Neuere Forschungen zum Verbot des Knochenzerbrechens," 700.

32. Pauli, *Alpen*, 176 ff.

33. Ibid., 45.

34. St. Zilkens, *Die Karner-Kapellen in Deutschland*, (Ph.D. dissertation, Cologne, 1983); Günter Binding, "Karner," in *Lexikon des Mittelalters*, vol. 5 (Munich, 1991), col. 1001.

35. Johann Nepomuk Ritter von Alpenburg, *Österreichische Alpensagen*, ed. Lothar Borowsky (Vienna, 1860), 212.

9. The Good Society

1. Lutz, *Vollständige Beschreibung des Schweizerlandes* (1827), vol. 1, 316–20.

2. R. Feller and E. Bonjour, *Geschichtsschreibung der Schweiz. Vom Spätmittelalter zur Neuzeit*, 2 vols. (2d ed., Basel, 1979), 286; Renward Cysat, *Collectanea chronica und denkwürdige Sachen pro chronica Lucernensi et Helvetiae*, ed. Josef Schmid, 2 vols. (Lucerne, 1969).

3. *DSWH*, 112; Cantonal Library of Lucerne (Kantonsbibliothek) "Cysat-Chronik," vol. B, fol. 97b.

4. *DSWH*, 118 f.; Cantonal Library of Lucerne, "Cysat-Chronik," vol. G, fol. 270a.

5. This whole complex is discussed in Julio Caro Baroja, *Die Hexen und ihre Welt* (Stuttgart, 1967), 83–92. Trans. O. N. V. Glendinning, *The World of the Witches* (Chicago, 1964), 60–66.

6. Regino of Prüm, *De synodalibus causis et ecclesiaticis disciplinis*, in *Patrologia Latina*, ed. Jacques-Paul Migne, vol. 132, 185–400, part 2, 364, at 352.

7. Wolfgang Behringer, ed., *Hexen und Hexenprozesse in Deutschland* (Munich, 1993), 60 f., trans. from Joseph Hansen, ed., *Quellen und Untersuchungen*, 38 f.

8. Hansen, *Zauberwahn, Inquisition und Hexenprozeß im Mittelalter*; Hansen, *Quellen*.

9. Flint, *Rise of Magic in Early Medieval Europe*, 122–26.

10. Patrizia Castelli, "'Donnaiole, amiche de li sogni' ovvero i sogni delle streghe," in *Bibliotheca Lamiarum. Documenti e immagini della stregoneria dal Medioevo all' Eta Moderna* (Pisa, 1994), 35–85, at 38.

11. Hansen, *Quellen* (1901).

12. *Tr. note: Unholden* was one of the German words for witches that became common by the sixteenth century. The text is printed in Hansen, *Quellen* (1901), 40; Claude Lecouteux, "Hagazussa—Striga—Hexe," *Hessische Blätter für Volks- und Kulturforschung* 18 (1985): 57–70, at 59 ff.

13. Ginzburg, *Ecstasies*, 96–109.

14. R. Magnen, *Epona déesse gauloise des cheveaux protectrice des chevaliers* (Bordeaux, 1953); Jan de Vries, *Keltische Religion* (Stuttgart, 1961); R. Maccana, *Celtic Mythology* (Feltham, 1970); "Epona," in *Reallexikon der Germanischen Altertumskunde*, vol. 7 (Berlin, 1989), 414–23.

15. It may be seen in the Vorarlberger Landesmuseum in Bregenz. Pictures of it are reproduced in Alfred Weitnauer, *Keltisches Erbe in Schwaben und Baiern* (Kempten, 1961), 31; Hans-Jörg Kellner, *Die Römer in Bayern* (Munich, 1971), ill. 104–7, explanation, 114 f.

16. Ginzburg, *Ecstasies*, 104–5.

17. Diana's annual festival was 13 August. H. Le Bonniec, "Diana," in *Lexikon der Alten Welt* (Zurich, 1990; orig. ed. 1965), col. 726; K. H. Roloff, "Artemis," in ibid., cols. 336–38.

18. *Tr. note:* Maria im Ährenkleid was the figure of Mary, dressed in a robe sewn with ears of wheat

19. "Maria," in *Lexikon des Mittelalters*, 2d ed. (Munich and Zurich, 1992), vol. 6 (243–75, for the iconography see 255–62. The figure of Maria lactans is here specifically derived from the Egyptian goddess Isis, while influences from the Greek goddess Nike (standing or enthroned) are also evident.

20. Gregory of Tours, *Zehn Bücher Geschichten* (Darmstadt, 1974), vol. 2, 179 ff. (book 8, chap. 15).

21. A. K. Michels, "Diana," in *Reallexikon für Antike und Christentum. Sachwörterbuch zur Auseinandersetzung des Christentums mit der antiken Welt*, vol. 3 (1955), cols. 963–72; Friedrich von Bezold, *Das Fortleben der antiken Götter im mittelalterlichen Humanismus* (Bonn, 1922), 38, 57, 96, 100.

22. K.-H. Roloff, "Artemis," in *Lexikon der Alten Welt*, cols. 336–38.

23. Harmening, *Zauberei im Abendland* (1991), 54 f., 63 f.

24. Caro Baroja, *World of the Witches*, 66.

25. A. Vernet, "Bernardus Guidonis," in *Lexikon des Mittelalters*, vol. 1 (1980), cols. 1,976–78.

26. Hansen, *Zauberwahn, Inquisition und Hexenprozeß im Mittelalter* (1900), 136.

27. Emmanuel LeRoy Ladurie, *Montaillou. Ein Dorf vor dem Inquisitor, 1294–1324,* (Frankfurt a.M., 1980; orig. ed. Paris, 1975), 35, 111, 351 f.

28. Arno Borst, *Die Katharer,* Schriften der Monumenta Germaniae Historica no. 12, (Stuttgart, 1953), 240 ff.

29. Martin Erbstösser, *Ketzer im Mittelalter* (Leipzig, 1984), 210 ff.

30. Bernardo Gui, *Interrogatoria ad sortilegos et divinos et invocatores demonum* (1315), in Hansen, *Quellen* (1901), 48.

31. The original Latin here is unclear. Perhaps the phrase (cum bacheta quam portat in manu cum pomo) implies an imitation or travesty of the imperial orb and scepter, or perhaps it merely means a staff with a knobbed pommel.

32. In the original (omitting later interpolations) the poor Latin runs: "Nos frater Beltramus de Cernuschillo . . . examinavimus quamdam confessionem factam per te, Petrinam...continentem quod tu Petrina . . . annorum sedecim tue etatis usque tunc ea die confessionis tue semper fuisti ad ludum Diane quam vos apelatis Hero-

diadem, et quod . . . semper fecisti eidem reverentiam inclinando sibi caput . . . et salutando eam dicendo: 'Bene stetis domina Horiens,' et ipsa vobis respondendo: 'Bene stetis, bona gens.' . . . Item dixisti quod in ea societate occidunt animalia et eorum carnes comedunt, ossa autem reponunt in coyris et ipsa domina cum bacheta quam portat in manu cum pomo percutit coyra animalium occisiorum et statim resurgunt, sed unquam sunt bona pro labore. Item dixisti quod illa domina cum societate vadunt per diversas domos diversarum personarum et maxime . . . ibi comedunt et bibunt et multum letantur quando inveniunt domos bene spaziatas et ordinatas et tunc dat illa domina benedictionem dicte domui. . . . Item dixisti quod illa domina docet vos de illa societate virtutes herbarum et etiam per signa que sibi hostenditis hostendit vobis omnia que sibi queritis de morbis et de furtis et de malleficiis et sic vos operam sichut docet vos et invenitis veritatem de omnia hostendit vobis. Item dixisti quod illa domina non vult quod vos publicetis aliquod de predictos et pro predicta. . . . Item dixisti quod tu credis ipsam Horientem ita fore dominam sue sotietatis sicut Christus est dominus mundi." Muraro, *La signora del gioco. Episodi della caccia alle streghe* (Milan, 1976), 242 f. Ginzburg provides an error-plagued translation in *Ecstasies*, 91–94.

33. Girolamo Visconti, *Lamiarum sive striarum opusculum* [ca. 1460] (Milan, 1490): "quia secundum communem theologorum sententiam demon non potest resuscitare mortuos." Citing Hansen, *Quellen* (1901), 203 ff.

34. Ginzburg, *Ecstasies*, 89–94.

35. Ibid., 96 f., following *Nicolai Cusae Cardinalis Opera*, vol. 2 (Paris, 1514), fols. 170v–172r.

36. Giuseppe Bonomo, *Caccia alle streghe* (Palermo, 1959), 74–84; Muraro, *La signora del gioco*, 55 f.

37. Otto Löhmann, "Die Entstehung der Tannhäusersage," *Fabula* 3 (1960): 224–53, at 243.

38. *Tr. note:* The Ladins are the people of southestern Switzerland, northern Italy, and a part of the Tyrol, who speak Ladin, a Rhaeto-Romanic dialect.

39. Johann Geiler von Kaisersberg, *Die Emeis* (Strasbourg, 1516), repr. in Hansen, *Quellen* (1901): 284 ff.

40. *Die elsässische Legenda Aurea*, ed. Werner Williams and Ulla Williams-Krapp (Tübingen, 1980), 480.

41. Julio Caro Baroja, *The World of the Witches,* trans. O. N. V. Glendinning (Chicago, 1964), 63–64.

42. Johannes Nider, *Formicarius* (1437), repr. in Hansen, *Quellen* (1901), 90.

43. Hansen, *Quellen* (1901), 235.

44. Johann Weyer, *De praestigiis daemonum* (Frankfurt a.M., 1586), 555 f.; George Mora et al., eds., *Witches, Devils, and Doctors in the Renaissance: Johann Weyer, "De praestigiis daemonum"* (Binghamton NY, 1991), 202–3.

45. Muraro, *La signora del gioco. Episodi della caccia alle streghe* (1976): 46–123, at 58 f., 64 f., 67 ff., 74 f.; the quotation is at 68; "Donna del Bon Zogo" at 75.

46. Ibid., 107.

47. Marina Cometta, "Il 'Laurin' nella tradizione tedesca del 15 e 16 secolo," *Acme* (Milan) 37 (1984): 29–74; J. Heinzle, "Laurin," in *Lexikon des Mittelalters*, vol. 5 (Munich, 1991), col. 1762.

48. Heide Dienst, "Hexenprozesse im Landgericht Völs im ersten Jahrzehnt des 16. Jahrhunderts," in *Völs am Schlern 888–1988. Ein Gemeindebuch* (1988), 249–56.

49. Heinrich Institoris (Heinrich Kramer), *Malleus Maleficarum*, trans. Montague Summers (London, 1928), part 3, question 15, 230.

50. Bernardo da Como, *Tractatus de strigibus* (Rome, 1584), 141 f.

51. Adriano Prosperi, "Credere alle streghe: inquisitori e confessori davanti alla 'superstizione,'" in *Bibliotheca Lamiarum. Documenti e immagini della stregoneria dal Medioevo all' Età Moderna* (Pisa, 1994), 17–34, at 22, citing Bernard of Como, *Lucerna inquisitorum haereticae pravitatis* (Milan, 1546), fols. 92–94.

52. Bartholomäus Anhorn, *Magiologia Das ist: Christlicher Bericht Von dem Aberglauben und Zauberey. Der Welt / ohne einige Passion der Religionen / fürgestellt / durch Philonem*, Augustae Rauracum Druckts Johann Heinrich Mayer. Zufinden Bey Matthias Enderlin von Isny (orig. ed. 1674, here I cite the Basel edition, 1675), 747–67, chapter titled "Helffende und Schaden heilende Zauberer und Hexen." Nicolas Remy, *Daemonolatria* (Lyon, 1593), book 1, chap. 13, fol. 44 (German tr. Frankfurt, 1598; English tr. London, 1930); Henry Boguet, *Discours des Sorciers* (Lyon, 1602), chaps. 35–37; English trans. London, 1929, 99–117.

53. Bartolomeo de Spina, *De strigibus* (Milan, 1525), vol. 2, part. 11, chap. 17; Francesco Guazzo, *Compendium Maleficarum* (Milan, 1608, 1626), book 1, chaps. 12, 14, 17 ; English trans., London, 1929, 38, 41, for the story according to Spina, and 53–72; Remy, *Daemonolatria* (1593 / 1930), 51.

54. Visconti, *Lamiarum sive striarum opusculum* [ca. 1460] (1901), 203; Bernardo da Como, *De strigis* [1510] (Milan, 1566), fol. U8; Bartolomeo de Spina, *Quaestio de strigibus* [1513] (Rome, 1576), chap. 4; Remy, *Daemonolatria* (1593 / 1930), foreword, 86–92.

55. Anhorn, *Magiologia*, 636.

56. Ibid., 636 f.

57. Remy, *Daemonolatria* (1593), foreword; Boguet, *Discours des Sorciers* (1602), foreword.

58. *Historisch-biographisches Lexikon der Schweiz*, vol. 1 (Neuenburg, 1921), 379.

59. Anhorn, *Magiologia*, 643 ff.

60. Martin Antoine Delrio, *Disquisitiones magicarum libri sex* (Louvain, 1599–1600), book 2, question 16.; trans. in Baroja, *World of the Witches*, 119–21.

61. Edda Fischer, *Die 'Disquisitionum Magicarum Libri Sex' von Martin Delrio als gegenreformatorische Exempel-Quelle*, Ph.D. dissertation, Frankfurt a.M., 1975.

62. Fischer, *Die 'Disquitionum Magicarum*, 245, example 39; Anhorn, *Magiologia*, 300 f. for the assemblies on the Venusberg.

63. Anhorn *Magiologia*, 645.

64. Keith Thomas, *Religion and the Decline of Magic* (Harmondsworth, 1980; 1st ed. London, 1971), 724.

65. M. W. Latham, *The Elizabethan Fairies* (New York, 1930).

66. "The Wife of Bath's Tale," ll. 857–74, Geoffrey Chaucer, *The Canterbury Tales: A Prose Version in Modern English,* ed. David Wright (New York, 1964), 190; translation slightly modified to clarify the meaning of "limiter."

67. *Der Prozeß der Jeanne d'Arc. Akten und Protokolle 1431–1456,* trans. Ruth Schirmer-Imhoff (Munich, 1978; 1st ed. 1961), 26 f.

68. Ibid., 69.

69. Ibid., 131–39.

70. Georges Duby and Andrée Duby, *Les procès de Jeanne d'Arc* (Paris, Gallimard, 1973).

71. Thomas, *Religion and the Decline of Magic,* 726.

72. Ibid., 727 ff.

73. Ibid., 732 ff.

74. J. Penry, *Three Treatises Concerning Wales* (Cardiff, 1960), 33.

75. Thomas, *Religion and the Decline of Magic,* 728 f. And see above, 54–55.

76. Ibid., 731 f.

77. *Tr. note:* The *benandanti* were those Friulian peasants who thought that they went forth in their dreams to fight off the witches and preserve the fertility of their fields. They ran into trouble with the Venetian Inquisition in the late sixteenth century and were occasionally accused of witchcraft themselves. The classic account is Carlo Ginzburg's *The Night Battles: Witchcraft and Agrarian Cults in the Sixteenth and Seventeenth Centuries,* trans. John Tedeschi and Anne Tedeschi (Baltimore, 1983).

78. Delrio, *Disquisitiones magicarum libri sex,* book 1, chap. 3, question 4; Fischer, *Die 'Disquisitionum Magicarum Libri Sex' von Martin Delrio,* 29.

79. Muraro, *La signora del gioco,* 160–71, at 167.

80. Ginzburg, *Benandanti* (Berlin, 1980), 194 f., 200; 1st ed., *I Benandanti,* Turin, 1966, trans. Tedeschi and Tedeschi, *Night Battles* (see n. 77).

81. Walter Niess, *Hexenprozesse in der Grafschaft Büdingen. Protokolle, Ursachen, Hintergründe* (Büdingen, 1982), 153–82.

82. *Tr. Note:* Locally, these maidens were also called *Gitschen, Antrischen,* and *Holden,* names that have no English equivalents.

83. Hans Fink, *Verzaubertes Land. Volkskult und Ahnenbrauch in Südtirol* (Innsbruck, 1969), 152 ff.

84. Zingerle, *Sagen aus Tirol,* 32 ff.

85. Ibid., 35–47.

86. Anhorn, *Magiologia*, 299.

87. Eva Pócs, *Fairies and Witches at the Boundary of South-Eastern and Central Europe*, Folklore Fellows Communications no. 243, (Helsinki, 1989).

88. *DSWH*, 115.

89. Ibid., 117; Cantonal Library of Lucerne, "Cysat-Chronik," vol. E, fol. 333a–b.

90. Cysat, cited in *DSWH*, 116.

91. Ibid., 112 f.; Cantonal Library of Lucerne, "Cysat Chronik," vol. B, fol. 100b.

92. Lutz, *Vollständige Beschreibung des Schweizerlandes* (1827), vol. 1, 401 f.

93. Eduard Hoffmann-Krayer, ed., "Luzerner Akten zum Hexen- und Zauberwesen II," *Schweizerisches Archiv für Volkskunde* 3 (1899): 81–123, at 95 ff.

94. Wolfgang Behringer, "Das Wetter, der Hunger, die Angst: Gründe der europäischen Hexenverfolgungen in Klima-, Sozial- und Mentalitätsgeschichte. Das Beispiel Süddeutschlands," in *Acta Ethnographica Academiae Scientarum Hungaricae* 37 (1991–92): 27–50. For Spain see Henry Kamen, *The Phoenix and the Flame. Catalonia and the Counter Reformation* (New Haven, 1993), 236–45.

95. Joseph Schacher von Inwil, *Das Hexenwesen im Kanton Luzern nach den Prozessen von Luzern und Sursee, 1400–1675* (Luzern, 1947), 86.

96. PA, VP, 15 Nov. 10. 1586, answer 15.

10. Wuotas

1. Reiser, *Sagen, Gebräuche und Sprichwörter des Allgäus,* vol. 1 (1895): 47 f. (the night people of Tiefenbach), 54 (The night people in Mittelberg in the Walser Valley); Beitl, "Die Sage vom Nachtvolk," 17.

2. Reiser, *Sagen, Gebräuche und Sprichwörter des Allgäus,* vol. 1, 39 (Rubi), 40 (Rettenherg), 41 (Burgberg), 41 (Kranzegg), 48 (Albers), 48 (Ottobeuren), 54 (Oberstaufen).

3. *Tr. note: Wut* means rage or fury.

4. Schacher von Inwil, *Das Hexenwesen im Kanton Luzern,* 21, citing J. Baechtold, *Hans Salat* (Basel, 1876), 123; P. Cuoni, *Hans Salat. Leben und Werk* (Stans, 1938).

5. Ludwig Lavater, *Von Gespänsten, unghüren, fälen und andern wunderbarlichen dingen* (Zurich, 1569). Repr. in *Theatrum de Veneficis* (Frankfurt, 1586), 115–92, quotations on 146 and 156.

6. Richard Beitl, "Die Sagen Vorarlbergs," in Hans Koren and Leopold Kretzenbacher, eds., *Volk und Heimat. Festschrift für Viktor von Geramb* (Graz, 1949), 193–208, at 193.

7. Ignaz Vinzenz Zingerle, ed., *Sagen aud Tirol* (1st ed., 1860; 2d ed., Innsbruck, 1891); Franz Josef Vonbun, *Volkssagen aus Vorarlberg* (Innsbruck, 1847); Beitl, "Sagen Vorarlbergs," (1949), 196.

8. Note the regional synonyms: "Der Reiter" (Vinschgau), "Der wilde Jäger" (Lana, Welschnofen), "Wilde Jagd" (Fersinatal), "Wilde Fahrta" (Innsbruck, Münster, Alpach/Wildschönau, Mals/Vinschgau, Glurns/Vinschgau, Stilfs), "Die wilde Fuhr" (Lienz/Drautal), "Wüthige Fahrt" (Lechtal), "Die Temper" (Ulten), "Wilde Leute" (Castelruth); see Zingerle "Die Sagen Vorarlbergs," (1891), 1–15, 23.

9. *Tr. note: Guotas* suggests *Gut* or, in English, "the Good."

10. Beitl, "Sagen Vorarlbergs," (1949), 201.

11. Reiser, *Sagen, Gebräuche und Sprichwörter des Allgäus,* vol. 1 (1897): "Section 1: Myths of the Gods: Wotan, Donar, The Procession of the Gods, Legendary Male Figures." Here Reiser placed all the stories concerning Muetes, the night people, and "the journey" (*die Fahrt*).

12. R. Brandstetter, "Die Wuotansage im alten Luzern," *Der Geschichtsfreund. Mitteilungen des Historischen Vereins der fünf Orte* 62 (1907): 101 ff.

13. *Ionae Vitae Columbani liber primus. Jonas erstes Buch vom Leben Columbans,* trans. Herbert Haupt, in *Quellen zur Geschichte des 7. und 8. Jahrhunderts* (Darmstadt, 1982), 402–98, at 483 ff.

14. Ibid., 488 f.

15. *DSVBL*, 229.

16. For the background, see Hermann Bausinger, "Volksideologie und Volksforschung. Zur nationalsozialistischen Volkskunde," *Zeitschrift für Volkskunde* 61 (1965): 177–204; Wolfgang Emmerich, *Germanistische Volkstumsideologie. Genese und Kritik der Volksforschung im Dritten Reich* (Tubingen, 1968); Helge Gerndt, ed., *Volkskunde und Nationalsozialismus* (München, 1987).

17. Barbara Schier, "Hexenwahn und Hexenverfolgung. Rezeption und politische Zurichtung eines kulturwissenschaftlichen Themas im Dritten Reich," *Bayerisches Jahrbuch für Volkskunde* (1990): 43–115.

18. Olaf Bockhorn, "Der Kampf um die Ostmark. Ein Beitrag zur Geschichte der nationalsozialistischen Volkskunde in Österreich," in *Willfährige Wissenschaft. Die Universität Wien 1938–1945,* Gernot Heiß et al., eds. (Vienna, 1989), 17–38.

19. Edmund Mudrak, *Das wütende Heer und der Wilde Jäger,* Bausteine zur Geschichte, Völkerkunde und Mythenkunde, no. 6 (Berlin, 1937).

20. Schier "Hexenwahn und Hexenverfolgung. Rezeption und politische Zurichtung eines kulturwissenschaftlichen Themas im Dritten Reich," 61–65; Bockhorn, "Der Kampf um die Ostmark," 19–23, 28–31; Hansjost Lixfeld, "Matthes Ziegler und die Erzählforschung des Amtes Rosenberg. Ein Beitrag zur Ideologie der nationalsozialistischen Volkskunde," in *Rheinisches Jahrbuch für Volkskunde* 26 (1985–86): 37–59.

21. HDA 6 (1936): cols. 806 ff.

22. Friedrich Ranke, "Das Wilde Heer und die Kultbünde der Germanen. Eine Auseinandersetzung mit Otto Höfler," *Niederdeutsche Zeitschrift für Volkskunde* 18 (1940): 1 ff.

23. Helmut Birkhan, "Nachruf Otto Höfler," *Almanach der Österreichischen Akademie der Wissenschaften* 138 (1988): 383–406.

24. *DSVBL.*

25. Richard Beitl, ed., *Im Sagenwald. Neue Sagen aus Vorarlberg* (Feldkirch, 1953).

26. *DSVBL,* 230.

27. Ibid., 233.

28. Elsbeth Liebl, "Geisterheere und ähnliche Erscheinungen," in *Atlas der schweizerischen Volkskunde* (1971), 768–84.

29. *DSWH,* 19–21, 25–27.

30. Ibid., 42, 53.

31. Ibid., 56.

32. *DSWH,* 72. *Tr. note:* Drude in Germanic mythology was a female spirit of the night, usually evil. *Truten* was a sixteenth-century word for witches.

33. Ibid., 96 f.

34. Ibid., 101, 95–129.

35. Guntern, "Gratzug und Totenprozession," in *Volkserzählungen aus dem Oberwallis,* 504 f.

11. Healing and Prophecy

1. Emmanuel Le Roy Ladurie, *Montaillou: The Promised Land of Error,* trans. Barbara Bray (New York, 1978). See the new examination of this material, Matthias Benad, *Domus und Religion in Montaillou* (Tübingen, 1990), 184 f.

2. G. Lammert, *Volksmedizin und medizinischer Aberglaube in Bayern und den angrenzenden Bezirken, begründet auf die Geschichte der Medizin und Cultur,* (Würzburg, 1869), 13; *HDA* 4 (1931), cols. 124–39.

3. Robert Jütte, *Ärzte, Heiler und Patienten. Medizinischer Alltag in der frühen Neuzeit* (Munich and Zurich, 1991), 17 ff.

4. Torunn Selberg, "Personal Narratives of Healing," *Fabula* 31 (1990): 284–88.

5. PA, VP, Konrad Stoecklin, 29 July 1586, fol. 4.

6. Thomas, *Religion and the Decline of Magic,* 209–301.

7. On this see the classic Edward Evan Evans-Pritchard, *Witchcraft, Oracles and Magic among the Azande* (Oxford, 1937).

8. *Malleus Maleficarum,* ed. Summers, part 2, question 2, 160–64.

9. E. William Monter, *Witchcraft in France and Switzerland* (Ithaca NY, 1976), 167 ff.

10. *HB*, 93, 180, 198 f. After the end of witchcraft trials, the concept of "reversing" was obviously transferred generally to folk medicine and lost its original connotation: Klaus Bayr, "Das Wenden im Raume Gmunden," *Österreichische Zeitschrift für Volkskunde* 76 (1973), 38–42, with references to further literature.

11. *Landtgebott wider die Aberglauben, Zauberey, Hexerey und andere sträffliche Teuffelkünste* (Munich, 1611), fol. 8 f.; MFLT, 170.

12. PA, VP, Konrad Stoeckhlin, 29 July 1586, fol. 3v.

13. *HB*, 89–96.

14. *Malleus Maleficarum*, ed. Summers, 159.

15. Robert J. W. Evans, *Rudolf II and His World: A Study in Intellectual History, 1576–1612* (Oxford, 1973), 196–242; Robert J. W. Evans, *The Making of the Habsburg Monarchy, 1550–1700: An Interpretation* (Oxford, 1979), 346–80.

16. Ivo Striedinger, *Der Goldmacher Marco Bragadino. Archivkundliche Studie zur Kulturgeschichte des 16. Jahrhunderts* (Munich, 1928).

17. Will-Erich Peuckert, ed., *Der Alchymist und sein Weib. Gauner- und Ehescheidungsprozesse des Alchymisten Thurneysser* (Stuttgart, 1956).

18. Germana Ernst, "I poteri delle streghe tra cause naturali e interventi diabolici. Spunti di un dibattito," in *Giovan Battista della Porta nell' Europa del suo tempo* (Naples, 1990), 167–97.

19. *DTF*, 231 f.

20. Bodin, *De magorum daemonomania*, 114.

21. Michel de Montaigne, *The Complete Essays*, ed. and trans. Michael Screech (London, 1991), xlvi–xlviii; book 1, chap. 3, 13; book 3, chap. 11, 1168–69; book 3, chap. 13, 1266–68. See also Alan Boase, *The Fortunes of Montaigne: A History of the Essays in France, 1580–1669* (New York, 1970), 23, 38–43, 244–46.

22. Hartmut Heinrich Kunstmann, *Zauberwahn und Hexenprozeß in der Reichsstadt Nürnberg* (Nürnberg, 1970), 65–72.

23. *HB*, 182 f.

24. Wolfgang Behringer, ed., *Hexen und Hexenprozesse in Deutschland* (Munich, 1993), 15 f., 39–50; Hartmann Amman, "Die Hexenprozesse im Fürstenthum Brixen," *Forschungen und Mitteilungen zur Geschichte Tirols und Vorarlbergs* 34 (1890): 144–66.

25. StA Augsburg: Hochstift Augsburg, Neuburger file, doc. 1214, fols. 285v–286v. Cf. Eva Labouvie, *Verbotene Künste* (St. Inghert, 1992).

26. Ginzburg, *Night Battles*, 78.

27. A. Marienescu, "Az áldozatok. Rumén népmythológiai képek és szokások," *Ethnographia* 2 (1891): 2–12, 53–58; cited in Pócs, *Fairies and Witches*, 47.

28. Th. Vlachos, "Geister und Dämonenvorstellungen im südosteuropäischen Raum griechischer Sprachzugehörigkeit," *Österreichische Zeitschrift für Volkskunde* 25 (1971): 217–48.

29. Pócs, *Fairies and Witches*, 47 f.; Maja Boskovič-Stulli, "Kresnik-krsnik, ein Wesen aus der kroatischen und slowenischen Volksüberlieferung," *Fabula* 3 (1959–60): 275–98.

30. Gábor Klaniczay, "Shamanistic Elements in Central European Witchcraft," in *The Uses of Supernatural Power: The Transformation of Popular Religion in Medieval and Early-Modern Europe*, trans. Susan Singerman, ed. Karen Margolis (Cambridge, U.K., 1990), 129–50, 227–30.

31. StA Augsburg: Hochstift Augsburg, Neuburger file, doc. 1199, fols. 39v–40.

12. Witches' Flight

1. For this pehenomenon in general, see Sigfried Hardung, *Die Vorladung vor Gottes Gericht* (Bühl, 1934); Louis Carlen, "Die Vorladung vor Gottes Gericht nach Walliser Quellen," *Schweizerisches Archiv für Volkskunde* 52 (1956): 10–18.

2. StA Augsburg, Hochstift Augsburg, Neuburger file, document 6737, fol. 126 (Pfleggericht Rettenberg, 1583).

3. Alan Macfarlane, *Witchcraft in Tudor and Stuart England: A Regional and Comparative Study* (London, 1970).

4. For this mechanism, see *HB*, 89–96.

5. M. R. Buck, "Hexenprozesse aus Oberschwaben," *Alemannia* 11 (1883): 108–35, at 110 f. and 113, for a witchcraft trial in the lordship Königsegg in 1665.

6. Anhorn, *Magiologia*, 411–65: "Concerning the Summons to the Valley of Josaphat." Anhorn (425) derives his notion of the summons from a misunderstood Scriptural passage (Jl. 3.2).

7. PA, letter to the councillors in Dillingen, 4 May 1583; letter to the sheriff of Rettenberg, 11 May 1583. A man named Johann Huber from Oberstdorf matriculated in 1563 at the University of Dillingen. Thomas Specht, *Die Matrikel der Universität Dillingen* (Dillingen, 1909–1911), vol. 1, 40.

8. Keyser and Stoob, eds., *Bayerisches Städtebuch*, 502. For the comparison with Vorarlberg, see Karl Heinz Burmeister, "Die ländliche Gemeinde in Vorarlberg bis 1800," in *Die ländliche Gemeinde—Il comune rurale. Historikertagung in Bad Ragaz. Convegno Storico di Bad Ragaz* (Bolzano, 1988), 139–57.

9. StA Augsburg: Hochstift Augsburg, Neuburger file, document 1199, fol. 413v (report of the Hofrat from 1586).

10. Bosl, ed., *Bayern*, 200 f.

11. *HB*, 130 ff.

12. StA Augsburg: Hochstift Augsburg, Neuburger file, document 1199, Index under 'C': "Conrad Stöckhlin."

13. StA Augsburg, Hochstift Augsburg, Neuburger file, document 6737, fols. 2 f.

14. Gustav Henningsen, *The Witches' Advocate* (Reno, Nevada, 1980).

15. PA, VP, interrogatoria for Konrad Stoeckhlin (146 questions), n.d., questions 15–40.

16. Ibid., questions 29–36, fols. 5–7v.

17. Ursula Lange, *Untersuchungen zu Bodins Demonomanie* (Frankfurt a.M., 1970).

18. Bodin, *De magorum daemonomania,* 109; PA, interrogatoria for Konrad Stoeckhlin (146 questions), n.d., question 96.

19. Bodin, *De magorum daemonomania,* 32–34.

20. Ibid., 112 ff.

21. Ibid., 100–118.

22. Weyer, *De Praestigiis daemonum* (1586), 167; Mora et al., eds., *Witches, Devils, and Doctors,* 186–89.

23. PA, VP, Konrad Stoeckhlin, 15 Nov. 1586, answer 15.

24. Ibid., answers 35–63.

25. Lavater *Von Gespänsten, unghüren, fälen und andern wunderbarlichen dingen* (1586), 138 ff.: "Daily Experience Teaches That There Are Many Monsters: The Fifteenth Chapter." and 144 f.

26. Bodin, *De magorum daemonomania,* 155.

27. PA, VP, Konrad Stoeckhlin, 29 July 1586, fol. 3v.

28. Bodin, *De magorum daemonomania,* 116.

29. PA, VP, Konrad Stoeckhlin, 15 Nov. 1586 answers 35–63.

30. PA, interrogatoria for Konrad Stoeckhlin (146 questions), n.d.

31. *DTF,* 174–78.

32. Dieter Harmening, *Superstitio. Überlieferungs- und theoriegeschichtliche Untersuchungen zur kirchlich-theologischen Aberglaubensliteratur des Mittelalters* (Berlin, 1979).

33. Alex Scobie, "Strigiform Witches in Roman and Other Cultures," *Fabula* 19 (1978): 74–101.

34. Johannes Franck, "Geschichte des Wortes 'Hexe,'" in Hansen, *Quellen,* 614–70, at 627 ff.

35. Fritz Byloff, *Hexenglaube und Hexenverfolgung in den österreichischen Alpenländern* (Berlin and Leipzig, 1934), 26, following L. Schönach, "Zur Geschichte des älteren Hexenwesens in Tirol," *Forschungen und Mitteilungen zur Geschichte Tirols und Vorarlbergs* 1 (1904): 62.

36. Franck, "Geschichte des Wortes 'Hexe,'" 617.

37. Mircea Eliade, "Some Observations on European Witchcraft," in *Occultism, Witchcraft and Cultural Fashions: Essays in Comparative Religions* (Chicago, 1976), 69–92, at 78 f.

38. Rudolf Endres, "Heinrich Institoris, sein Hexenhammer und der Nürnberger Rat," in Peter Segl, ed., *Der Hexenhammer. Entstehung und Umfeld des Malleus maleficarum von 1487* (Cologne and Berlin, 1988), 195–216.

39. Emil Allgäuer, "Zeugnisse zum Hexenwahn des 17. Jahrhunderts. Ein Beitrag zur Volkskunde Vorarlbergs," in *Programm des K.K. Staatsgymnasiums in Salzburg, Salzburg* (1914), 3–38, at 27; Manfred Tschaikner, *Damit das Böse ausgerottet werde: Hexenverfolgungen in Vorarlberg im 16. und 17. Jahrhundert* (Bregenz, 1992), 47 ff. For Mittelberg, see J. Fink and H. v. Klenze, *Der Mittelberg. Geschichte, Landes– und Volkskunde des ehemaligen gleichnamigen Gerichts* (Mittelberg, 1891).

40. Allgäuer, "Zeugnisse zum Hexenwahn des 17. Jahrhunderts," 24.

41. Thomas Platter, *Hirtenknabe, Handwerker, Humanist. Die Selbstbiographie, 1499 bis 1582*, ed. Heinrich Boss, afterword by Ralph–Rainer Wuthenow (Nördlingen, 1989), 15.

42. *DTF*, 152, 155, 218, 238 f.

13. Heuberg

1. PA, interrogation schema, question 72.

2. PA, interrogation report for Anna Luzin, 26 Aug. 1586.

3. On the general topic of accusing witch doctors as witches, see Monter, *Witchcraft in France and Switzerland*, 184 f.

4. PA, interrogatory for Stoeckhlin with 146 questions, n.d., questions 72 and 83.

5. Ibid., question 70.

6. PA, VP, confrontation of 19 Dec. 1586, testimony of Anna Weberin.

7. Johannes Prätorius, *Blockes-Berges Verrichtung* (Leipzig, 1669).

8. Andrcas Blauert, ed., *Ketzer, Zauberer, Hexen. Die Anfänge der europäischen Hexenverfolgungen* (Frankfurt a.M., 1990); Robert Muchembled, *Le roi et la sorcière. L'Europe des bûchers, XVe–XVIIIe siècle* (Paris, 1993), 76–80.

9. Franck, "Geschichte des Wortes 'Hexe,'" 635.

10. Anhorn, *Magiologia*, 637.

11. Hansen, *Quellen*, 437. *Tr. note:* On the evolution of the term *Unholden* for witches, see 50–51.

12. Ibid., 609, following the *Bichtbücher* in the Staatsarchiv of Zurich.

13. Ibid., 260, 437, 609; Byloff, *Hexenglaube und Hexenverfolgung in den österreichischen Alpenländern*, 60.

14. Robert Dengler, *Das Hexenwesen im Stift Obermarchthal von 1581–1756* (Ph.D. dissertation, Erlangen, 1953).

15. *HB*, 132; Jutta Novosadtko, *Scharfrichter und Abdecker in Bayern (1500–1800). Der Alltag zweier unehrlicher Berufe in Theorie, Literatur und Sozialgeschichte* (Ph.D. dissertation, Essen, 1992).

16. On this, see *HB*, 131 f.

17. PA, VP, Konrad Stoeckhlin, "guet- und peinliche bekhentnuß" (Confession without and with torture), 23 Dec. 1586, with answers to 119 questions.

18. Ibid., answer 62.

19. Ibid., answer 98.

20. PA, VP, interrogatoria for Konrad Stoeckhlin (146 questions), n.d.

21. Beitl, *Wörterbuch der deutschen Volkskunde,* 970–72.

22. Bodin, *De magorum daemonomania,* 109.

23. Franceso de Ossuna, *Flagellum diaboli, oder: Deß Teufels Geißel,* trans. Aegidius Albertinus (Munich, 1602), fol. 6; Anhorn, *Magiologia,* 637.

14. Witch Hunt

1. PA, report to the court, 3 Feb. 1587.

2. *Malleus Maleficarum,* ed. Summers, part 2, question 1, chap. 2, 100–101; chap. 13, 141–44; part 3, question 6, 211–12.

3. PA, confrontation, 19 Dec. 1586.

4. Tschaikner *Damit das Böse ausgerottet werde,* 47.

5. Schwendiger, *Der Große Widderstein erzählt. Historisches, Glaubwürdiges und Merkwürdiges aus dem Kleinwalsertal,* 88 ff.

6. StA Augsburg: Hochstift Augsburg, Neuburger file, doc. 1200, fols. 126v–128.

7. PA, testimony of Barbara Erbin, 7 and 10 April 1587.

8. PA, testimony of Barbara Erbin, 11 April 1587.

9. PA, copy of the report to court, 13 April 1587.

10. PA, order from the government, 22 April 1587.

11. Richard van Dülmen, *Theater des Schreckens* (Munich, 1985), 145 f. See English trans. by Elisabeth Neu, *Theater of Horror: Crime and Punishment in Early Modern Germany* (Oxford, 1990).

12. Tschaikner, *Damit das Böse ausgerottet werde,* 54 f., 64 f., 72 ff.

13. PA, report, 20 May 1587.

14. PA, inventory, 26 June 1592.

15. PA, report of the Pfleggericht, 13 May 1587.

16. PA, order of the government, 20 May 1587.

17. PA, order, 16 July 1587.

18. PA, report, 23 July 1587; answer to communication of 16 July.

19. PA, order, 31 July 1587; answer to communication of 23 July.

20. PA, communication, Sonthofen, 1 Sept. 1587.

21. StA Augshurg: Hochstift Augsburg, Neuburger file, doc. 1200, fol. 431, 451v–52 (Monday, 12 Oct. 1587).

22. Ibid., document 1199, fol. 413.

23. Ibid., document 1200, fol. 464v.

24. Ibid., fol. 479v–80.

25. Ibid., fol. 502v–503.

26. Ibid., fol. 516.

27. Ibid., doc. 1202, fol. 92; concerning the assets of the executed, fols. 666, 691.

28. On this see Manfred Tschaikner, "'Also schlecht ist das Weib von Natur . . .' Grundsätzliches zur Rolle der Frau in den Vorarlberger Hexenverfolgungen," in Alois Niederstätter and Wolfgang Schefflknecht, eds., *Hexe oder Hausfrau. Das Bild der Frau in der Geschichte Vorarlbergs* (Sigmaringendorf, 1991), 57–76.

29. Schwendiger, *Der Große Widderstein erzählt,* 90 ff., following Köberle, *Volksgenealogie des Kleinen Walsertals,* published by the Heimatmuseum Riezlern.

30. StA Augsburg: Hochstift Augsburg, Neuburger file, doc. 1200, fol. 431.

31. *HB,* 436 (with source references).

32. StA Augsburg: Hochstift Augsburg, Neuburger file, doc. 1200, fol. 301v.

33. *HB,* 436–40.

34. Population figures were estimated on the basis of data in Keyser and Stoob, eds., *Bayerisches Städtebuch,* 356: in 1812 Oberdorf had ca. 780 inhabitants.

35. Österreichische Nationalbibliothek Vienna, cod. 8963, fols. 751 f.

15. Peasant Rebellion

1. StA Augsburg: Hochstift Augsburg, Neuburger file, doc. 1199, fol. 53.

2. Bilgeri, *Geschichte Vorarlbergs,* vol. 3 (1977), 20–61.

3. Weitnauer, *Allgäuer Chronik,* vol. 1, 226–34.

4. Hipper and Kolb, *Sonthofen im Wandel der Geschichte,* 261 f.

5. Peter Blickle, *Landschaften im Alten Reich. Die staatliche Funktion des gemeinen Mannes in Oberdeutschland* (Munich, 1973), 321 ff.; Weitnauer, *Allgäuer Chronik,* vol. 1, 240, 244, 273, 277, 295 ff. *Tr. note:* The heavy peasant's clog, the *Bundschuh,* was the rallying symbol for a series of planned peasant rebellions in southwestern Germany in the fifteenth and early sixteenth centuries.

6. Günter Franz, *Der deutsche Bauernkrieg* (11th ed., Darmstadt, 1977), 113–34.

7. Günther Franz, *Quellen zur Geschichte des Bauernkrieges* (Darmstadt, 1963), 163 f.

8. Claudia Ulbrich, "Oberschwaben und Württemberg," in Horst Buszello, Peter Blickle, Rudolf Endres, eds., *Der deutsche Bauernkrieg* (2d ed., Paderborn, 1991), 97–134, at 104.

9. Peter Blickle, *The Revolution of 1525: The German Peasants' War from a New Perspepctive,* trans. Thomas A. Brady Jr. and H. C. Erik Midelfort (Baltimore, 1981), 18–22.

10. Franz, *Quellen zur Geschichte des Bauernkrieges,* 199.

11. Weitnauer, *Allgäuer Chronik,* vol. 2, 118–20, 134–36; GMO 2-1974, 159.

12. GMO 2–1974, 160 f.; Hipper and Kolb, *Sonthofen im Wandel der Geschichte,* 133–47.

13. PA, report of the sheriff (Pfleger) to the government in Dillingen, 3 Feb. 1587.

14. *GMO* 2-1974, 163.

15. Hipper and Kolb, *Sonthofen im Wandel der Geschichte*, 136 f.

16. Ibid., 138.

17. *GMO* 2-1974, 165 f.

18. *Tr. note:* An imperial ban would have had the effect of declaring the rebels outlaws. Hipper and Kolb, *Sonthofen im Wandel der Geschichte*, 141.

19. Ibid., 142.

20. Felix Stieve, "Ein Bauernaufstand in der Herrschaft Rettenberg," *Zeitschrift des Historischen Vereins für Schwaben und Neuburg* 11 (1884): 32–52; Weitnauer, *Allgäuer Chronik*, vol. 2 (1984), 140–43. On 15 Jan. 1608 the rebellion ended with formal prostration and oaths of obedience to the bishop.

21. Hipper and Kolb, *Sonthofen im Wandel der Geschichte*, 145.

22. *GMO* 2-1974, 172 and 181.

23. Ibid., 172.

16. Folk Beliefs

1. Weitnauer, *Allgäuer Chronik*, vol. 2 (1984), 130 f.

2. *HB*, 130–37.

3. Stieve, "Ein Bauernaufstand in der Herrschaft Rettenberg" (article 8), 38.

4. *MFLT*, 153 ff.

5. Richard Weiss, *Das Alpwesen Graubündens. Wirtschaft, Sachkultur, Recht, Älplerarbeit und Älplerleben* (Zürich, 1941), 350–58.

6. K. Weinhold, "Der Wildemännlestanz von Oberstdorf," *Zeitschrift des Vereins für Volkskunde* (1897): 427–37; E. Rausch, *Wilde Männle im Allgäu* (Kempten, 1967).

7. Reiser, *Sagen, Gebräuche und Sprichwörter des Allgäus*, vol. 1 (1895), 129–40 (Wild women), 141–47 (Wild men); Karl Haiding, "Sagen von Wildleuten," in *Österreichischer Volkskundeatlas* (Graz, 1959–1979), map 117.

8. Leander Petzoldt, *Volkstümliche Feste. Ein Führer zu Volksfesten, Märkten und Messen in Deutschland* (Munich, 1983), 18 ff.

9. Weitnauer, *Allgäuer Chronik*, vol. 2 (1984), 111 ff.

10. "Funkalied," in *Montafoner Heimatbuch* (Schruns, 1980), 149.

11. Lutz, *Vollständige Beschreibung des Schweizerlandes* (1827), vol. 2, 246 f.

12. Arno Borst, "Die Anfänge des Hexenwahns in den Alpen," in *Barbaren, Ketzer und Artisten* (Munich, 1988), 262–86.

13. Blauert, *Frühe Hexenverfolgungen*, 50; on Fründs Chronicle, 67 ff.

14. Borst, "Die Anfänge des Hexenwahns in den Alpen," 271.

15. Borst, "Anfänge des Hexenwahns in den Alpen," 279. For a different view see

Euan Cameron, *The Reformation of the Heretics. The Waldenses of the Alps, 1480–1580* (Oxford, 1984), 111–13.

16. Felicien Gamba, "Die Hexe von Saint-Vincent. Ein Ketzer- und Hexenprozeß im 15. Jahrhundert," in *Ketzer, Zauberer, Hexen,* Blauert, ed., 160–81.

17. Claude Tholosan, *Ut magorum et maleficiorum errores,* appendix to Pierette Paravy, "Zur Genesis der Hexenverfolgungen im Mittelalter: Der Traktat des Claude Tholosan, Richter in der Dauphine (um 1436)," in *Ketzer, Zauberer, Hexen,* Blauert, ed., 118–60, at 145.

18. Paravy, "Zur Genesis der Hexenverfolgungen im Mittelalter," 130.

19. Walter Rummel, "Gutenberg, der Teufel und die Muttergottes von Eberhardklausen. Erste Hexenverfolgung im Trierer Land," in *Ketzer, Zauberer, Hexen,* Blauert, ed., 91–117, 101 f.

20. Joseph Hansen, *Zauberwahn, Inquisition und Hexenprozeß im Mittelalter.*

21. Joseph Kämpfen, *Hexen und Hexenprocesse im Wallis* (Stans, 1867); Peter Kamber, "La chasse aux sorciers et aux sorcières dans le pays de Vaud. Aspects quantitatifs (1581–1620)," in *Revue historique vaudoise* 90 (1982): 21–33.

22. *HB,* Tschaikner, *Damit das Böse ausgerottet werde,* 223–32.

23. Gustav Henningsen and John Tedeschi, eds., *The Inquisition in Early Modern Europe: Studies on Sources and Methods* (Dekalb IL, 1986); Stephen Haliczer, ed., *Inquisition and Society in Early Modern Europe* (London, 1987).

24. Petzoldt, *Volkstümliche Feste. Ein Führer zu Volksfesten, Märkten und Messen in Deutschland,* 57 f.

25. Richard Wolfram, "Jahresfeuer-Termine," in *Österreichischer Volkskundeatlas* (Graz, 1959–1979), map 74; Richard Wolfram, "Jahresfeuer II," in ibid., map 75 d: on burning figures in effigy.

26. *Der tanzende Tod. Mittelalterliche Totentänze,* tr. Gert Kaiser (Frankfurt a.M., 1983).

27. *Tr. note:* These lines are in crude verse:
"Hupff auf, du hessigs kammelthier, / Im fewr muest du jetz schwitzen schier, / dein gabel reitten hat ein endt, / vom hewberg hol ich dich gar geschwendt."

28. Reinhold Böhm, *'Sagt ja, Sagt nein—Getanzt Muess Sein.' Der Füssener Totentanz* (Füssen, 1978).

29. Michael Petzet, *Die Kunstdenkmäler von Schwaben* vol. 8, *Landkreis Sonthofen* (München, 1964), 628 ff.; GMO 3-1976, 272 f.

30. Ginzburg, *Night Battles.*

31. Tschaikner, *Damit das Böse ausgerottet werde,* 227 ff.

32. Bartholomaeus Anhorn, *Magiologia* (I cite the Basel, 1675 ed.).

33. Otto Seger and Peter Putzer, *Hexenprozesse in Liechtenstein und das Salzburger Rechtsgutachten 1682* (Vienna, 1987).

34. Ferdinand Sprecher, "Der letzte Hexenprozeß in Graubünden," *Bündner Monatsblatt* (1936): 321–31; Kaspar Freuler, *Die Geschichte der letzten Hexe in der Schweiz* (3d ed., Glarus, 1976); Werner Kundert, "Die Hexenprozesse im Puschlav, 1631–1753," *Zeitschrift für Schweizerisches Recht* (NF) 104 (1985): 301–43.

35. Kundert, "Die Hexenprozesse im Puschlav, 1631–1753," 310; following C. Camenisch, *Carlo Borromeo und die Gegenreformation im Veltlin* (Chur, 1901); Paolo d'Allessandri, ed., *Atti di S. Carlo riguardanti la Svizzeria e i suoi territorii* (Locarno, 1909); Rinaldo Boldini, "Un incidente poco diplomatico durante la visita di S. Carlo in Mesolcina," *Quaderni Grigionitaliani* 26 (1956/57), 215–22; Massimo Bormetti, *Al tempo delle streghe* (2d ed., Sondrio, 1981).

36. Schmid and Sprecher, "Zur Geschichte der Hexenverfolgung in Graubünden," 133, 201; quotation in Schacher von Inwil, *Das Hexenwesen im Kanton Luzern*, 16 f.

37. Paul Beck, "Ein Hexenprozeß aus Vorarlberg vom Jahr 1597," *Ausgewählte Aufsätze zur Geschichte Oberschwabens* (Bad Buchau, 1985), 135–44, 136. Repr. from *Anzeiger für Kunde der deutschen Vorzeit*, Neue Folge 26 (1879): 345–54.

38. Allgäuer, "Zeugnisse zum Hexenwahn des 17. Jahrhunderts," 22.

39. Schmid and Sprecher, "Zur Geschichte der Hexenverfolgung in Graubünden," 133.

40. Schacher von Inwil, *Hexenwesen im Kanton Luzern*, 15.

41. Caro Baroja, *World of the Witches*, 112–21.

42. *Tr. note: Rumplklausen* are wild figures associated with the violent celebrations held on the eve of Saint Nicholas, that is, 5 Dec. Günter Kapfhammer, ed., *Sagen aus Altbayern, Schwaben und Franken* (Munich, 1978), 68 (the male witch); 80 (the army of Muetas at Sonthofen); 84 (the one-too-many on Saint Nicholas's Day in Berghofen, near Sonthofen).

43. Ibid., 70 (revenants), 78 (wild men), 89 f. (revenants in Harbatshofen).

44. Kapfhammer, ed., *Sagen aus Altbayern, Schwaben und Franken*, 85 f.

45. *HDA* 4 (1931), cols. 128 f.

46. Leza Uffer, "Das Bild des Hirten in der volkstümlichen Literatur der Rätoromanen," in *Alpes Orientales* 4 (Munich, 1972), 115–21; Klaniczay, *Uses of Supernatural Power*, 144.

47. *HDA* 6 (1934), cols. 1598–1684.

48. Cf. the discussion of Cysat's concepts in *DSWH*, 112 f.; Cantonal Library of Lucerne, "Cysat-Chronik," vol. B, fol. 100b.

49. *DSWH*, 112 f. Cantonal Library of Lucerne, "Cysat-Chronik," vol. E, fol. 333b.

50. Walter Brandmüller, ed., *Handbuch der Bayerischen Kirchengeschichte*, vol. 2, *Von der Glaubensspaltung bis zur Säkularisation* (St. Ottilien, 1993), see the essays by Wolfgang Wüst on Swabia, 65–122, 357–90.

51. Maja Boskovič-Stulli, "Kresnik-krsnik, ein Wesen aus der kroatischen und slowenischen Volksüberlieferung," *Fabula* 3 (1959–60): 275–98.

52. Klaus Graf, "Carlo Ginzburgs 'Hexensabbat'—Herausforderung an die Methodendiskussion der Geschichtswissenschaft," *kea. Zeitschrift für Kulturwissenschaften* 5 (1993): 1–17.

53. Willem de Blécourt, "Spuren einer Volkskultur oder Dämonisierung? Kritische Bemerkungen zu Ginzburgs 'Benandanti,'" *kea. Zeitschrift für Kulturwissenschaften* 5 (1993): 17–30, at 24.

54. *Le Sabbat des Sorciers,* ed. Nicole Jacques Chaquin and Maxime Preaud (Grenoble, 1993).

55. Karl Hofmann, *Oberstdorfer Hexen auf dem Scheiterhaufen* (Oberstdorf, 1931).

56. Ginzburg, *Benandanti,* 77 f.

57. Tschaikner, *Damit das Böse ausgerottet werde,* 174.

58. *MFLT,* 196 ff.

59. StA Augsburg: Hochstift Augsburg, Neuburger file, document 1202, fol. 216 f.

60. *HB,* 175 ff.

61. Harmening, *Superstitio*; Harmening, *Zauberei im Abendland*; Christoph Daxelmüller, *Zauberpraktiken. Eine Ideengeschichte der Magie* (Zurich, 1993).

62. Peter Dinzelbacher, "Zur Erforschung der Geschichte der Volksreligion," in *Volksreligion im hohen und späten Mittelalter,* ed. Peter Dinzelbacher and Dieter R. Bauer (Paderborn, 1990), 9–28, at 20 f.

63. Jean-Claude Schmitt, *The Holy Greyhound: Guinefort, Healer of Children since the Thirteenth Century,* trans. Martin Thom (Cambridge, U.K., 1983. Originally published as *Le saint levrier* (Paris, 1979).

64. Boskovic[special c]-Stulli, "Kresnik-krsnik," 293–97.

65. Klaniczay, *Uses of Supernatural Power,* 137.

66. Baroja, *World of the Witches,* 126–28.

67. Gustav Henningsen, "Die 'Frauen von außerhalb.' Der Zusammenhang von Feenkult, Hexenwahn und Armut im 16. und 17. Jahrhundert auf Sizilien," in Hans Peter Duerr, ed., *Die Mitte der Welt. Aufsätze zu Mircea Eliade* (Frankfurt a.M., 1984), 164–83.

68. Klaniczay, *Uses of Supernatural Power,* p. 149.

69. Siegfried Müller, *Drei 'Wunderheiler' aus dem Vorarlberger Oberland* (Feldkirch, 1986), 56–69.

70. Manfred Tschaikner, "Von 'bösen zauberischen Leuten' in Braz um 1750. Aus der Familiengeschichte des berühmten Exorzisten Johann Joseph Gassner," *Bludenzer Geschichtshlätter* 5 (1989): 15–34.

71. Tschaikner, *Damit das Böse ausgerottet werde,* 61 f. For Vandans see Hans Barbisch, *Vandans. Eine Heimatkunde aus dem Tale Montafon in Vorarlberg* (Innsbruck, 1922). Barbisch was related by marriage to Schoder, and ancestors of his were executed as witches in 1597; on this Tschaikner, *Damit das Böse ausgerottet werde,* 200.

72. Müller, *Drei 'Wunderheiler,'* 79–117.

73. Ebermuth Rudolf, *Die geheimnisvollen Ärzte: Von Gesundbetern und Spruchheil-ern* (Olten, 1977); Inge Schöck, *Hexenglaube in der Gegenwart. Empirische Untersuchungen in Südwestdeutschland* (Tübingen, 1978).

17. Shamanism

1. Wilhelm Radloff, *Das Schamanentum und sein Kultus* (St. Petersburg, 1885); Sergej M. Shirokogoroff, "General Theory of Shamanism among the Tungus," *Journal of the North China Branch of the Royal Asiatic Society* 57 (1923): 246–49.

2. Vladimir N. Basilov, "Zur Erforschung der Überreste des Schamanismus in Zentralasien," in *Sehnsucht nach dem Ursprung. Zu Mircea Eliade*, ed. Hans Peter Duerr, (Frankfurt a.M., 1983), 207–25, at 208.

3. Eliade, *Schamanismus und archaische Ekstasetechnik*, 461.

4. Basilov, "Zur Erforschung der Überreste des Schamanismus in Zentralasien," 215 f.

5. Klaniczay, *Uses of Supernatural Power*, 95–110, 129–50.

6. Sergej M. Shirokogoroff, *Psychomental Complex of the Tungus* (London, 1935), 279 ff.

7. Ginzburg, *Ecstasies*.

8. Eliade, *Schamanismus und archaische Ekstasetechnik*, 441.

9. Mircea Eliade, "Der magische Flug," *Antaios* 1 (1959): 1–12.

10. Hansjost Lixfeld, "Die Guntramsage (AT 1645a). Volkserzählungen und Alter Ego in Tiergestalt und ihre schamanistische Herkunft," *Fabula* 13 (1972): 60–107.

11. Kathrin Utz-Tremp, "Waldenser und Wiedergänger: Das Fegefeuer im Inquisitionsregister des Bischofs Jacques Fournier von Pamiers (1317–1326)," in *Himmel, Hölle, Fegefeuer. Das Jenseits im Mittelalter. Katalog des Schweizer Landesmuseums*, Jezler, ed., 125–34, 129 ff. (for a sharp critique of Le Roy Ladurie's *Montaillou*, see 368–79); Kirsten Hastrup, "Iceland: Sorcerers and Paganism," in *Early Modern European Witchcraft: Centres and Peripheries*, ed. Bengt Ankarloo and Gustav Henningsen (Oxford, 1990), 383–402, at 390 f; Gustav Henningsen,"'The Ladies from Outside': An Archaic Pattern of the Witches' Sabbath," in *Early Modern European Witchcraft*, ed. Ankarloo and Henningsen, 191–218; Klaniczay, *Uses of Supernatural Power*, 129–50; Boskovič-Stulli, "Kresnik-krsnik" 275–98.

12. Bonomo, *Caccia alle streghe*, 65.

13. Henningsen, "'Ladies from Outside,'" 193 ff.

14. Vladimir Propp, *Die historischen Wurzeln des Zaubermärchens* (Munich, 1987; orig. ed. Leningrad, 1946), 461 f.

15. Basilov, "Zur Erforschung der Überreste des Schamanismus in Zentralasien," 215 f.

18. Bricolage

1. Karl-Heinz Kohl, *Ethnologie—die Wissenschaft vom kulturell Fremden: Eine Einführung* (Munich, 1993), 132.

2. Assmann et al., *Schrift und Gedächtnis*, 277.

3. On functionalism and structuralism, see Kohl, *Ethnologie—die Wissenschaft vom kulturell Fremden: Eine Einführung*, 137–45.

4. David Sabean, "A Prophet in the Thirty Years' War: Penance as a Social Metaphor," in *Power in the Blood. Popular Culture and Village Discourse in Early Modern Germany* (Cambridge, UK, 1984), 61–93, at 85–91.

5. Claude Lévi-Strauss, *The Savage Mind* (Chicago, 1966), 17.

6. Jack Goody, ed., *Literacy in Traditional Societies* (Cambridge, 1968.)

7. Anhorn, *Magiologia*, 93–96.

8. Lévi-Strauss, *Savage Mind*, 17–21.

9. PA, VP, Konrad Stoeckhlin, 29 July 1586, fol. 3v. For Mathies as an old Walser Name, see *Montafoner Heimatbuch* (1980), 171.

10. Ilg, *Walser in Vorarlberg*, part 2, 62 ff.

11. Ibid., 73.

12. For example, "The Nocturnal Banquet," in Jegerlehner, *Sagen aus dem Unterwallis*, or "The Dance of Death," in Johannes Jegerlehner, *Was die Sennen erzählen. Märchen aus dem Wallis. Aus dem Volksmund gesammelt* (Bern, 1916).

13. Alfred Weitnauer, *Keltisches Erbe in Schwaben und Baiern*, (Kempten, 1961).

14. Pócs, *Fairies and Witches*, 13; Ginzburg, *Ecstasies*, 109; following Jacob Grimm, *Irische Elfenmärchen* (Leipzig, 1826).

15. *Montafoner Heimtbuch* (Schruns, 1980), 129–35; Hans Kreis, *Ein Stück Siedlungsgeschichte der Zentralalpen* (2d ed., Bern, 1966), 109–12. In the appendix of *Ein Stück* is a map of the distribution of Walser settlement.

16. *Historisch-biographisches Lexikon der Schweiz*, vol. 6 (1931), 722. In German he was also called Saint Joder and Saint Jodro, although he is sometimes listed as Saint Theodorus in dictionaries of the church. François-O. Dubuis, "Theodor von Octodurus," in *Lexikon für Theologie und Kirche*, vol. 10 (1963), cols. 28 f. Louis Carlen, "Theodul," in Wolfgang Braunfels, ed., *Lexikon der christlichen Ikonographie*, vol. 8 (Freiburg, 1976), 456–58.

17. Zirkel, *Geschichte des Marktes Oberstdorf*, part 2, 271 f. See also Werner Grundmann, "Der hl. Theodul, seine Wetterglocke und Weintraube im Spiegel schwäbischer Kunst," in *Das schöne Allgäu* (1970), no. 3; G. Breuss, "Die Verehrung des St. Theodul bei den Walsern in Vorarlberg," *Walserheimat in Vorarlberg* 16 (1975): 242–50.

18. Lévi-Strauss, *Savage Mind*, 18 ff.

19. Alois Senti, *Sagen aus dem Sarganserland* (Basel, 1974), 239. And generally for Switzerland, Liebl, "Geisterheere und ähnliche Erscheinungen."

20. Guntern, *Volkserzählungen aus dem Oberwallis,* 250.

21. University of Munich Library (Universitätsbibliothek), Manuscript Division, "Kemptener Chronik," 2 cod. ms. 500, fols. 139 ff.

22. A description offered by Augsburg folklorist Günter Kapfhammer (d. 1993) in a discussion of the Stoeckhlin case.

19. Private Revelations

1. Eliade, *Schamanismus und archaische Ekstasetechnik,* 464.

2. Sabean, *Power in the Blood,* 86.

3. Sara T. Nalle, "Popular religion in Cuenca on the Eve of the Catholic Reformation," in *Inquisition and Society in Early Modern Europe,* ed. Haliczer 67–68; Jean Pierre Dedieu, "The Inquisition and Popular Culture in New Castile," in ibid., 129–46; Mary Elizabeth Perry, "Beatas and the Inquisition in Early Modern Seville," in ibid., 147–70; Jaime Contreras and Gustav Henningsen, "Forty-thousand Cases of the Spanish Inquisition (1540–1700): Analysis of a Historical Data Bank," in *The Inquisition in Early Modern Europe. Studies on Sources and Methods,* ed. Henningsen and Tedeschi, 100–129; E. William Monter and John Teschedi, "Toward a Statistical Profile of the Italian Inquisitions, Sixteenth to Eighteenth Centuries," in ibid., 130–57; Henningsen, "'The Ladies from Outside,'" 191–215.

4. Hilda Graef, "Ekstase," in *Lexikon für Theologie und Kirche,* vol. 3 (1959), cols. 788–91.

5. Clive Hart, *Images of Flight* (Berkeley, 1988), 193–210; *DFT,* 262 ff.; David Gentilcore, *From Bishop to Witch: The System of the Sacred in Early Modern Terra d'Otranto* (Manchester, 1992).

6. Karl Rahner, "Privatoffenbarung," in *Lexikon für Theologie und Kirche,* vol. 8 (1963), cols. 772–73; Hans Wulf, "Unterscheidung der Geister," in *Lexikon für Theologie und Kirche,* vol. 10 (1963), cols. 533–35.

7. Bodin, *De magorum daemonomania,* 17–35.

8. Anhorn, *Magiologia,* 24, citing in addition the discussion of Delrio, *Disquisitiones magicarum libri sex,* book 4, chap. 3, question 6; Sabean, *Power in the Blood.* 70–76.

9. *HB,* 181–84; Wolfgang Behringer, "Die große Schongauer Hexenverfolgung und ihr historischer Kontext," in *Der Welf. Jahrbuch des Historischen Vereins Schongau* 1 (1993): 1–17.

10. HStAM, Witchcraft Trial Records 1, prod. 1, fol. 7v. Edited in *MFLT,* 97–108, at 103.

11. Anhorn, *Magiologia,* 36–57, quotations at 37 and 45.

12. In additon to Olaus Magnus, Anhorn based his description of the "magic flight" of the Eskimo shamans (47 f.), on the Jesuits Martin Delrio (lib. 2, quaest. 25) and Caspar Schott (*Physica curiosa*, m. 25).

13. Anhorn, *Magiologia*, 55.

14. Burke, *Popular Culture in Early Modern Europe*, 207 f.

15. Henningsen, "'The Ladies from Outside,'" 207.

16. *DSWH*, 112 f.; Cantonal Library of Lucerne, "Cysat-Chronik," vol. E, fol. 333b.

20. The End of the Dreamtime

1. Clifford Geertz, "Common Sense as a Cultural System," in *Local Knowledge. Further Essays in Interpretive Anthropology* (New York, 1983), 73–93.

2. Jean Bodin, *Les six livres de la république* (1576). German trans. *Sechs Bücher über den Staat*, books 1–3, trans. by B. Wimmer, ed. R.-C. Mayer-Tasch (Munich, 1981), book 1: 8, 205.

3. Hans Peter Duerr, *Dreamtime: Concerning the Boundary between Wilderness and Civilization*, trans. Felicitas D. Goodman (Oxford, 1985).

4. Karin Baumann, *Aberglaube für Laien. Zur Programmatik und Überlieferung mittelalterlicher Superstitionenkritik* (Würzburg, 1989), 361–66.

5. Jacques Chiffoleau, *La compatibilité de l'au-delà. Les hommes, la mort, et la religion dans la region d'Avignon à la fin du moyen âge (vers 1320–vers 1480* (Rome, 1980); Pócs, *Fairies and Witches*, 65 f.; Henningsen, "'The Ladies from Outside,'"; Carlo Ginzburg, "Deciphering the Sabbath," in *Early Modern European Witchcraft*, ed. Ankarloo and Henningsen, 121–38.

6. Perry Anderson, "Witchcraft. Storia notturna: Una decifrazione del Sabba," *London Review of Books*, 8 Nov. 1990, 6–11.

Index

Index

Index

Index

Index

Studies in Early Modern German History

H. C. Erik Midelfort, *Mad Princes of Renaissance Germany*

Arthur E. Imhof, *Lost Worlds: How Our European Ancestors Coped with Everyday Life and Why Life Is So Hard Today,* translated by Thomas Robisheaux

Peter Blickle, *Obedient Germans? A Rebuttal: A New View of German History,* translated by Thomas A. Brady Jr.

Wolfgang Behringer, *Shaman of Oberstdorf: Chonrad Stoeckhlin and the Phantoms of the Night,* translated by H. C. Erik Midelfort